Molière
Five Plays

The School for Wives, Tartuffe, The Misanthrope,
The Miser, The Hypochondriac

This volume offers five of Molière's finest and best-known
comedies in superb modern translations that have won widespread
critical favour. The three verse plays, *The Misanthrope*, *Tartuffe* and
The School for Wives, have been rendered into sparkling English
verse by the poet Richard Wilbur. The two prose comedies,
The Miser and *The Hypochondriac*, have been translated by the
playwright Alan Drury. All five have been the basis of acclaimed
productions in major theatres, notably Tom Courtenay's
Misanthrope for the Royal Exchange Theatre in Manchester and
London and the National Theatre's *Hypochondriac* with Daniel
Massey. Completing the volume are a chronology of Molière's life
and work and an authoritative introduction to the plays by Donald
Roy.

Methuen World Classics
include

Jean Baptiste Poquelin de
MOLIERE

Five Plays

The School for Wives
Tartuffe
The Misanthrope
Translated into English verse by Richard Wilbur

The Miser
The Hypochondriac
Translated into English prose by Alan Drury

With an introduction by Donald Roy

METHUEN DRAMA

Methuen World Classics

This collection first published as a paperback original in 1982 by Methuen
London Ltd
Reprinted in 1989 by Methuen Drama
215 Vauxhall Bridge Road, London SW1V 1EJ

Methuen Publishing Limited Reg. No. 3543167

Reprinted 1990, 1991, 1992
Reissued with a new cover design 1994

7 9 10 8

ISBN 0 413 49760 7

Printed and bound in Great Britain by
Cox & Wyman Ltd, Reading, Berkshire

Contents

Molière: A Chronology

15 January 1622	Jean-Baptiste Poquelin baptized at Saint-Eustache church, near Les Halles, Paris, the firstborn (of six children) to a prosperous upholsterer and his wife, whose family background is similar.
1631	His father purchases the office of upholsterer-in-ordinary to the king, giving him an entrée to the court and a hereditary position for his eldest son.
1632	His mother dies and his father remarries in the following year.
1636–1640(?)	He attends the Collège de Clermont, a reputable Jesuit school for the sons of noblemen and well-to-do bourgeois, mixing with school-friends who are later to be known as free-thinkers.
1641	According to tradition, he takes a degree in Law at Orléans University.
1642	Exercising the family business he accompanies the court to Narbonne as a replacement for his father.
1643	He abandons upholstery and becomes founder member of a new acting company, the Illustre Théâtre, adopting the stage name of Molière.
1645	The company goes bankrupt, Molière's debts are discharged by his father and he leaves Paris with Madeleine Béjart and other surviving members to join a touring company.
1646–1658	On tour in the southern provinces, playing at such towns as Nantes, Bordeaux, Agen, Toulouse, Carcassonne, Narbonne, Montpellier, Avignon, Grenoble, Dijon and in particular Pézenas and Lyon. Molière becomes director of the company, possibly in 1650, and writes his first plays for them, *La Jalousie du Barbouillé*, *Le Médecin volant*, *L'Etourdi* (performed in 1655) and *Dépit amoureux* (performed in 1656).
1658	After a brief sojourn in Rouen the company gives a successful command performance before Louis XIV at the Louvre. They secure the protection of Monsieur, the king's brother, together with the promise of a pension, and are granted the use of the Salle du Petit-Bourbon, which they share with an Italian company led by Tiberio Fiorelli (Scaramouche).

1659	Fiorelli returns home, leaving Molière in sole possession of the theatre. Molière writes and performs *Les Précieuses ridicules*, an immediate success but temporarily withdrawn, possibly under pressure from rivals or indignant 'précieux'.
1660	He presents *Sganarelle* with equal success. The Petit-Bourbon is scheduled for demolition, doubtless in response to intrigues against him, and Molière spends three months giving private performances for the king and various members of the court.
1661	His company occupies the Palais-Royal, formerly the private theatre of Cardinal Richelieu and refurbished for them at the king's behest. Performance of *Don Garcie de Navarre* is a failure, that of *L'Ecole des maris* a great success, as is *Les Fâcheux*, commissioned for a private entertainment by Fouquet and later transferred to Paris, with Molière playing seven roles.
1662	He marries Armande Béjart, daughter or sister of Madeleine. Triumph of *L'Ecole des femmes* at the Palais-Royal and subsequently at court.
1663	Molière is at the height of his success, despite charges of bad taste and immorality in his latest play, to which he replies confidently in *La Critique de l'Ecole des femmes* and *L'Impromptu de Versailles*. Scurrilous offerings at a rival theatre depict him, variously, as a cuckolded or incestuous husband.
1664	His son Louis is born, to whom the king acts as godfather but who dies within the year. *Le Mariage forcé* performed by royal command at the Louvre and then at the Palais-Royal. *La Princesse d'Elide* and *Le Tartuffe* form part of a royal fête at Versailles; only the former is publicly performed. First attacks in the long campaign of vilification against *Le Tartuffe* and its author, denounced as a blasphemous libertine.
1665	*Don Juan* becomes an instant success in Paris, but is withdrawn under pressure at end of season and never revived in Molière's lifetime. Further attacks on him for impiety. A daughter, Esprit-Madeleine, is born. His company receives an annual pension from the king, adopting the new title of the Troupe du Roi. *L'Amour médecin* performed at Versailles and in Paris.
1666	First signs of serious (pulmonary?) disorder and estrangement from his wife. At the Palais-Royal *Le Misanthrope* is received with some interest, *Le Médecin malgré lui* with enthusiasm. The company is invited to Saint-Germain-en-Laye for a royal fête to which Molière contributes *Mélicerte* (unfinished).

1667   *Pastorale comique*, a substitute for *Mélicerte*, and *Le Sicilien, ou l'Amour peintre* performed at Saint-Germain. Molière's illness worsens, forcing him to give up acting for several months. *L'Imposteur*, a lengthened and modified version of *Le Tartuffe*, receives one public performance and is promptly banned by the Parlement and condemned by the Archbishop of Paris.

1668   Both *Amphitryon*, at the Palais-Royal, and *Georges Dandin*, at Versailles and later at Paris, meet with success, but *L'Avare* is a failure with the public.

1669   Permission granted to perform *Le Tartuffe* in full in public; it is a prodigious success. Molière's father dies. *Monsieur de Pourceaugnac* performed for the king at Chambord and transferred to the Palais-Royal.

1670   Two further royal entertainments presented, *Les Amants magnifiques* at Saint-Germain and *Le Bourgeois gentilhomme* at Chambord; the latter is also well received in Paris.

1671   *Psyché*, written in collaboration with Corneille and Quinault, performed for the court at the 'théâtre des machines' in the Tuileries, and later at the Palais-Royal, where *Les Fourberies de Scapin* enjoys little success. Invited again to Saint-Germain for a fête, Molière presents *La Comtesse d'Escarbagnas*, which is revived there and in Paris the following year.

1672   Death of Madeleine Béjart. *Les Femmes savantes* successfully presented at the Palais-Royal. Reconciliation with Armande and birth of another son, who also fails to survive.

1673   Intended for performance at court, *Le Malade imaginaire* is rejected through Lulli's machinations, but is enthusiastically received at the Palais-Royal. Already ill, Molière is overcome by convulsive coughing during the fourth performance on February 17th and dies soon afterwards. At first, interment in consecrated ground is refused but, on the king's intercession, he is buried at night and without ceremony. Lulli takes possession of the Palais-Royal for his Opera and Molière's company is amalgamated with that of the Théâtre du Marais.

1680   By royal decree this joint company is merged with that of the Hôtel de Bourgogne to form the Comédie-Française.

Introduction

At once the most obvious and most necessary consideration to bear in mind in reading Molière is that he was a complete man of the theatre – playwright, actor, director, company manager, publicist and apologist. From the age of 21, when he abandoned a prosperous bourgeois background with prospects of advancement in the family upholstery business in order to throw in his lot with a group of ambitious young actors, until his early death at 51, less than an hour after appearing in his last play as a genuinely sick hypochondriac, the stage was his entire world. He was dedicated to creating his own inimitable performances, supervising those of his fellow players, scripting a stream of new work for them to act in and generally guiding the fortunes of his company in the face of the bitter professional jealousy of rivals, the hostility of churchmen, doctors and others in positions of power, and a royal patronage that could be as unpredictable as it was enthusiastic. The traces, and indeed the scars, of this intensive involvement in the daily rough and tumble of theatrical activity are everywhere apparent in his plays and provide the surest way of approaching one of the acknowledged comic geniuses of European theatre whose work can nonetheless seem strangely tame, even banal, on the translated page.

It was in June 1643 that Molière signed a contract of association with nine friends, in all probability a mixture of erstwhile amateurs like himself and struggling young professionals (among them three members of the remarkable Béjart family, Madeleine, Geneviève and Joseph), and launched his first theatrical enterprise on borrowed capital. But the so-called Illustre Théâtre, a name chosen to match their youthful aspirations, soon proved an inglorious failure. Opening their first Paris season in a rented tennis-court on 1 January 1644 they withstood the competition of the two established professional companies, at the Hôtel de Bourgogne and the Théâtre du Marais, for less than two years. By August 1645 Molière was in prison for debt. Before the end of the year he and the surviving members of the company had left Paris to join a group of strolling players led by the actor Dufresne. Thereafter his life was to divide itself into two roughly equal but quite distinct phases: first came a period of virtually continuous touring in the provinces for the best part of thirteen years; then a speculative return to Paris in October 1658 and the subsequent fourteen-year success story. The success was compounded with freaks of fortune, conflict with many enemies and a herculean expenditure of energy in the writing and mounting of plays, but it brought Molière wealth, renown, a permanent theatre of his own and the ultimate cachet of playing regularly at court as one of Louis XIV's accredited entertainers. This latter phase is by far the better chronicled, not least in the meticulous daily register of performances kept by his right-hand man in the company, La Grange, but the earlier phase is arguably the more interesting in that it taught Molière his craft and allowed him to flex his theatrical muscles to the full. It was of a touring company that he first emerged clearly as director and for the same company that he wrote his first plays. Moreover, throughout their peregrinations across a wide area of southern France, from Bordeaux, Toulouse and Carcassonne in the west to Avignon, Lyon and Grenoble in the east, it was a question of travelling light over rough country roads, of playing on a fit-up stage with few material or technical resources, of adjusting to a mixture of environments and to constantly changing audiences. Having digested the lesson of the Illustre Théâtre, namely that he did not possess the qualities then expected of a tragic actor, Molière now learnt how to please an audience with his remarkable gifts as a comedian and to capitalize on them by evolving a distinctive comic method as a playwright. Thereafter he was only to refine and elaborate it, never to abandon it: it is at the heart of his densest, most opaque comedies like *Tartuffe* and *The Misanthrope* just as it informs the early touring farces or a limpid farcical confection like *The Tricks of Scapin* towards the end of his career.

The method is intensely physical in a number of ways, one that takes account of the physical possibilities and limitations of stage performance. First and foremost it relies heavily on the physical presence of the actor. Without benefit of sophisticated staging the major responsibility for success always falls on the actor, on his ability to use his body to create effect, through movement, gesture, facial expression and voice, his talent for individualizing a character or underlining a comic point by means of physical resources alone. In these circumstances nothing can be overlooked that might be turned to profit, not even physical deformities or afflictions, such as Louis Béjart's limp, which so irritates Harpagon about his servant La Flèche in *The Miser*, or indeed Molière's own hacking cough to which he refers explicitly in the same play and which he undoubtedly used to particularly good purpose some five years later as the hypochondriac before actually dying of it. In fact, the word commonly employed by his contemporaries to describe Molière's acting and that of his company was 'naïf', which we should not take to mean 'natural' (as has sometimes been supposed) but just what it says: forthright, energetic, unfussy, apparently artless in the sense that it was not bound by the rhetorical conventions of delivery and bodily expression that tragic actors then considered necessary and appropriate to the rhetorical devices embedded in the language of tragedy. That Molière's approach to acting was anything but artless, however, is evident from an examination of the infrastructure of his comic dialogue. A clear example is provided by the scene between Marianne and Valère in Act II of *Tartuffe*, where what starts as mutual lovers' pique gets progressively out of hand and forces the two young people into ever more extreme positions of disaffection, physically separated from each other on opposite sides of the stage, with Valère at the door and threatening to walk out for ever – a situation which the maid-servant Dorine has to resolve by dragging the two together again, bodily as well as verbally. Here the dialogue is a blueprint for contrived movement in performance or, more accurately, it represents a kind of chemical precipitate of movement, the fossilized remains of the movement choreographed by Molière for this scene, as perfectly preserved in the text as in the stage directions of any French's acting edition.

The scene in question is of course a standard lovers' quarrel of the type that abounds in commedia dell'arte – from which Molière may well have lifted it – and it serves as little more than an agreeable diversion from the main thrust of the action, adding nothing to the play's central concerns and not shedding much light on human nature except to show that love can, in its way, make people behave as short-sightedly and unreasonably as any other obsession. However, the same principle may be seen at work time and time again in Molière's writing, where the patterning of dialogue (in terms of phrasing, cadence, length of line, repetition and so forth) reflects a patterning of physical movement on stage and at the same time contributes to our understanding of situation or character, or both. Two consecutive scenes in the first act of *The Hypochondriac* demonstrate this very clearly. In the first the contrast between Angélique's fulsome praises of the young man she has recently met and Toinette's curt, even monosyllabic replies invite a distinction in action and posture while underlining Toinette's realism as opposed to Angélique's romantic singlemindedness, which is thus gently satirized out of her own mouth. There follows Argan's announcement of the offer of marriage he has received, entailing a lengthy comic quid pro quo between father and daughter before the misunderstanding is revealed and Angélique dissolves into speechlessness and tears. Coming to her mistress's rescue, Toinette then proceeds to pit her realism against Argan's obsession with his own health, which is so extreme as to determine his choice of a doctor's son as a suitable husband for his daughter. This confrontation of attitudes is exquisitely paralleled in the cross-talk repartee, rising to a climax in which Argan is forced by the momentum of the exchange to make his classic outburst of petulance:

TOINETTE: I can read you like a book. You are naturally good.
ARGAN: I am not naturally good. I can be absolutely horrid when I want to.

This is a perfectly logical remark for Argan to make in the context, as the whole exchange between them has been constructed on the pattern of his denying each one of Toinette's assertions in turn, yet it is a piece of absurd self-condemnation for him to claim that he can act against his nature if he tries hard enough. Toinette's use of the word 'naturally' is no accident: in a comic flash we are made to see the opposition between natural fatherly feeling and the rigid posture of tyranny that Argan aims to assume at will, and the idea preposterous enough to make us laugh while at the same time recognizing the danger of such wilful abuse of authority. Having taken this progression as far as it will go Molière now changes tack. Argan, in full flow as strident paterfamilias, has the ground cut from under him by Toinette's reminder that he is supposed to be unwell and, rediscovering the illness which the heavy-father act has momentarily dispelled from his mind, he relapses into the earlier pose again, wailing in the pitiable voice of the invalid at death's door: 'I absolutely command her to take the husband I decide,' to which Toinette replies, doubtless imitating his tone of voice as well as his phrasing: 'And I absolutely forbid her to do it.' Out of this a further progression emerges and builds to a climax. Stung as much by her parody as by the retort itself, Argan suddenly regains all his strength, enough to yell at her and then to pass from mere invective to action. Now that Molière has wrung every ounce of potential from the verbal exchange between them the comic routine bursts out of words into deeds and Argan, oblivious once more to his feigned illness, proceeds to chase Toinette round the room, attempting to batter her with his walking-stick. Yet again the respective patterns of dialogue and movement echo each other palpably, Argan thrusting with his imprecations as with his stick, Toinette parrying with her replies as she dodges him with her nimble steps, until after one last despairing lunge Argan misses and collapses in a heap, alternately appealing to his daughter for help, threatening her and bemoaning his imaginary complaint.

The whole sequence is a perfect illustration of Ramon Fernandez's astute observation that in Molière's plays 'the dialogue (with, likewise, the structure of the scenes) resembles dance figures, and even more closely the figures of calisthenics'.* The artfulness of the scene's design even extends to the contrivance of a mirror-image effect between its two main sections, with Toinette taking the initiative and Argan doing the answering back in the first and then reversing roles in the second. However, these two consecutive scenes contribute far more than a skilfully shaped, highly entertaining episode to the plot; they provide one elaboration of the play's theme, which is not hypochondria as such but enslavement to the mystique of medical science and the social repercussions of

*R. Fernandez: *Molière. The Man Seen Through the Plays*, p. 24.

such an obsession. Hitherto, Argan has been shown as an individual sufferer, pathetically deluding himself about his state of health: the very first scene of the play significantly presents him alone on stage, marooned in the chair in which he spends most of his life, apostrophizing his apothecary's bills and the phoney but euphonious remedies they prescribe; the second shows him haranguing his servant for inadequate attention to his personal needs. Only when Angélique appears and he uses his condition to browbeat and to control her future conduct for selfish ends does the threat to others become apparent, a danger to the family unit that is further explored in the scenes immediately following, with the calculating second wife, Béline, who positively encourages his hypochondria, and the crooked lawyer she has summoned to redraft his will in her favour. All these scenes are very funny, and very physically so, but such hilarity should not blind us to their thematic relevance which is as great as that of the (textually) more recognizable satire on medical practice and the exploiters of hypochondria in Act II.

The opening scenes of *The Hypochondriac* also illustrate very clearly two other recurrent features of Molière's comic method. The first is the supreme importance of stage properties and particular elements of dress or personal props used by the actors. Either because of the unsophisticated stages to which he grew accustomed during his apprentice years in the provinces or because of the reductive effect of a preoccupation with unity of place in the accepted dramatic theory of the day, the settings of Molière's plays are almost immaterial to the action that takes place within them: apart from providing a necessary location for events and a number of entrances, exits and strategic acting positions, they make no real theatrical statement. This is, however, more than offset by the eloquence of props. Few are mentioned in the text or in Molière's infrequent stage directions but, when used, they have a function which goes well beyond mere stage dressing. When the curtain rises on Argan we see an apparently healthy man in night-cap and fur cloak hunched in an armchair over a table littered with apothecary's bills and counters which he is using to tot up the sums of money involved. As an image this neatly encapsulates the subject of the play, and the coexistence of the last two items in particular serves to reflect Argan's twin concerns, which are to loom so large in the subsequent action: maximum medical attention at minimum financial cost. They even show that he has a quantitative, almost mechanistic, attitude to physical well-being, as is confirmed moments later in his monologue when he discovers that he has taken fewer injections and doses of medicine this month than he did last and attributes to this the fact that he feels less well. Later in the act when he flails about him with his stick in attempting to strike Toinette, it is clear that the very aid without which he says he is unable to walk and which has acted as a prop to his illness has now become an aggressive weapon, just as his illness itself has become a weapon to be used against his daughter: the stick is, as it were, an objective correlative of his incipient tyranny. Similarly, in the following scene, a precise equation is suggested between Béline's excessive solicitude, engulfing her husband in cushions, and her covert desire to inhibit his freedom of action in legal matters and thereby make herself sole beneficiary of his estate. Toinette's placing of the last cushion over his face, as if to smother him altogether, shows what she thinks of the whole procedure; it is an act of physical sarcasm. At its best Molière's treatment of stage props is truly emblematic.

The other characteristic device in these scenes is the part played by the maidservant, Toinette. As in most traditional comedy, Molière's servants follow a partly supportive, partly subversive line towards their masters. They are invariably on the side of young love, especially when it is pitted against parental authority or financial interest, as it usually is. In particular, his soubrettes act as a foil to their overbearing, self-opinionated masters, endeavouring in vain to bring home to them the enormity of their behaviour or exercising their superior intelligence and resourcefulness to mitigate its worst effects. Toinette is no exception, but what is particularly illuminating about her long altercation with Argan in this act is that it represents her first and last attempt to reason him out of his folly, an attempt which predictably fails; hereafter she will resort to theatrical stratagems. In almost the last line of the act in Molière's original she proposes to seek the help of 'my lover, Punchinello' from the commedia dell'arte, an obvious cue for the *intermède* which follows, but one that also looks forward to her own comic turn in Act III where she masquerades as a doctor specializing in hopeless cases and the scarcely less improbable charade a little later in which Argan, at her instigation, pretends to be dead and is thus permitted to discover the true feelings towards him of his deceitful wife and his affectionate daughter. It is therefore a farcical scheme of hers that brings about the resolution of the action and ensures the triumph of love, not the lengthy homily of Béralde, the 'reasonable man', whose support for Angélique and distrust of Béline cut as little ice with his brother as his condemnation of conventional medicine and its opportunistic practitioners. In fact, the importance of the *raisonneur* in Molière's plays has often been exaggerated by literary critics, probably because what these characters say tends to bulk large on the printed page and appears to expound a cogent viewpoint; it has even been assumed that they are an embodiment of Molière's own 'philosophy'. What seems much more likely is that the *raisonneur* is there to supply a necessary antithesis to the entrenched prejudice of the leading character, to prompt the latter into revealing the full extent of his absurdity, to provide a source of dramatic conflict and comic potential – in other words, for predominently theatrical purposes. Certainly, their views can at times be highly questionable: Béralde's dismissal of medical science is as excessive and as pig-headed as his brother's infatuation with it, while in *The Misanthrope*, for example, it is not difficult to imagine circumstances which would make Philinte's acquiescence in the corruption of society and advocacy of compromise and discretion appear more contemptible than Alceste's intransigence. In the last analysis what perhaps serves best to undermine the importance of the *raisonneurs* is their ineffectuality: their rational arguments have little or no impact on the action or on the folly of their respective antagonists. Significantly, Béralde, seeing that Argan's obsession with doctors is impervious to reason, finally resolves to indulge it and his last act is to take a leaf out of Toinette's book: he gets a troupe of actors to perform the concluding *intermède*, a mock graduation ceremony in which Argan is received into the learned company of doctors and becomes the ideal, self-sufficient medical unit, both patient and doctor in one – the apotheosis of his affliction. Molière seems to accept that his plays are ultimately powerless to unseat the eternal follies of mankind and that they are at their weakest in this respect when at their most reasonable. What Toinette says about her own mock-doctor act, in a passage whose double meanings are virtually impossible to capture in translation,

'It's an old trick, but it might just work.' *

could even be taken to epitomise his view of comedy as a whole.

Molière's admiration for the commedia dell'arte is of course legendary and the evidence of it is plain to see in almost all his work. Admittedly he owed an inescapable debt to the native farce tradition as well, with its robust, often lewd antics and its preoccupation with conjugal strife of one kind or another, which enjoyed a brief period of metropolitan glory in the 1620s and early 1630s in the inspired collaboration of three ageing farceurs, Hugues Guéru, Robert Guérin and Henri Legrand (better known as Gaultier-Garguille, Gros-Guillaume and Turlupin), whom Molière could well have seen at the Hôtel de Bourgogne in his youth and whose last great heir, Julien Bedeau (known as Jodelet), was a member of his company in 1659-1660, appearing alongside the author in *Les Précieuses ridicules* in a part specially written for him. But the single most pervasive influence on Molière was undoubtedly the Italian commedia, which was very well known and fairly ubiquitous in France in Molière's day. The presence of commedia troupes in Paris is recorded as early as the mid-16th century and the welcome accorded to them was given additional impetus by the enthusiasm of successive French kings (or their Italian consorts) from the time of Henri II to that of Louis XIV. As a boy Molière could have seen them playing on open-air stages at the annual fair at the Saint-Germain market where the family business had a couple of stalls and he must have encountered them quite frequently during his travels as an actor in the southern provinces, particularly after 1651 when his company seems to have used Lyon (the residence of its patron, the Prince de Conti) as a quasi-permanent base. Lyon, then at the upstream limit of navigation in the Rhône, was an important gateway to France for road and river traffic alike, and therefore wide open to transalpine influences of all kinds, including that of the commedia dell'arte. This

* 'C'est une imagination burlesque. Cela sera peut-être plus heureux que sage.'

familiarity was renewed and reinforced as soon as Molière arrived in Paris in 1658. He was commanded to give a private performance for Louis XIV and his court at the Louvre and decided to follow up a coolly received rendering of Corneille's *Nicomède* with a farce of his own entitled *Le Docteur amoureux,* in which, according to his first biographer Grimarest, 'he was quite confident of success . . . for his company were trained to extemporize short comic pieces in the manner of the Italian actors'.* The young king so enjoyed it that he gave permission for the unknown provincial company to present public performances at the nearby Salle du Petit-Bourbon, where they opened on 2 November calling themselves the Troupe de Monsieur after the king's brother, whose protection they had obtained. The theatre was already occupied by a highly successful Italian company playing on the customary days (Sunday, Tuesday and Friday), so Molière had to be content with the remainder of the week, but the company was led by Tiberio Fiorelli, one of the greatest of all commedia players in the rôle of Scaramouche, and the experience of sharing a theatre and performing in alternation with so masterly an exponent of the tradition clearly had a profound effect on Molière. His enemies were even to suggest that his whole style of acting was but a pale copy of Scaramouche, as slavishly imitated as the comic plots that he took from commedia scenarios. The evident jealousy behind such attacks deters us from taking them at face value, but there is a grain of truth in them. Molière was deeply impressed by the agility and disciplined movement of the Italian actors, by their powers of mime, their vocal range and controlled patter, and in the case of Fiorelli (who, unlike previous Scaramouches, played without a mask) the mobility and expressiveness of his features. Much of this was absorbed or, more accurately perhaps, transmuted into his own comic acting and, thanks to his industry as director and company manager, into that of his fellows. La Grange, from his privileged position, saw it thus: 'He was inimitable both in the way in which he created the characters of his comedies, and in the unique quality that he endowed them with, through the precision of his actors' performance. Facial expressions, gesture, movement, everything showed a shrewdness of

* *La Vie de M. de Molière* (1705) ed. G. Mongrédien, pp. 99–100.

observation and an attention to detail never before seen on the Paris stage.'*

Similarly, his borrowings from the commedia, in terms of basic intrigue, *lazzi* or *burle* and character masks, are unmistakable and in some cases, in the choice of names for instance, openly acknowledged, as if it were a conscious act of homage. Many of his characters, be they masters, servants, lovers, doctors or other purveyors of jargon, bear the imprint of commedia 'masks'; although they do not wear actual masks (at least not after Mascarille of *L'Etourdi*), it is as if they wore invisible, psychological masks, fixing them into certain attitudes. What Molière does with them, however, is entirely his own. He will, for example, annex to them particular word-patterns or catch-phrases, like Orgon's 'Poor fellow' in *Tartuffe*, Harpagon's 'But without a dowry' in *The Miser*, or perhaps most hilariously of all Géronte's 'What the devil did he want to go in the galley for?' in *The Tricks of Scapin*. Or he will force us to laugh at the very fixity of the mask only to let it slip and reveal something quite different underneath, making us laugh still more at the incompatibility between what a character wishes or professes to be and what he is. Or again, he will multiply the masks, have them put on or dropped at will and contrive that the assumption of one shall reveal the truth behind another. Yet this persistent, and at times complex, exercise in rôle-playing is conducted with such vigour and such effortless ease as never to compromise the sense of real life in a situation or a character.

The process can be seen at work admirably in a play like *Tartuffe*, where the idea of the mask has obvious relevance and manifold possibilities, particularly of course in the central characters of the holy man, Tartuffe, and his zealous disciple, Orgon. But it extends to other characters and other parts of the play, as for instance the scene in Act II where Dorine and Marianne are discussing Orgon's plan to marry his daughter to Tartuffe rather than to Valère, whom she loves and to whom he has previously promised her. Dorine, sensing that her mistress is not sufficiently determined to defy her father's command, tries to arouse her indignation by assuming the mask of complaisance, pretending that she approves of Orgon's scheme and that Marianne probably deserves a monster like Tar-

*Preface to Molière, *Œuvres* (1682).

tuffe. The imposture has the desired effect of strengthening Marianne's resolve and the mask adopted by one person brings out the true feelings of another. Orgon himself is depicted as someone who has lost all sense of proportion and judgment, who has been reduced to the status of a mindless puppet by his infatuation with Tartuffe and the man's display of piety. Out of this delusion comes his determination to act in a way that is consistent with it, even to the extent of overlooking or denying the truth. Our first sight of him in Act I shows him to be oblivious to Dorine's graphic account of his wife's real illness, muttering instead an absurd litany about the sufferings he fondly imputes to Tartuffe; and later, when he insists that his daughter marry Tartuffe and say she is glad to do so, it is

Because I am resolved it shall be true.
That it's my wish should be enough for you.

Neither his wife nor his brother can understand the change that has overcome him since Tartuffe's arrival and the lengths to which his wilful assumption of a different persona may go are highlighted when he tries to explain it to Cléante, condemning himself out of his own mouth in the process:

Yes, thanks to him I'm a changed man indeed.
Under his tutelage my soul's been freed
From earthly loves, and every human tie:
My mother, children, brother, and wife could die,
And I'd not feel a moment's pain.

In what is tantamount to a Freudian slip he is unable to find words adequately to express his adulation of Tartuffe other than to say, 'He is a man who . . . a man who . . . an excellent man.' We are warned in advance and the irony is subsequently not lost on us.

Molière's treatment of Tartuffe is even more skilful. We see the man manipulating one mask after another. His first appearance – shrewdly delayed until Act III – is a deliberately theatrical entry, making it obvious to us that he is giving a performance, putting on a public show of piety for anyone who is listening, and we soon discover that the professed revulsion for Dorine's over-exposed bosom is nothing but a sham. In the first conversation with Elmire, the wife of his host and benefactor, his ostensible solicitude for her welfare and reputation gradually stands revealed as sensual lust. When Elmire resists the attempted seduction and expresses surprise at such conduct in a man of God he quickly readjusts the mask and presents his lust as a display of spiritual love and respect, though the true nature of his passion keeps peeping through, and the ultimate masquerade of virtue concealing depravity is offered to Elmire when he suggests that an affair with him would be perfectly safe as 'men of my sort' are above suspicion. As soon as Damis attempts to unmask him to his father Tartuffe quickly dons another mask and escapes through a crafty display of repentance and mortification, even pushing Orgon to the limit by inviting him to distrust the appearance of such virtuous self-abasement and thus destroying any possible case against him. One is irresistibly reminded of Eisenring's classic exposition of the ploy in Max Frisch's *The Fire Raisers*: 'the best way of all of deceiving people is to tell them the plain, unvarnished truth. Strangely enough they never believe it.' Here Molière inverts the whole procedure to which the audience has by now grown accustomed and has real infamy worn self-consciously, as a mask to imply the existence of a non-existent virtue underneath.

The result of this first threat to his security is that Tartuffe ends up in a stronger position than before, with an even more enslaved Orgon begging him to stay and resolving to make Tartuffe his heir, upon which the latter's comment is a superbly hypocritical 'let the will of Heaven be done'. Finally the come-uppance required by comedy is achieved by the singularly apt expedient of Elmire, the virtuous wife, adopting a mask of wantonness with Tartuffe: a fairly standard device of Molière's, the villain hoist by his own petard and the mask assumed voluntarily, as with Argan's shamming dead, in order to uncover the truth. Throughout the second tête-à-tête between them the offended husband Orgon is concealed beneath a table to overhear Tartuffe's reaction – a familiar farcical situation, perhaps, but one in which it is not too fanciful to see the table as a larger version of the mask he has worn hitherto, an emblem of his wooden insensitivity to all but his spiritual mentor. As he emerges from under it all pretence to spirituality falls from him and genuine human wrath is laid bare. Interestingly, Orgon then goes on to attack Tartuffe with as much blind vehemence as he has used to defend him earlier in the play, as extreme now in his condemnation of godliness as he has been in his adulation. Despite the apparent volte-face Orgon is unchanged by his experience: he represents a clever study in fanaticism. That this was the play's centre of interest for Molière is suggested by the fact that he himself played the part of Orgon, not Tartuffe.

The traditional comic impulse tends to set up a manichean division in characters between villains and fools, those who deceive others and those who deceive themselves. In these terms Tartuffe is presented unmistakably as a villain, so that his final unmasking makes for a resolution which is ethically and socially satisfying (even though engineered by a *deus ex machina* in the shape of the monarch) as well as theatrically entertaining. But in a play like *The Misanthrope* the opposition between mask and face, between what the eponymous character professes to be and what he is, becomes, morally speaking, less clear-cut, and Molière's handling of the opposition reaches its comic maturity (and, some have argued, impinges on tragedy). At face value Alceste would appear to be an idealist, a man who prizes the truth above all things and is determined to speak his mind openly and sincerely on all issues, while his friend Philinte urges restraint and the necessity for compromise, without which civilized social intercourse would be impossible. It is tempting to take Alceste as the hero in more than a merely technical sense, and a romantic view of the play would see it as presenting the dilemma of a noble soul beset by conformism in matters of taste, manners and morality, protesting against the artificiality of contemporary society and the authoritarian spirit of the establishment. However, closer scrutiny will not support such a simplistic reading: what we find, to use W. G. Moore's judicious phrase, is Molière's delight in 'situations in which constructions of the mind are opposed to act and fact'.* For one thing Alceste is nattily dressed in 'green ribbons', which suggests that, despite all his disclaimers, he is a slave to conformity at least in matters of dress. Moreover, when asked for his opinion on Oronte's sonnet and thus faced in person with a challenge to his sincerity, he temporises, speaks obliquely and does his hypocritical best to avoid stating his

*W. G. Moore: *Molière. A New Criticism*, p. 116.

frank opinion for fear of giving offence. So much for sincerity in the real world, we conclude – or conversely, perhaps, that Alceste is capable of being a kinder person in practice than in theory. But there are yet more dimensions to his temperament than this and Molière in effect shows that Alceste's professed attitude of mind is at odds with his true nature. The excessiveness of his concern for sincerity is established from the outset, as are his bad temper, his impetuosity and his sheer wilfulness. The subsequent action of the play progressively reveals the quality of calculation, even fanaticism, that is present in his concern for sincerity. He wants to be singled out, not only to be different from other people but to be seen to be different: what interests him in fact is not so much sincerity itself as the *éclat*, the reputation for being the only sincere person in a corrupt society, which is why he is fundamentally not displeased to find evidence of villainy in others. A genuine idealist, one who was well disposed towards his fellow men, would be saddened to see justice thwarted. On the contrary, when Alceste loses a just lawsuit through bribery of the judges, he first rails eloquently against a corrupt world, eliciting some sympathy from us, but then forfeits it by declining to appeal. Clearly he prefers to be unjustly treated because it confirms him in his misanthropy, it allows him the self-indulgent pleasure of despising the world, the entire human race.

However, it is perhaps through his relationship with Célimène that Alceste is revealed most transparently. His love for her is shown to be quite illogical, for she is the incarnation of those aspects of human nature and social life, like superficiality and deceit, which he professes most to despise. Yet he loves her: neither effort of will nor intellectual disapproval is proof against natural inclination, though he rationalises the anomaly by pretending that he will be able to 'convert' her to his cause, to force her nature as he has forced his own. Of course he wishes his love for her to be remarked upon by other people and predictably enough he intends to be the sole source of happiness and comfort to her. When he discovers her infidelity – the fact that she has several men in tow – he insists that she make a choice between them, and do so publicly, which is symptomatic of his innate preference for 'show'. His final solution is to propose to forgive her provided that she will join him in fleeing Parisian society and virtually abjuring the company of other people. Far from being a mark of love, as he claims, this is a token of his selfish desire to 'colonise' her for his one-man campaign. When she refuses he goes to the opposite extreme of rejecting her completely and transferring the offer to Eliante. His final exit shows him unchanged, impetuous and uncompromising as ever. Molière has used the play to explore an obsession that renders its victim fundamentally unequipped for life in any society: he calls insincerity a mask, yet aspires to put in its place something equally artificial, an inhuman perfection that is no less a mask. When he cannot achieve it he rejects everything else and his last appearance is that of the disillusioned hero *and* petulant fool, preserving the play's tension between sincerity and vanity to the very end.

The Misanthrope is Molière's most open-ended play, the very last remark of Philinte holding out some faint, if forlorn, hope of persuading Alceste to see reason and accept the world as it is. But in the majority of cases reason is an elusive commodity: the end of the play indicates that the central character has learnt nothing, leaving him, if anything, more firmly entrenched in his folly than ever before. In a sense, Molière's endings accomplish little of substance, apart from the union of young lovers and the necessary discomfiture of a villain, both of which are brought about in a deliberately factitious manner, in accord with what Louis Jouvet called 'the purest, most exquisite theatrical convention'. Similarly the plots themselves are flimsy and fairly predictable, because Molière's interest does not lie in telling a story as such but in elaborating a theme: he will take an abstract human trait like avarice or sexual chauvinism or fanaticism, embody it in a character, and situate that character in a succession of scenes which subject him to pressures, show him responding to stimuli in a way that illuminates the abstraction from various angles and in its various ramifications. The articulation of those scenes into a plausibly coherent whole does not seem to have been a matter of overriding concern with Molière any more than their uniformity of tone. Some adequately satisfy the demands of psychological realism, some emphatically do not; some maintain an air of narrative probability, some are extravagant or fantastical; some are content with the idiom of conversational dialogue, some employ devices normally associated with opera, musical comedy, revue, burlesque and of course knockabout farce: the mode fluctuates wildly from the acceptably realistic to the utterly unrealistic, at times even within a single scene. This heterogeneity contributes to an ultimate ambivalence in Molière's plays, for while he clearly conceived of them as comedies and intended them above all to provoke laughter, the subjects which most of them treat with such lightness of touch are nothing if not weighty and the conclusions that they reach, with the main character unchanged by his experiences, exude a comic fatalism that suggests a tragic view of life in their creator (and seems to carry a vestigial echo of those pretensions to tragedy which the public found unacceptable in him both as actor and as playwright). There are moments in his plays when the ambivalence is palpable, like the breathtakingly theatrical scene in *The Miser* where Harpagon, unhinged by the loss of his precious casket, searches for the thief and imagines he has found him when he catches his own arm – which in a luminously metaphorical sense is true since it is his excessive concern for money that has impoverished him, robbed him of all humanity – and then appeals directly to the audience to help him:

If any of you know anything, on bended knees I beg you to tell me. You all look at me and snigger behind your hands. You're all involved in it. Accomplices.

At such moments thought obtrudes in the midst of our laughter: they operate with an audience on a plane where the categories of comedy and tragedy seem to merge in a single perspective of response and incline one to dub Molière, at his most distinctive, an inventor of philosophical slapstick.

The five plays in this collection are a convenient index to the vicissitudes of reception that Molière encountered at the hands of the theatregoing public and to the critical attacks and quarrels that they were apt to provoke. *The School for Wives* was first performed on 26 December 1662 at the Palais-Royal theatre, where it became an immediate and resounding success. Presented at court soon after, on 6 January 1663, it made Louis XIV 'hold his sides' with laughter according to one report. It was printed in the same month and held the boards until the following Christmas, in over 60 performances. Molière played Arnolphe; the part of Agnès, though perhaps modelled on his very young wife Armande Béjart whom he had married only months earlier (in February 1662), was taken by Catherine de Brie. The very success of the play gave rise to attacks from jealous enemies who accused Molière of perpetrating, apart from faults of construction and characterisation, some obscene double-entendres (particularly in the famous 'ribbon' sequence in Act II) and allusions of an irreverent nature (in Arnolphe's ten maxims on marriage). Molière took the novel step of rebutting these accusations in dramatic form in his *Critique of the School for Wives* (presented on 1 June 1663), where Uranie says of Agnès that 'she speaks not a word that isn't perfectly decent in itself and if you wish to understand something else underneath, then you are the one who's making it dirty, not her . . .'. This spirited response led to further attacks on the play's vulgarity and immorality, some in dramatic form, and further counter-attacks (including Molière's own *Impromptu of Versailles*, first performed there for the court on 14 October 1663 and in Paris on 4 November), which kept the quarrel simmering for the rest of the year. All this was unquestionably good for business, especially as Molière eventually came off better than his opponents, but it also served to sour his relations with many influential people and probably prompted the imputations of incest – that Armande was not Madeleine Béjart's youngest sister but her daughter, possibly by Molière himself.

Within a year he found himself embroiled in an even more virulent dispute over *Tartuffe*. Along with two others by Molière, the play was first presented (in three-act form) at Versailles as part of a royal entertainment entitled *Les Plaisirs de L'Ile Enchantée* on 12 May 1664, with Molière as Orgon and Du Croisy as Tartuffe. It is likely that the three acts in question were, to all intents and purposes, the first three acts of the existing text and that Tartuffe was played as a man of the cloth, complete with clerical collar. Either at the discreet suggestion of the king or as a result of the intervention of the Compagnie du Saint-Sacrement, the play was not transferred to Paris for public performance. This did not prevent the publication of a vitriolic pamphlet which denounced Molière as 'a demon made flesh' and his play as 'a crime of divine *lèse-majesté*' aimed at discrediting the church and its curacy of souls. Religious contention was rife in France at the time, particularly over the condemnation of the Jansenists, and it seems probable that Molière may have brought down on his individual head a deal of accumulated wrath against heretics and free-thinkers in general. Perhaps he may even have courted it. At all events his *Don Juan*, staged in 1665, and *The Misanthrope*, staged in 1666, can be interpreted, at least in part, as reflections on the continuing '*Tartuffe* affair'. The play's notoriety, together with private readings of the text, redoubled the desire to see it publicly performed, until in the summer of 1667, almost certainly with the connivance of the king who was piqued by ecclesiastical censure of his illicit 'amours' and perhaps glad to sanction anything that might be construed as anti-Jansenist, it was billed for performance at the Palais-Royal theatre, where it opened on 5 August shortly after Louis's departure for the war in Flanders. It was now in its five-act form, retitled *The Impostor* and toned down in certain particulars (such as the precise nature of Tartuffe's calling). On the very next day it was suppressed by order of the president of the Paris Parlement and this temporal ban was followed on the 11th by a letter from the Archbishop of Paris to all the city's parish priests instructing them to denounce the play from their pulpits and to forbid their parishioners either to perform or to see it under threat of excommunication. Molière immediately addressed an appeal to the king but it was not until 1669, after the 'Peace of the Church' had ostensibly put an end to the Jansenist controversy and restored good relations between the king and Pope Clement IX, that the ban was lifted. Re-opening on 5 February, *Tartuffe* ran for 33 consecutive performances (28 public, 5 private) until the end of the season at Easter and was revived immediately afterwards, subsequently becoming one of the playwright's greatest financial successes; it has remained the most frequently performed of his plays at the Comédie-Française.

The Misanthrope was first staged at the Palais-Royal theatre on 4 June 1666, with Molière in the title rôle, his wife as Célimène, and La Thorillière as Philinte. Initial audience response seems to have been cool, if not unfavourable, and takings began to fall away after the first nine performances. That it was certainly not a failure is borne out by the fact that its first run consisted of 21 consecutive performances and it received 34 performances in all in the course of the year, a reasonable number for that period, though it was occasionally accompanied by a farce as tail-piece. The relative indifference of the public at large was offset by acclaim from critics and the cultivated elite, particularly Boileau for whom Molière was ever to remain the author of *The Misanthrope* and who found it hard to forgive him for the grosser buffooneries in other plays: even one of his adversaries called it 'an inimitable masterpiece'.

The first performance of *The Miser*, with Molière as Harpagon, took place on 9 September 1668 at the Palais-Royal and met with a distinctly frigid reception, Boileau being reportedly the only member of the audience to laugh unreservedly. This apathy is normally attributed to its prose dialogue, which disconcerted spectators who were accustomed to full-length plays in verse. Whatever the reason, the play was withdrawn after only nine performances with dwindling receipts; it fared slightly, but not significantly, better when revived in December and in January 1669 for a further eleven performances in harness with a farce – a standard practice of Molière's for plays enjoying only a moderate success. It was not until after his death that *The Miser* became really popular and it is now the second most frequently performed of his plays at the Comédie-Française.

As is evident from its structure, with a prologue and three *intermèdes* all sung and danced to orchestral accompaniment, *The Hypochondriac* was designed for performance at court: Louis XIV was particularly enamoured of such *divertissements* and Molière had evolved the form of the comedy-ballet expressly to satisfy this predilection. That it was not, in fact, presented at court has been interpreted as the sign of a fall from royal grace by Molière or of some intrigue by Lulli, formerly his collaborator on these entertainments but now his rival for the king's favour. Instead the play was presented at the Palais-Royal on 10 February 1673 at the height of carnival time and Molière spared no expense on its staging or on the engagement of musical talent (to be precise, twelve violinists, seven other musicians and twelve dancers) for the realisation of Charpentier's score. That his confidence in the enterprise was not misplaced is indicated by the size of the takings at the first four performances, but his personal success was to be short-lived. Having declined the advice of his fellow actors to cancel the fourth performance on Friday 17 February because of his state of health, he was seized by a fit of coughing on stage and, while endeavouring to control it, began to spit blood. He carried on until the end of the show, but took to his bed immediately afterwards and died within the hour. Despite the confusion into which the company was thrown they reopened the theatre exactly a week later with *The Misanthrope* and resumed performances of *The Hypochondriac* on the following Friday, with La Thorillière replacing Molière as Argan. There is some uncertainty about the remaining cast for the première, but it seems likely that Armande played Angélique and Jeanne Beauval Toinette. The play was eventually presented before the king at Versailles on 21 August 1674, more than a year after the amalgamation of Molière's company with that of the Théâtre du Marais, but with the irony still undimmed of Argan's mock death and Toinette's ascription of all his trouble to 'the lungs'.

DONALD ROY

The School for Wives

Comedy in Five Acts

Translated into English verse by Richard Wilbur

CHARACTERS

ARNOLPHE, also known as MONSIEUR DE LA SOUCHE
AGNES, an innocent young girl, Arnolphe's ward
HORACE, Agnès' lover, Oronte's son
ALAIN, a peasant, Arnolphe's manservant
GEORGETTE, a peasant woman, servant to Arnolphe
CHRYSALDE, a friend of Arnolphe's
ENRIQUE, Chrysalde's brother-in-law, Agnès' father
ORONTE, Horace's father and Arnolphe's old friend
A NOTARY

The scene is a square in a provincial city.

*This translation first staged by the Phoenix Theatre,
New York, on 16 February 1971.*

Act One

CHRYSALDE So, you're resolved to give this girl your
                hand?

ARNOLPHE Tomorrow I shall marry her, as planned.

CHRYSALDE We're quite alone here, and we can discuss
                Your case with no one overhearing us:
                Shall I speak openly, and as your friend?
                This plan – for your sake – troubles me no
                   end.
                I must say that, from every point of view,
                Taking a wife is a rash step for you.

ARNOLPHE You think so? Might it be, friend, that you
                 base
                Your fears for me upon your own sad case?
                Cuckolds would have us think that all who
                 marry
                Aquire a set of horns as corollary.

CHRYSALDE Fate gives men horns, and fate can't be
                 withstood;
                To fret about such matters does no good.
                What makes me fear for you is the way you
                 sneer
                At every luckless husband of whom you hear.
                You know that no poor cuckold, great or
                 small,
                Escapes your wit; you mock them one and all,
                And take delight in making boisterous
                 mention
                Of all intrigues which come to your attention.

ARNOLPHE Why not? What other town on earth is known
For husbands so long-suffering as our own?
Can we not all too readily bring to mind
Ill-treated dupes of every shape and kind?
One husband's rich; his helpmeet shares the
    wealth
With paramours who cuckold him by stealth;
Another, with a scarcely kinder fate,
Sees other men heap gifts upon his mate –
Who frees his mind of jealous insecurity
By saying that they're tributes to her purity.
One cuckold impotently storms and rants;
Another mildly bows to circumstance,
And when some gallant calls to see his spouse,
Discreetly takes his hat and leaves the house.
One wife, confiding in her husband, mentions
A swain who bores her with his warm
    attentions;
The husband smugly pities the poor swain
For all his efforts – which are *not* in vain.
Another wife explains her wealthy state
By saying that she's held good cards of late;
Her husband thanks the Lord and gives Him
    praise,
Not guessing what bad game she truly plays.
Thus, all about us, there are themes for wit;
May I not, as an observer, jest a bit?
May I not laugh at –

CHRYSALDE   Yes; but remember, do,
That those you mock may someday mock at
    you.
Now, I hear gossip, I hear what people say
About the latest scandals of the day,
But whatsoever I'm told, I never hear it
With wicked glee and in a gloating spirit.

I keep my counsel; and though I may
   condemn
Loose wives, and husbands who put up with
   them,
And though I don't propose, you may be sure,
To endure the wrongs which some weak men
   endure,
Still, I am never heard to carp and crow,
For tables have been known to turn, you
   know,
And there's no man who can predict, in
   fact,
How in such circumstances he would act.
In consequence, should fate bestow on me
What all must fear, the horns of cuckoldry,
The world would treat me gently, I believe,
And be content with laughing up its sleeve.
There are, in fact, some kindly souls who
   might
Commiserate me in my sorry plight.
But you, dear fellow, with you it's not the
   same.
I say once more, you play a dangerous game.
Since with your jeering tongue you plague the
   lives
Of men who are unlucky in their wives,
And persecute them like a fiend from Hell,
Take care lest someday you be jeered as well.
If the least whisper about your wife were
   heard,
They'd mock you from the housetops, mark
   my word.
What's more —

ARNOLPHE   Don't worry, friend; I'm not a fool.
I shan't expose myself to ridicule.

I know the tricks and ruses, shrewd and sly,
Which wives employ, and cheat their husbands
    by;
I know that women can be deep and clever;
But I've arranged to be secure forever:
So simple is the girl I'm going to wed
That I've no fear of horns upon my head.

CHRYSALDE Simple! You mean to bind yourself for life –

ARNOLPHE A man's not simple to take a simple wife.
Your wife, no doubt, is a wise, virtuous
    woman,
But brightness, as a rule, is a bad omen,
And I know men who've undergone much
    pain
Because they married girls with too much
    brain.
I want no intellectual, if you please,
Who'll talk of nothing but her Tuesday teas,
Who'll frame lush sentiments in prose and
    verse
And fill the house with wits, and fops, and
    worse,
While I, as her dull husband, stand about
Like a poor saint whose candles have gone
    out.
No, keep your smart ones; I've no taste for
    such.
Women who versify know far too much.
I want a wife whose thought is not sublime,
Who has no notion what it is to rhyme,
And who, indeed, if she were asked in some
Insipid parlour game, 'What rhymes with
    drum?'
Would answer in all innocence, 'A fife.'
In short, I want an unaccomplished wife,

And there are four things only she must
    know:
To say her prayers, love me, spin, and sew.

CHRYSALDE Stupidity's your cup of tea, I gather.

ARNOLPHE I'd choose an ugly, stupid woman rather
Than a great beauty who was over-wise.

CHRYSALDE But wit and beauty –

ARNOLPHE   Virtue is what I prize.

CHRYSALDE But how can you expect an idiot
To know what's virtuous and what is not?
Not only would it be a lifelong bore
To have a senseless wife, but what is more,
I hardly think you could depend upon her
To guard her husband's forehead from
    dishonour.
If a bright woman breaks her wedding vow,
She knows what she is doing, anyhow;
A simpleton, however, can commit
Adultery without suspecting it.

ARNOLPHE To that fine argument I can but say
What Pantagruel says in Rabelais:
Preach and harangue from now till
    Whitsuntide
Against my preference for a stupid bride;
You'll be amazed to find, when you have
    ceased,
That I've not been persuaded in the least.

CHRYSALDE So be it.

ARNOLPHE   Each man has his own design
For wedded bliss, and I shall follow mine.
I'm rich, and so can take a wife who'll be
Dependent, in the least respect, on me –
A sweet, submissive girl who cannot claim
To have brought me riches or an ancient
    name.

The gentle, meek expression which she wore
Endeared Agnès to me when she was four;
Her mother being poor, I felt an urge
To make the little thing my ward and charge,
And the good peasant woman was most
    pleased
To grant my wish, and have her burden eased.
In a small convent, far from the haunts of
    man,
The girl was reared according to my plan:
I told the nuns what means must be employed
To keep her growing mind a perfect void,
And, God be praised, they had entire success.
As a grown girl, her simple-mindedness
Is such that I thank Heaven for granting me
A bride who suits my wishes to a T.
She's out of the convent now, and since my
    gate
Stands open to society, early and late,
I keep her here, in another house I own,
Where no one calls, and she can be alone:
And, to protect her artless purity,
I've hired two servants as naïve as she.
I've told you all this so that you'll understand
With what great care my marriage has been
    planned;
And now, to clinch my story, I invite
You, my dear friend, to dine with her tonight;
I want you to examine her, and decide
Whether or not my choice is justified.

CHRYSALDE Delighted.

ARNOLPHE   You'll gain, I think, a lively sense
Of her sweet person and her innocence.

CHRYSALDE As to her innocence, what you've related
Leaves little doubt —

ARNOLPHE   My friend, 't was understated.
           Her utter naïveté keeps me in stitches.
           I laugh so that I almost burst my breeches.
           You won't believe this, but the other day
           She came and asked me in a puzzled way,
           And with a manner touchingly sincere,
           If children are begotten through the ear.

CHRYSALDE I'm happy indeed, Monsieur Arnolphe –

ARNOLPHE   For shame!
           Why must you always use my former name?

CHRYSALDE I'm used to it, I suppose. What's more, I find
           That *de la Souche* forever slips my mind.
           What in the devil has persuaded you
           To debaptize yourself at forty-two
           And take a lordly title which you base
           On an old tree stump at your country place?

ARNOLPHE The name La Souche goes with the property
           And sounds much better than Arnolphe to me.

CHRYSALDE But why forsake the name your fathers bore
           For one that's fantasy and nothing more?
           Yet lately that's become the thing to do.
           I am reminded – no offence to you –
           Of a peasant named Gros-Pierre, who owned a small
           Parcel of land, an acre or so in all;
           He dug a muddy ditch around the same
           And took Monsieur de l'Isle for his new name.

ARNOLPHE I can dispense with stories of that kind.
           My name is de la Souche, if you don't mind.
           I like that title, and it's mine by right;
           To address me otherwise is impolite.

CHRYSALDE Your new name is employed by few, at best;
           Much of your mail, I've noticed, comes addressed –

ARNOLPHE I don't mind that, from such as haven't been
    told;
  But you –

CHRYSALDE   Enough. Enough. No need to scold.
  I hereby promise that, at our next meeting,
  'Good day, Monsieur de la Souche' shall be
    my greeting.

ARNOLPHE Farewell. I'm going to knock now on my door
  And let them know that I'm in town once
    more.

CHRYSALDE (*aside, as he moves off*).
  The man's quite mad. A lunatic, in fact.

ARNOLPHE (*alone*).
  On certain subjects he's a trifle cracked.
  It's curious to see with what devotion
  A man will cling to some quite pointless
    notion.
  Ho, there!

SCENE TWO: Alain, Georgette, Arnolphe

ALAIN (*within*).
      Who's knocking?

ARNOLPHE   Ho! (*Aside:*)
  They'll greet me, after
  My ten days' trip, with smiles and happy
    laughter.

ALAIN Who's there?

ARNOLPHE   It's I.

ALAIN   Georgette.

GEORGETTE   What?

ALAIN   Open

below!

GEORGETTE   Do it yourself!

ALAIN   You do it!

GEORGETTE   I won't go!

ALAIN   I won't go either!

ARNOLPHE   Gracious servants, these,

To leave me standing here. Ho! If you please!

GEORGETTE   Who's there?

ARNOLPHE   Your master.

GEORGETTE   Alain!

ALAIN   What?

GEORGETTE   Go lift the latch!

It's him.

ALAIN   You do it.

GEORGETTE   I'm getting the fire to catch.

ALAIN   I'm keeping the cat from eating the canary.

ARNOLPHE   Whoever doesn't admit me, and in a hurry,

Will get no food for four long days, and more.

Aha!

GEORGETTE   I'll get it; what are you coming for?

ALAIN   Why you, not me? That's a sneaky trick to

play!

GEORGETTE   Get out of the way.

ALAIN   No, *you* get out of the way.

GEORGETTE   I want to open that door.

ALAIN   I want to, too.

GEORGETTE   You won't.

ALAIN   And you won't either.

GEORGETTE   Neither will you.

ARNOLPHE   (*to himself*).

My patience with these two amazes me.

ALAIN   I've opened the door, Sir.

GEORGETTE   No, I did it! See?

'T was I.

ALAIN   If only the master, here, weren't present,
              I'd –

ARNOLPHE (*receiving a blow from* ALAIN, *meant for*
              GEORGETTE).
         Blast you!

ALAIN   Sorry, Sir.

ARNOLPHE   You clumsy peasant!

ALAIN It's her fault too, Sir.

ARNOLPHE   Both of you, stop this row.
         I want to question you; no nonsense, now.
         Alain, is everything going smoothly here?

ALAIN Well, Sir, we're –
         (ARNOLPHE *removes* ALAIN'*s hat;* ALAIN
              obliviously puts it back on.)
                     Well, Sir –
         (*Hat business again.*)
                     Well, thank God, Sir, we're –
         (ARNOLPHE *removes* ALAIN'*s hat a third time,
              and throws it to the ground.*)

ARNOLPHE Where did you learn, you lout, to wear a hat
         While talking to your master? Answer me
              that.

ALAIN You're right, I'm wrong.

ARNOLPHE   Now, have Agnès come down.
         (*To* GEORGETTE:)
         Was she unhappy while I was out of town?

GEORGETTE Unhappy? No.

ARNOLPHE   No?

GEORGETTE   Yes.

ARNOLPHE   For what reason, then?

GEORGETTE Well, she kept thinking you'd be back again,
         So that whatever passed on the avenue –
         Horse, mule, or ass – she thought it must be
         you.

SCENE THREE: Agnès, Alain, Georgette, Arnolphe

ARNOLPHE Her needlework in hand! That's a good sign.
Well, well, Agnès, I'm back and feeling fine.
Are you glad to see me?

AGNES   Oh, yes, Sir; thank the Lord.

ARNOLPHE I'm glad to see you too, my little ward.
I take it everything has been all right?

AGNES Except for the fleas, which bothered me last
night.

ARNOLPHE Well, there'll be someone soon to drive them
away.

AGNES I shall be glad of that.

ARNOLPHE   Yes, I dare say.
What are you making?

AGNES   A headpiece, Sir, for me;
Your nightshirts are all finished, as you'll see.

ARNOLPHE Excellent. Well, upstairs with you, my dear:
I'll soon come back and see you, never fear;
There's serious talk in which we must engage.
(*Exeunt all but* ARNOLPHE.)
O learned ladies, heroines of the age,
Gushers of sentiment, I say that you,
For all your verse, and prose, and billets-
doux,
Your novels, and your bright accomplishments,
Can't match this good and modest ignorance.

SCENE FOUR : Horace, Arnolphe

ARNOLPHE What does her lack of money matter to me?
What matters – Oh! What's this? No! Can it be?
I'm dreaming. Yes, it's he, my dear friend's boy.
Well!

HORACE Sir!

ARNOLPHE Horace!

HORACE Arnolphe!

ARNOLPHE Ah, what a joy!
How long have you been in town?

HORACE Nine days.

ARNOLPHE Ah, so.

HORACE I called at your house, in vain, a week ago.

ARNOLPHE I'd left for the country.

HORACE Yes, you were three days gone.

ARNOLPHE How quickly children grow! How time rolls on!
I am amazed that you're so big and tall.
I can remember when you were –
(*He makes a gesture of measuring from the floor.*)
that small.

HORACE Yes, time goes by.

ARNOLPHE But come now, tell me of
Oronte, your father, whom I esteem and love:
How's my old friend? Still spry and full of zest?
In all that's his, I take an interest.

Alas, it's four years since I talked with him,
And we've not written in the interim.

HORACE Seigneur Arnolphe, he's spry enough for two;
He gave me this little note to give to you,
But now he writes me that he's coming here
Himself, for reasons not entirely clear.
Some fellow-townsman of yours, whom you
    may know,
Went to America fourteen years ago;
He's come back rich. Do you know of whom I
    speak?

ARNOLPHE No. Did the letter give his name?

HORACE   Enrique.

ARNOLPHE No . . . no . . .

HORACE   My father writes as if I ought
To recognize that name, but I do not.
He adds that he and Enrique will soon set out
On some great errand that he's vague about.

ARNOLPHE I long to see your father, that sterling man.
I'll welcome him as royally as I can.
(*He reads the note from* ORONTE.)
A friendly letter needn't flatter and fuss.
All this politeness is superfluous,
And even without his asking, I'd have desired
To lend you any money you required.

HORACE I'll take you at your word, Sir. Can you
    advance
Fifty *pistoles* or so, by any chance?

ARNOLPHE I'm grateful that you let me be of use,
And what you ask, I happily can produce.
Just keep the purse.

HORACE   Here –

ARNOLPHE   Forget the I.O.U.
Now, how does our town impress you? Tell
    me, do.

HORACE It's rich in people, sublime in architecture,
    And full of fine amusements, I conjecture.

ARNOLPHE There's pleasure here for every taste; and
     those
    The world calls gallants, ladies' men, or beaux
    Find here the sport on which their hearts are
     set,
    Since every woman in town's a born coquette.
    Our ladies, dark or fair, are pliant creatures;
    Their husbands, likewise, have permissive
     natures;
    Oh, it's a capital game; it's often made
    Me double up with mirth to see it played.
    But you've already broken some hearts, I'd
     guess;
    Have you no gallant conquest to confess?
    Cuckolds are made by such as you, young
     man,
    And looks like yours buy more than money
     can.

HORACE Well, since you ask, I'll lay my secrets bare.
    I *have* been having a covert love affair –
    Which, out of friendship, I shall now unveil.

ARNOLPHE Good; good; 't will be another rakish tale
     Which I can put into my repertory.

HORACE Sir, I must beg you: don't divulge my story.

ARNOLPHE Of course not.

HORACE   As you know, Sir, in these matters,
    One word let slip can leave one's hopes in
     tatters.
    To put the business plainly, then, my heart's
    Been lost to a lady dwelling in these parts.
    My overtures, I'm very pleased to state,
    Have found her ready to reciprocate,
    And not to boast, or slur her reputation,

I think I'm in a hopeful situation.

ARNOLPHE *(laughing)*.
Who is she?

HORACE A girl whose beauty is past telling,
And yonder red-walled mansion is her
    dwelling.
She's utterly naïve, because a blind
Fool has sequested her from humankind,
And yet, despite the ignorance in which
He keeps her, she has charms that can
    bewitch;
She's most engaging, and conveys a sense
Of sweetness against which there's no defence.
But you, perhaps, have seen this star of love
Whose many graces I'm enamoured of.
Her name's Agnès.

ARNOLPHE *(aside)*.
            Oh, death!

HORACE   The man, I hear,
Is called La Zousse, La Source, or something
    queer;
I didn't pay much attention to the name.
He's rich, I gather, but his wits are lame,
And he's accounted a ridiculous fellow.
D'you know him?

ARNOLPHE *(aside)*.
        Ugh, what a bitter pill to swallow!

HORACE I said, do you know him?

ARNOLPHE   Yes, I do, in a way.

HORACE He's a dolt, isn't he?

ARNOLPHE   Oh!

HORACE   What? What did you say?
He is, I take it. And a jealous idiot, too?
An ass? I see that all they said was true.
Well, to repeat, I love Agnès, a girl

Who is, to say the least, an orient pearl,
And it would be a sin for such a treasure
To be subjected to that old fool's pleasure.
Henceforth, my thoughts and efforts shall
    combine
To break his jealous hold and make her
    mine;
This purse, which I made bold to borrow, will
    lend
Me great assistance toward that worthy end.
As you well know, whatever means one tries,
Money's the key to every enterprise,
And this sweet metal, which all men hanker
    for,
Promotes our conquests, whether in love or
    war.
You look disturbed, Sir; can it be that you
Do not approve of what I mean to do?

ARNOLPHE No; I was thinking –

HORACE   I'm boring you. Farewell, then.
I'll soon drop by, to express my thanks again.

ARNOLPHE (*to himself*).
How could this happen –

HORACE (*returning*).
                      Again, Sir, I entreat
You not to tell my secret; be discreet.
(*He leaves.*)

ARNOLPHE (*to himself*).
I'm thunderstruck.

HORACE (*returning*).
                   Above all, don't inform
My father; he might raise a dreadful storm.
(*He leaves.*)

ARNOLPHE (*he expects* HORACE *to return again; that not
    occurring, he talks to himself*).

Oh! . . . What I've suffered during this
   conversation!
No soul has ever endured such agitation.
With what imprudence, and how hastily
He came and told the whole affair . . . to me!
He didn't know I'd taken a new title;
Still, what a rash and blundering recital!
I should, however, have kept myself in hand,
So as to learn what strategy he's planned,
And prompt his indiscretion, and discover
To what extent he has become her lover.
Come, I'll catch up with him; he can't be far;
I'll learn from him precisely how things are.
Alas, I'm trembling; I fear some further blow;
One can discover more than one wants to
   know.

Act Two

SCENE ONE: Arnolphe

ARNOLPHE It's just as well, no doubt, that I should fail
To catch him – that I somehow lost his trail:
For I could not have managed to dissemble
The turbulence of soul which makes me
    tremble;
He'd have perceived my present near-despair,
Of which it's best that he be unaware.
But I'm not one to be resigned and meek
And turn this little fop the other cheek.
I'll stop him; and the first thing I must do
Is find out just how far they've gone, those
    two.
This matter involves my honour, which I
    prize;
The girl's my wife already, in my eyes;
If she's been tarnished, I am covered with
    shame,
And all she's done reflects on my good name.
Oh, why did I take that trip? Oh, dear, oh,
    dear.
(*He knocks at his door.*)

SCENE TWO: Alain, Georgette, Arnolphe

ALAIN Ah! *This* time, Sir –
ARNOLPHE   Hush! Both of you come here:
This way, this way. Come, hurry! Do as you're
    told!

GEORGETTE You frighten me; you make my blood run
cold.

ARNOLPHE So! In my absence, you have disobeyed me!
The two of you, in concert, have betrayed
me!

GEORGETTE (*falling on her knees*).
Don't eat me, Sir; don't eat me alive, I beg.

ALAIN (*aside*).
I'd swear some mad dog's nipped him in the
leg.

ARNOLPHE (*aside*).
Oof! I'm too tense to speak. I'd like to shed
These blasted clothes. I'm burning up with
dread.
(*To* ALAIN *and* GEORGETTE:)
You cursèd scoundrels, while I was gone you
let
A man into this house –
(*To* ALAIN, *who has made a move to flee:*)
No, not just yet!
Tell me at once – (*To* GEORGETTE:) Don't
move! I want you two
To tell me – Whff! I mean to learn from you –
(ALAIN *and* GEORGETTE *rise and try to escape.*)
If anyone moves, I'll squash him like a louse.
Now tell me, how did that man get into my
house?
Well, speak! Come, hurry. Quickly! Time is
fleeting!
Let's hear it! Speak!

ALAIN *and*
GEORGETTE (*falling on their knees*).
Oh! Oh!

GEORGETTE My heart's stopped
beating.

ALAIN I'm dying.

ARNOLPHE (*aside*).

I'm sweating, and I need some air.
I must calm down: I'll walk around the
    square.
When I saw him in his cradle, I didn't know
What he'd grow up and do to me. O woe!
Perhaps – yes, I'd do better to receive
The truth from her own lips, I now believe.
I'll mute my rage as well as I know how;
Patience, my wounded heart! Beat softly, now!
(*To* ALAIN *and* GEORGETTE *:*)
Get up, and go inside, and call Agnès.
Wait. (*Aside:*) That way her surprise would be
    the less.
They'd warn her of my anger, I don't doubt.
I'd best go in myself and bring her out.
(*To* ALAIN *and* GEORGETTE *:*)
Wait here.

SCENE THREE: *Alain, Georgette*

GEORGETTE God help us, but his rage is terrible!
The way he glared at me – it was unbearable.
He's the most hideous Christian I ever did
    see.

ALAIN He's vexed about that man, as I said he'd be.

GEORGETTE But why does he order us, with barks and
    roars,
Never to let the mistress go outdoors?
Why does he want us to conceal her here
From all the world, and let no man come
    near?

ALAIN It's jealousy that makes him treat her so.

GEORGETTE But how did he get like that, I'd like to know?

ALAIN It comes of being jealous, I assume.

GEORGETTE But why is he jealous? Why must he rage and
fume?

ALAIN Well, jealousy – listen carefully, Georgette –
Is a thing – a thing – which makes a man
upset,
And makes him close his doors to everyone.
I'm going to give you a comparison,
So that you'll clearly understand the word.
Suppose you were eating soup, and it
occurred
That someone tried to take what you were
eating:
Wouldn't you feel like giving him a beating?

GEORGETTE Yes, I see that.

ALAIN   Then grasp this, if you can.
Womankind is, in fact, the soup of man,
And when a man perceives that others wish
To dip their dirty fingers into his dish,
His temper flares, and bursts into a flame.

GEORGETTE Yes. But not everybody feels the same.
Some husbands seem to be delighted when
Their wives consort with fancy gentlemen.

ALAIN Not every husband is the greedy kind
That wants to have it all.

GEORGETTE   If I'm not blind,
He's coming back.

ALAIN   It's he; your eyes are keen.

GEORGETTE He's scowling.

ALAIN   That's because he's feeling mean.

SCENE FOUR: Arnolphe, Alain, Georgette

ARNOLPHE (*aside*).
    A certain Greek presumed once to advise
    The great Augustus, and his words were wise:
    When you are vexed, he said, do not forget,
    Before you act, to say the alphabet,
    So as to cool your temper, and prevent
    Rash moves which later on you might repent.
    In dealing with Agnès, I have applied
    That counsel, and I've bidden her come
       outside,
    Under the pretext of a morning stroll,
    So that I can relieve my jangled soul
    By seeking dulcetly to draw her out
    And learn the truth, and put an end to doubt.
    (*Calling:*) Come out, Agnès. (*To* ALAIN *and*
      GEORGETTE:*) Go in.

SCENE FIVE: Arnolphe, Agnès

ARNOLPHE   The weather's mild.
  AGNES Oh, yes.
ARNOLPHE   Most pleasant.
  AGNES   Indeed!
ARNOLPHE   What news, my child?
  AGNES The kitten died.

ARNOLPHE   Too bad, but what of that?
                All men are mortal, my dear, and so's a cat.
                While I was gone, no doubt it rained and
                    poured?
AGNES   No.
ARNOLPHE   You were bored, perhaps?
AGNES   I'm never bored.
ARNOLPHE During my ten days' absence, what did you
                    do?
AGNES   Six nightshirts, I believe; six nightcaps, too.
ARNOLPHE (*after a pause*).
                My dear Agnès, this world's a curious thing.
                What wicked talk one hears, what gossiping!
                While I was gone, or so the neighbours claim,
                There was a certain strange young man who
                    came
                To call upon you here, and was received.
                But such a slander's not to be believed,
                And I would wager that their so-called news –
AGNES   Heavens! Don't wager; you'd be sure to lose.
ARNOLPHE What! Is it true, then, that a man –
AGNES   Oh, yes.
                In fact, he all but lived at this address.
ARNOLPHE (*aside*).
                That frank reply would seem to demonstrate
                That she's still free of guile, at any rate.
                (*Aloud:*)
                But I gave orders, Agnès, as I recall,
                That you were to see no one, no one at all.
AGNES   I disobeyed you, but when I tell you why,
                You'll say that you'd have done the same as I.
ARNOLPHE Perhaps; well, tell me how this thing occurred.
AGNES   It's the most amazing story you ever heard.
                I was sewing, out on the balcony, in the
                    breeze,

When I noticed someone strolling under the
    trees.
It was a fine young man, who caught my eye
And made me a deep bow as he went by.
I, not to be convicted of a lack
Of manners, very quickly nodded back.
At once, the young man bowed to me again.
I bowed to him a second time, and then
It wasn't very long until he made
A third deep bow, which I of course repaid.
He left, but kept returning, and as he
    passed,
He'd bow, each time, more gracefully than the
    last,
While I, observing as he came and went,
Gave each new bow a fresh acknowledgment.
Indeed, had night not fallen, I declare
I think that I might still be sitting there,
And bowing back each time he bowed to me,
For fear he'd think me less polite than he.

ARNOLPHE Go on.

AGNES   Then an old woman came, next day,
And found me standing in the entryway.
She said to me, 'May Heaven bless you, dear,
And keep you beautiful for many a year.
God, who bestowed on you such grace and
    charm,
Did not intend those gifts to do men harm,
And you should know that there's a heart
    which bears
A wound which you've inflicted unawares.'

ARNOLPHE (*aside*).
    Old witch! Old tool of Satan! Damn her hide!

AGNES 'You say I've wounded somebody?' I cried.
'Indeed you have,' she said. 'The victim's he

Whom yesterday you saw from the balcony.'
'But how could such a thing occur?' I said;
'Can I have dropped some object on his head?'
'No,' she replied, 'your bright eyes dealt the
    blow;
Their glances are the cause of all his woe.'
'Good heavens, Madam,' said I in great
    surprise,
'Is there some dread contagion in my eyes?'
'Ah, yes, my child,' said she. 'Your eyes
    dispense,
Unwittingly, a fatal influence:
The poor young man has dwindled to a shade;
And if you cruelly deny him aid,
I greatly fear,' the kind old woman went on,
'That two days more will see him dead and
    gone.'
'Heavens,' I answered, 'that would be sad
    indeed.
But what can I do for him? What help does he
    need?'
'My child,' said she, 'he only asks of you
The privilege of a little interview;
It is your eyes alone which now can save him,
And cure him of the malady they gave him.'
'If that's the case,' I said, 'I can't refuse;
I'll gladly see him, whenever he may choose.'

ARNOLPHE (*aside*).

O 'kind old woman'! O vicious sorceress!
May Hell reward you for your cleverness!

AGNES And so I saw him, which brought about his
    cure.
You'll grant I did the proper thing, I'm
    sure.
How could I have the conscience to deny

The succour he required, and let him die –
I, who so pity anyone in pain,
And cannot bear to see a chicken slain?

ARNOLPHE (*aside*).

It's clear that she has meant no wrong, and I
Must blame that foolish trip I took, whereby
I left her unprotected from the lies
That rascally seducers can devise.
Oh, what if that young wretch, with one bold
    stroke,
Has compromised her? That would be no
    joke.

AGNES What's wrong? You seem a trifle irritated.
Was there some harm in what I just related?

ARNOLPHE No, but go on. I want to hear it all.
What happened when the young man came to
    call?

AGNES Oh, if you'd seen how happy he was, how
    gay,
And how his sickness vanished right away,
And the jewel-case he gave me – not to forget
The coins he gave to Alain and to Georgette,
You would have loved him also, and you too –

ARNOLPHE And when you were alone, what did he do?

AGNES He swore he loved me with a matchless
    passion,
And said to me, in the most charming fashion,
Things which I found incomparably sweet,
And never tire of hearing him repeat,
So much do they delight my ear, and start
I know not what commotion in my heart.

ARNOLPHE (*aside*).

O strange interrogation, where each reply
Makes the interrogator wish to die!
(*To* AGNES:)

Besides these compliments, these sweet
  addresses,
Were there not also kisses, and caresses?

AGNES Oh, yes! He took my hands, and kissed and
  kissed
Them both, as if he never would desist.

ARNOLPHE And did he not take – something else as well?
(*He notes that she is taken aback.*)
Agh!

AGNES   Well, he –

ARNOLPHE   Yes?

AGNES   Took –

ARNOLPHE   What?

AGNES   I dare not tell.
I fear that you'll be furious with me.

ARNOLPHE No.

AGNES   Yes.

ARNOLPHE   No, no.

AGNES   Then promise not to be.

ARNOLPHE I promise.

AGNES   He took my – oh, you'll have a fit.

ARNOLPHE No.

AGNES   Yes.

ARNOLPHE   No, no. The devil! Out with it!
What did he take from you?

AGNES   He took –

ARNOLPHE (*aside*).

                 God save me!

AGNES He took the pretty ribbon that you gave me.
Indeed, he begged so that I couldn't resist.

ARNOLPHE (*taking a deep breath*).
Forget the ribbon. Tell me: once he'd
  kissed
Your hands, what else did he do, as you
  recall?

AGNES Does one do other things?

ARNOLPHE   No, not at all;
But didn't he ask some further medicine
For the sad state of health that he was in?

AGNES Why, no. But had he asked, you may be sure
I'd have done anything to speed his cure.

ARNOLPHE (*aside*).
I've got off cheap this once, thanks be to God;
If I slip again, let all men call me clod.
(*To* AGNES:)
Agnès, my dear, your innocence is vast;
I shan't reproach you; what is past is past.
But all that trifler wants to do – don't doubt
    it –
Is to deceive you, and then boast about it.

AGNES Oh, no. He's often assured me otherwise.

ARNOLPHE Ah, you don't know how that sort cheats and
    lies.
But do grasp this: to accept a jewel-case,
And let some coxcomb praise your pretty face,
And be complaisant when he takes a notion
To kiss your hands and fill you with
    'commotion'
Is a great sin, for which your soul could die.

AGNES A sin, you say! But please, Sir, tell me why.

ARNOLPHE Why? Why? Because, as all authority states,
It's just such deeds that Heaven abominates.

AGNES Abominates! But why should Heaven feel so?
It's all so charming and so sweet, you know!
I never knew about this sort of thing
Till now, or guessed what raptures it could
    bring.

ARNOLPHE Yes, all these promises of love undying,
These sighs, these kisses, are most gratifying,
But they must be enjoyed in the proper way;

	One must be married first, that is to say.
AGNES	And once you're married, there's no evil in it?
ARNOLPHE	That's right.
AGNES	Oh, let me marry, then, this minute!
ARNOLPHE	If that's what you desire, I feel the same;
	It was to plan your marriage that I came.
AGNES	What! Truly?
ARNOLPHE	Yes.
AGNES	How happy I shall be!
ARNOLPHE	Yes, wedded life will please you, I foresee.
AGNES	You really intend that we two –
ARNOLPHE	Yes, I do.
AGNES	Oh, how I'll kiss you if that dream comes true!
ARNOLPHE	And I'll return your kisses, every one.
AGNES	I'm never sure when people are making fun.
	Are you quite serious?
ARNOLPHE	Yes, I'm serious. Quite.
AGNES	We're to be married?
ARNOLPHE	Yes.
AGNES	But when?
ARNOLPHE	Tonight.
AGNES	*(laughing).*
	Tonight?
ARNOLPHE	Tonight. It seems you're moved to laughter.
AGNES	Yes.
ARNOLPHE	Well, to see you happy is what I'm after.
AGNES	Oh, Sir, I owe you more than I can express!
	With him, my life will be pure happiness!
ARNOLPHE	With whom?
AGNES	With . . . him.
ARNOLPHE	With *him!* Well, think again.
	You're rather hasty in your choice of men.
	It's quite another husband I have in mind;
	And as for 'him', as you call him, be so kind,
	Regardless of his pitiable disease,

As never again to see him, if you please.
When next he calls, girl, put him in his place
By slamming the door directly in his face;
Then, if he knocks, go up and drop a brick
From the second-floor window. That should
   do the trick.
Do you understand, Agnès? I shall be hidden
Nearby, to see that you do as you are bidden.

AGNES Oh, dear, he's so good-looking, so –

ARNOLPHE   Be still!

AGNES I just won't have the heart –

ARNOLPHE   Enough; you will.
Now go upstairs.

AGNES   How can you –

ARNOLPHE   Do as I say.
I'm master here; I've spoken; go, obey.

Act Three

ARNOLPHE Yes, I'm most pleased; it couldn't have gone
better.
By following my instructions to the letter,
You've put that young philanderer to flight:
See how wise generalship can set things right.
Your innocence had been abused, Agnès;
Unwittingly, you'd got into a mess,
And, lacking my good counsel, you were well
Embarked upon a course which leads to Hell.
Those beaux are all alike, believe you me:
They've ribbons, plumes, and ruffles at the
knee,
Fine wigs, and polished talk, and brilliant
teeth,
But they're all scales and talons underneath –
Indeed, they're devils of the vilest sort,
Who prey on women's honour for their sport.
However, owing to my watchful care,
You have emerged intact from this affair.
The firm and righteous way in which you
threw
That brick at him, and dashed his hopes of
you,
Persuades me that there's no cause to delay
The wedding which I promised you today.
But first, it would be well for me to make
A few remarks for your improvement's sake.
(*To* ALAIN, *who brings a chair:*)
I'll sit here, where it's cool.

(*To* GEORGETTE:) Remember, now –

GEORGETTE Oh, Sir, we won't forget again, I vow.

That young man won't get round us any
   more.

ALAIN I'll give up drink if he gets through that door.

Anyway, he's an idiot; we bit

Two coins he gave us, and they were
   counterfeit.

ARNOLPHE Well, go and buy the food for supper, and
   then

One of you, as you're coming home again,

Can fetch the local notary from the square.

Tell him that there's a contract to prepare.

SCENE TWO: *Arnolphe, Agnès*

ARNOLPHE (*seated*).

Agnès, stop knitting and hear what I have to
   say.

Lift up your head a bit, and turn this way.

(*Putting his finger to his forehead:*)

Look at me *there* while I talk to you, right
   there,

And listen to my every word with care.

My dear, I'm going to wed you, and you
   should bless

Your vast good fortune and your happiness.

Reflect upon your former low estate,

And judge, then, if my goodness is not great

In raising you, a humble peasant lass,

To be a matron of the middle class,

To share the bed and the connubial bliss

Of one who's shunned the married state till this,

Withholding from a charming score or two
The honour which he now bestows on you.
Be ever mindful, Agnès, that you would be,
Without this union, a nonentity;
And let that thought incline your heart to
    merit
The name which I shall lend you, and to
    bear it
With such propriety that I shall never
Regret my choice for any cause whatever.
Marriage, Agnès, is no light matter; the role
Of wife requires austerity of soul,
And I do not exalt you to that station
To lead a life of heedless dissipation.
Yours is the weaker sex, please realize;
It is the beard in which all power lies,
And though there are two portions of
    mankind,
Those portions are not equal, you will find:
One half commands, the other must obey;
The second serves the first in every way;
And that obedience which the soldier owes
His general, or the loyal servant shows
His master, or the good child pays his sire,
Or the stern abbot looks for in the friar,
Is nothing to the pure docility,
The deep submission and humility
Which a good wife must ever exhibit toward
The man who is her master, chief, and lord.
Should he regard her with a serious air,
She must avert her eyes, and never dare
To lift them to his face again, unless
His look should change to one of tenderness.
Such things aren't understood by women
    today,

But don't let bad example lead you astray.
Don't emulate those flirts whose indiscretions
Are told all over town at gossip-sessions,
Or yield to Satan's trickery by allowing
Young fops to please you with their smiles and
    bowing.
Remember that, in marrying, I confide
To you, Agnès, my honour and my pride;
That honour is a tender, fragile thing
With which there can be no light dallying;
And that all misbehaving wives shall dwell
In ever-boiling cauldrons down in Hell.
These are no idle lessons which I impart,
And you'll do well to get them all by heart.
Your soul, if you observe them, and abjure
Flirtation, will be lily-white and pure;
But deviate from honour, and your soul
Will forthwith grow as vile and black as coal;
All will abhor you as a thing of evil,
Till one day you'll be taken by the Devil,
And Hell's eternal fire is where he'll send you –
From which sad fate may Heaven's grace
    defend you.
Make me a curtsey. Now then, just as a
    novice,
Entering the convent, learns by heart her
    office,
So, entering wedlock, you should do the same.
(*He rises.*)
I have, in my pocket, a book of no small fame
From which you'll learn the office of a wife.
'T was written by some man of pious life.
Study his teaching faithfully, and heed it.
Here, take the book; let's hear how well you
    read it.

AGNES (*reading*).

The Maxims of Marriage
or
The Duties of a Married Woman,
Together with Her Daily Exercises.

First Maxim:
A woman who in church has said
She'll love and honour and obey
Should get it firmly in her head,
Despite the fashions of the day,
That he who took her for his own
Has taken her for his bed alone.

ARNOLPHE I shall explain that; doubtless you're
perplexed.
But, for the present, let us hear what's next.
AGNES (*continuing*).

Second Maxim:
She needs no fine attire
More than he may desire
Who is her lord and master.
To dress for any taste but his is vain;
If others find her plain,
'T is no disaster.

Third Maxim:
Let her not daub her face
With paint and patch and powder-base
And creams which promise beauty on the
label.
It is not for their husbands' sake
But vanity's, that women undertake
The labours of the dressing table.

Fourth Maxim:

Let her be veiled whenever she leaves the
    house,
So that her features are obscure and dim.
If she desires to please her spouse,
She must please no one else but him.

Fifth Maxim:

Except for friends who call
To see her husband, let her not admit
    Anyone at all.
    A visitor whose end
Is to amuse the wife with gallant wit
Is *not* the husband's friend.

Sixth Maxim:

To men who would confer kind gifts upon
    her,
She must reply with self-respecting nays.
Not to refuse would to be court dishonour.
Nothing is given for nothing nowadays.

Seventh Maxim:

She has no need, whatever she may think,
Of writing table, paper, pen, or ink.
In a proper house, the husband is the one
To do whatever writing's to be done.

Eighth Maxim:

At those licentious things
    Called social gatherings,
Wives are corrupted by the worldly crowd.
Since, at such functions, amorous plots are
    laid
    And married men betrayed,
    They should not be allowed.

Ninth Maxim:

Let the wise wife, who cares for her good
name,
Decline to play at any gambling game.
In such seductive pastimes wives can lose
Far more than coins, or bills, or I.O.U.'s.

Tenth Maxim:

It is not good for wives
To go on gay excursions,
Picnics, or country drives.
In all such light diversions,
No matter who's the host,
The husbands pay the most.

Eleventh Maxim –

ARNOLPHE Good. Read the rest to yourself. I'll clarify
Whatever may confuse you, by and by.
I've just recalled some business I'd forgot;
'T will only take a moment, like as not.
Go in, and treat that precious book with care.
If the notary comes, tell him to have a chair.

SCENE THREE: Arnolphe

ARNOLPHE What could be safer than to marry her?
She'll do and be whatever I prefer.
She's like a lump of wax, and I can mould her
Into what shape I like, as she grows older.
True, she was almost lured away from me,
Whilst I was gone, through her simplicity;
But if one's wife must have some
imperfection,

It's best that she should err in that direction.
Such faults as hers are easy to remove:
A simple wife is eager to improve,
And if she has been led astray, a slight
Admonitory talk will set her right.
But a clever wife's another kettle of fish:
One's at the mercy of her every wish;
What she desires, she'll have at any cost,
And reasoning with her is labour lost.
Her wicked wit makes virtues of her crimes,
Makes mock of principle, and oftentimes
Contrives, in furtherance of some wicked
    plan,
Intrigues which can defeat the shrewdest man.
Against her there is no defence, for she's
Unbeatable at plots and strategies,
And once she has resolved to amputate
Her husband's honour, he must bow to fate.
There's many a decent man could tell that
    story.
But that young fool will have no chance to
    glory
In my disgrace: he has too loose a tongue,
And that's a fault of Frenchmen, old or
    young.
When they are lucky in a love affair,
To keep the secret's more than they can bear;
A foolish vanity torments them, till
They'd rather hang, by Heaven, than be still.
What but the spells of Satan could incline
Women to favour men so asinine?
But here he comes; my feelings must not show
As I extract from him his tale of woe.

SCENE FOUR: Horace, Arnolphe

HORACE I've just been at your house, and I begin
To fear I'm fated never to find you in.
But I'll persist, and one day have the joy –

ARNOLPHE Ah, come, no idle compliments, my boy.
All this fine talk, so flowery and so polished,
Is something I'd be glad to see abolished.
It's a vile custom: most men waste two-
thirds
Of every day exchanging empty words.
Let's put our hats on, now, and be at ease.
Well, how's your love life going? Do tell me,
please.
I was a bit distrait when last we met,
But what you told me I did not forget:
Your bold beginnings left me much
impressed,
And now I'm all agog to hear the rest.

HORACE Since I unlocked my heart to you, alas,
My hopes have come to an unhappy pass.

ARNOLPHE Oh, dear! How so?

HORACE   Just now – alas – I learned
That my beloved's guardian has returned.

ARNOLPHE That's bad.

HORACE   What's more, he's well aware that we've
Been meeting secretly, without his leave.

ARNOLPHE But how could he so quickly find that out?

HORACE I don't know, but he has, beyond a doubt.
I went at my usual hour, more or less,
To pay my homage to her loveliness,

And found the servants changed in attitude.
˙They barred my way; their words and looks
    were rude.
'Be off!' they told me, and with no good
    grace
They slammed the door directly in my face.

ARNOLPHE Right in your face!

HORACE   Yes.

ARNOLPHE   Dreadful. Tell me more.

HORACE I tried to reason with them through the door,
But whatsoever I said to them, they cried,
'The master says you're not to come inside.'

ARNOLPHE They wouldn't open it?

HORACE   No. And then Agnès,
On orders from her guardian, as one could
    guess,
Came to her window, said that she was sick
Of my attentions, and threw down a brick.

ARNOLPHE A brick, you say!

HORACE   A brick; and it wasn't small.
Not what one hopes for when one pays a
    call.

ARNOLPHE Confound it! That's no mild rebuff, my lad.
I fear your situation's pretty bad.

HORACE Yes, that old fool's return has spoiled my
    game.

ARNOLPHE You have my deepest sympathy; it's a shame.

HORACE He's wrecked my plans.

ARNOLPHE   Oh, come; you've lost some ground,
But some means of recouping will be
    found.

HORACE With a little inside help, I might by chance
Outwit this jealous fellow's vigilance.

ARNOLPHE That should be easy. The lady, as you say,
Loves you.

HORACE   Indeed, yes.

ARNOLPHE   Then you'll find a way.

HORACE   I hope so.

ARNOLPHE   You must not be put to flight
By that ungracious brick.

HORACE   Of course you're right.
I knew at once that that old fool was back
And secretly directing the attack.
But what amazed me (you'll be amazed as
    well)
Was something else she did, of which I'll tell –
A daring trick one wouldn't expect to see
Played by a girl of such simplicity.
Love is indeed a wondrous master, Sir,
Whose teaching makes us what we never
    were,
And under whose miraculous tuition
One suddenly can change one's disposition.
It overturns our settled inclinations,
Causing the most astounding transformations:
The miser's made a spendthrift overnight,
The coward valiant, and the boor polite;
Love spurs the sluggard on to high endeavour,
And moves the artless maiden to be clever.
Well, such a miracle has changed Agnès.
She cried, just now, with seeming bitterness,
'Go! I refuse to see you, and don't ask why;
To all your questions, here is my reply!' –
And having made that statement, down she
    threw
The brick I've mentioned, and a letter, too.
Note how her words apply to brick *and* letter:
Isn't that fine? Could any ruse be better?
Aren't you amazed? Do you see what great
    effect

True love can have upon the intellect?
Can you deny its power to inspire
The gentlest heart with fortitude and fire?
How do you like that trick with the letter, eh?
A most astute young woman, wouldn't you
    say?
As for my jealous rival, isn't the role
He's played in this affair extremely droll?
Well?

ARNOLPHE   Yes, quite droll.

HORACE   Well, laugh, if that's the case!
    (ARNOLPHE *gives a forced laugh.*)
My, what a fool! He fortifies his place
Against me, using bricks for cannon balls,
As if he feared that I might storm the walls;
What's more, in his anxiety he rallies
His two domestics to repulse my sallies;
And then he's hoodwinked by the girl he
    meant
To keep forever meek and innocent!
I must confess that, though this silly man's
Return to town has balked my amorous plans,
The whole thing's been so comical that I find
That I'm convulsed whenever it comes to
    mind.
You haven't laughed as much as I thought you
    would.

ARNOLPHE (*with a forced laugh*).
I beg your pardon; I've done the best I could.

HORACE But let me show you the letter she wrote, my
    friend.
What her heart feels, her artless hand has
    penned
In the most touching terms, the sweetest
    way,

With pure affection, purest naïveté;
Nature herself, I think, would so express
Love's first awakening and its sweet distress.

ARNOLPHE (*aside*).

Behold what scribbling leads to! It was quite
Against my wishes that she learned to write.

HORACE (*reading*).

I am moved to write to you, but I am much at a loss as to how to begin. I have thoughts which I should like you to know of; but I don't know how to go about telling them to you, and I mistrust my own words. I begin to perceive that I have always been kept in a state of ignorance, and so I am fearful of writing something I shouldn't, or of saying more than I ought. In truth, I don't know what you have done to me, but I know that I am mortally vexed by the harsh things I am made to do to you, that it will be the most painful thing in the world to give you up, and that I would be happy indeed to be yours. Perhaps it is rash of me to say that; but in any case I cannot help saying it, and I wish that I could have my desire without doing anything wrong. I am constantly told that all young men are deceivers, that they mustn't be listened to, and that all you have said to me is mere trickery; I assure you, however, that I have not yet been able to think that of you, and your words so touch me that I cannot believe them false. Please tell me frankly what you intend; for truly, since my own intentions are blameless, it would be very wicked of you to deceive me, and I think that I should die of despair.

ARNOLPHE (*aside*).
          The bitch!
  HORACE   What's wrong?
ARNOLPHE   Oh, nothing: I was sneezing.
  HORACE Was ever a style so amiable, so pleasing?
          Despite the tyranny she's had to bear,
          Isn't her nature sweet beyond compare?
          And is it not a crime of the basest kind
          For anyone to stifle such a mind,
          To starve so fine a spirit, and to enshroud
          In ignorance a soul so well-endowed?
          Love has begun to waken her, however,
          And if some kind star favours my endeavour
          I'll free her from that utter beast, that
              black
          Villain, that wretch, that brute, that
              maniac –
ARNOLPHE Good-bye.
  HORACE   What, going?
ARNOLPHE   I've just recalled that I'm
          Due somewhere else in a few minutes' time.
  HORACE Wait! Can you think of someone who might
              possess
          An entrée to that house, and to Agnès?
          I hate to trouble you, but do please lend
          Whatever help you can, as friend to friend.
          The servants, as I said, both man and maid,
          Have turned against my cause, and can't be
              swayed.
          Just now, despite my every blandishment,
          They eyed me coldly, and would not relent.
          I had, for a time, the aid of an old woman
          Whose talent for intrigue was superhuman;
          She served me, at the start, with much
              success,

But died four days ago, to my distress.
Don't you know someone who could help me
out?

ARNOLPHE I don't; but you'll find someone, I don't
doubt.

HORACE Farewell, then, Sir. You'll be discreet, I know.

SCENE FIVE: *Arnolphe*

ARNOLPHE In that boy's presence, what hell I undergo,
Trying to hide my anguish from his eye!
To think that an innocent girl should prove so
sly!
Either she's fooled me, and never *was* naïve,
Or Satan's just now taught her to deceive.
That cursèd letter! I wish that I were dead.
Plainly that callow wretch has turned her
head,
Captured her mind and heart, eclipsed me
there,
And doomed me to distraction and despair.
The loss of her entails a double hell:
My honour suffers, and my love as well.
It drives me mad to see myself displaced,
And all my careful planning gone to waste.
To be revenged on her, I need but wait
And let her giddy passion meet its fate;
The upshot can't be anything but bad.
But oh, to lose the thing one loves is sad.
Good Lord! To rear her with such calculation,
And then fall victim to infatuation!
She has no funds, no family, yet she can dare

Abuse my lavish kindness and my care;
And what, for Heaven's sake, is my reaction?
In spite of all, I love her to distraction!
Have you no shame, fool? Don't you resent
   her crimes?
Oh, I could slap my face a thousand times!
I'll go inside for a bit, but only to see
How she will face me after her treachery.
Kind Heaven, let no dishonour stain my
   brow;
Or if it is decreed that I must bow
To that misfortune, lend me at least, I pray,
Such patient strength as some poor men
   display.

Act Four

SCENE ONE: Arnolphe

ARNOLPHE (*entering from the house, alone*).

I can't hold still a minute, I declare.
My anxious thoughts keep darting here and
    there,
Planning defences, seeking to prevent
That rascal from achieving his intent.
How calm the traitress looked when I went in!
Despite her crimes, she shows no sense of sin,
And though she's all but sent me to my grave,
How like a little saint she dares behave!
The more she sat there, cool and unperturbed,
The less I thought my fury could be curbed;
Yet, strange to say, my heart's increasing ire
Seemed only to redouble my desire.
I was embittered, desperate, irate,
And yet her beauty had never seemed so great.
Never did her bright eyes so penetrate me,
So rouse my spirit, so infatuate me;
Oh, it would break the heart within my breast
Should fate subject me to this cruel jest.
What! Have I supervised her education
With loving care and long consideration,
Sheltered her since she was a tiny creature,
Cherished sweet expectations for her future,
For thirteen years moulded her character
And based my hopes of happiness on her,
Only to see some young fool steal the prize
Of her affection, under my very eyes,

And just when she and I were all but wed?
Ah, no, young friend! Ah, no, young
    chucklehead!
I mean to stop you; I swear that you shall not
Succeed, however well you scheme and plot,
And that you'll have no cause to laugh at me.

SCENE TWO: *The Notary, Arnolphe*

NOTARY   Ah, here you are, Sir! I am the notary.
      So, there's a contract which you'd have me
        draw?

ARNOLPHE *(unaware of the notary)*.
      How shall I do it?

NOTARY   According to the law.

ARNOLPHE *(still oblivious)*.
      I must be prudent, and think what course is
        best.

NOTARY   I shall do nothing against your interest.

ARNOLPHE *(oblivious)*.
      One must anticipate the unexpected.

NOTARY   In my hands, you'll be thoroughly protected.
      But do remember, lest you be betrayed,
      To sign no contract till the dowry's paid.

ARNOLPHE *(oblivious)*.
      I must act covertly; if this thing gets out,
      The gossips will have much to blab about.

NOTARY   If you're so anxious not to make a stir,
      The contract can be drawn in secret, Sir.

ARNOLPHE *(oblivious)*.
      But how shall she be dealt with? Can I
        condone –

NOTARY   The dowry is proportional to her own.

ARNOLPHE (*oblivious*).
>It's hard to be strict with one whom you
>>adore.

NOTARY In that case, you may wish to give her more.

ARNOLPHE (*oblivious*).
>How should I treat the girl? I must decide.

NOTARY As a general rule, the husband gives the bride
>A dowry that's one-third the size of hers;
>But he may increase the sum, if her prefers.

ARNOLPHE (*oblivious*).
>If –

NOTARY (ARNOLPHE *now noticing him*).
>>As for property, and its division
>In case of death, the husband makes provision
>As he thinks best.

ARNOLPHE   Eh?

NOTARY   He can make certain of
>His bride's security, and show his love,
>By jointure, or a settlement whereby
>The gift is cancelled should the lady die,
>Reverting to her heirs, if so agreed;
>Or go by common law; or have a deed
>Of gift appended to the instrument,
>Either by his sole wish, or by consent.
>Why shrug your shoulders? Am I talking rot?
>Do I know contracts, Sir, or do I not?
>Who could instruct me? Who would be so
>>bold?
>Do I not know that spouses jointly hold
>Goods, chattels, lands, and money in their two
>>names,
>Unless one party should renounce all claims?
>Do I not know that a third of the bride's
>>resources
>Enters the joint estate –

ARNOLPHE   All that, of course, is
         True. But who asked for all this pedantry?

NOTARY   You did! And now you sniff and shrug at me,
         And treat my competence with ridicule.

ARNOLPHE   The devil take this ugly-featured fool!
         Good day, good day. An end to all this
           chatter.

NOTARY   Did you not ask my aid in a legal matter?

ARNOLPHE   Yes, yes, but now the matter's been deferred.
         When your advice is needed, I'll send word.
         Meanwhile, stop blathering, you blatherskite!

NOTARY   He's mad, I judge; and I think my judgment's
           right.

SCENE THREE: *The Notary, Alain, Georgette, Arnolphe*

NOTARY   (*to* ALAIN *and* GEORGETTE).
         Your master sent you to fetch me, isn't that
           so?

ALAIN   Yes.

NOTARY   How you feel about him I don't know,
         But I regard him as a senseless boor.
         Tell him I said so.

GEORGETTE   We will, you may be sure.

SCENE FOUR : Alain, Georgette, Arnolphe

ALAIN   Sir –

ARNOLPHE   Ah, come here, my good friends, tried and
true:
You've amply proved that I may count on
you.

ALAIN   The notary –

ARNOLPHE   Tell me later, will you not?
My honour's threatened by a vicious plot;
Think, children, what distress you'd feel, what
shame,
If some dishonour touched your master's
name!
You wouldn't dare to leave the house, for
fear
That all the town would point at you, and
sneer.
Since we're together, then, in this affair,
You must be ever watchful, and take care
That no approach that gallant may adopt –

GEORGETTE   We've learned our lesson, Sir; he shall be
stopped.

ARNOLPHE   Beware his fine words and his flatteries.

ALAIN   Of course.

GEORGETTE   We can resist such talk with ease.

ARNOLPHE   (*to* ALAIN).
What if he said, 'Alain, for mercy's sake,
Do me a kindness' – what answer would you
make?

ALAIN   I'd say, 'You fool!'

ARNOLPHE   Good, good. (*To* GEORGETTE*:*)
      'Georgette, my dear,
      I'm sure you're just as sweet as you appear.'

GEORGETTE   'Fathead!'

ARNOLPHE   Good, good. (*To* ALAIN*:*) 'Come, let
      me in. You know
      That my intent is pure as the driven snow.'

ALAIN   'Sir, you're a knave!'

ARNOLPHE   Well said. (*To* GEORGETTE*:*)
      'Unless you take
      Pity on my poor heart, it's sure to break.'

GEORGETTE   'You are an impudent ass!'

ARNOLPHE   Well said, Georgette.
      'I'm not the sort of person to forget
      A favour, or begrudge the *quid pro quo*,
      As these few coins, Alain, will serve to
       show.
      And you, Georgette, take this and buy a
       dress.
      (*Both hold out their hands and take the
       money*.)
      That's but a specimen of my largesse.
      And all I ask is that you grant to me
      An hour of your young mistress' company.'

GEORGETTE   (*giving him a shove*).
      'You're crazy!'

ARNOLPHE   Good!

ALAIN   (*shoving* ARNOLPHE).
        'Move on!'

ARNOLPHE   Good!

GEORGETTE   (*shoving* ARNOLPHE).
         'Out of my sight!'

ARNOLPHE   Good, good – but that's enough.

GEORGETTE   Did I do it right?

ALAIN   Is that how we're to treat him?

ARNOLPHE   You were fine;
Except for the money, which you should
    decline.

GEORGETTE We didn't think, Sir. That was wrong
    indeed.

ALAIN Would you like to do it over again?

ARNOLPHE   No need;
Go back inside.

ALAIN   Sir, if you say the word, we —

ARNOLPHE No, that will do; go in at once; you heard
    me.
Just keep the money; I shall be with you
    shortly.
Be on your guard, and ready to support me.

SCENE FIVE: Arnolphe

ARNOLPHE The cobbler at the corner is sharp of eye;
I think that I'll enlist him as a spy.
As for Agnès, I'll keep her under guard,
And all dishonest women shall be barred —
Hairdressers, glovers, handkerchief-makers,
    those
Who come to the door with ribbons, pins, and
    bows,
And often, as a sideline to such wares,
Are go-betweens in secret love affairs.
I know the world, and the tricks that people
    use;
That boy will have to invent some brand-new
    ruse
If he's to get a message in to her.

SCENE SIX: *Horace, Arnolphe*

HORACE What luck to find you in this quarter, Sir!
I've just had a narrow escape, believe you me!
Just after I left you, whom did I chance to see
Upon her shady balcony, but the fair
Agnès, who had come out to take the air!
She managed, having signalled me to wait,
To steal downstairs and open the garden gate.
We went to her room, and were no sooner
    there
Than we heard her jealous guardian on the
    stair;
In which great peril I was thrust by her
Into a wardrobe where her dresses were.
He entered. I couldn't see him, but I heard
Him striding back and forth without a word,
Heaving deep sighs of woe again and again,
Pounding upon the tables now and then,
Kicking a little dog, who yipped in fright,
And throwing her possessions left and right.
What's more, to give his fury full release,
He knocked two vases off her mantelpiece.
Clearly the old goat had some vague,
    dismaying
Sense of the tricks his captive had been
    playing.
At last, when all his anger had been spent
On objects which were dumb and innocent,
The frantic man, without a word, went
    striding

Out of the room, and I came out of hiding.
Quite naturally, we didn't dare extend
Our rendezvous, because our jealous friend
Was still about; tonight, however, I
Shall visit her, quite late, and on the sly.
Our plan is this: I'll cough, three times,
    outside;
At that, the window will be opened wide;
Then, with a ladder and the assistance of
Agnès, I'll climb into our bower of love.
Since you're my old friend, I tell you this –
For telling, as you know, augments one's
    bliss.
However vast the joy, one must confide
In someone else before one's satisfied.
You share, I know, my happy expectations.
But now, farewell; I must make preparations.

SCENE SEVEN: *Arnolphe*

ARNOLPHE The evil star that's hounding me to death
    Gives me no time in which to catch my
      breath!
    Must I, again and again, be forced to see
    My measures foiled through their complicity?
    Shall I, at my ripe age, be duped, forsooth,
    By a green girl and by a harebrained youth?
    For twenty years I've sagely contemplated
    The woeful lives of men unwisely mated,
    And analysed with care the slips whereby
    The best-planned marriages have gone awry;
    Thus schooled by others' failures, I felt
      that I'd

Be able, when I chose to take a bride,
To ward off all mischance, and be protected
From griefs to which so many are subjected.
I took, to that end, all the shrewd and wise
Precautions which experience could devise;
Yet, as if fate had made the stern decision
That no man living should escape derision,
I find, for all my pondering of this
Great matter, all my keen analysis,
The twenty years and more which I have spent
In planning to escape the embarrassment
So many husbands suffer from today,
That I'm as badly victimized as they.
But no, damned fate, I challenge your decree!
The lovely prize is in my custody,
And though her heart's been filched by that
    young pest,
I guarantee that he'll not get the rest,
And that this evening's gallant rendezvous
Won't go as smoothly as they'd like it to.
There's one good thing about my present fix —
That I'm forewarned of all my rival's tricks,
And that this oaf who's aiming to undo me
Confesses all his bad intentions to me.

SCENE EIGHT: *Chrysalde, Arnolphe*

CHRYSALDE Well, shall we dine, and then go out for a
    stroll?
ARNOLPHE No, no, the dinner's off.
CHRYSALDE   Well, well, how droll!
ARNOLPHE Forgive me: there's a crisis I must face.

CHRYSALDE Your wedding plans have changed? Is that the
case?

ARNOLPHE I have no need of your solicitude.

CHRYSALDE Tell me your troubles, now, and don't be
rude.
I'd guess, friend, that your marriage scheme
has met
With difficulties, and that you're upset.
To judge by your expression, I'd almost swear
it.

ARNOLPHE Whatever happens, I shall have the merit
Of not resembling some in this community,
Who let young gallants cheat them with
impunity.

CHRYSALDE It's odd that you, with your good intellect,
Are so obsessive in this one respect,
Measure all happiness thereby, and base
On it alone men's honour or disgrace.
Greed, envy, vice, and cowardice are not
Important sins to you; the one grave blot
You find on any scutcheon seems to be
The crime of having suffered cuckoldry.
Now, come: shall a man be robbed of his good
name
Through an ill chance for which he's not to
blame?
Shall a good husband lacerate his soul
With guilt for matters not in his control?
When a man marries, why must we scorn or
praise him
According to whether or not his wife betrays
him?
And if she does so, why must her husband see
The fact as an immense catastrophe?
Do realize that, to a man of sense,

There's nothing crushing in such accidents;
That, since no man can dodge the blows of fate,
One's sense of failure should not be too great,
And that there's no harm done, whatever they
 say,
If one but takes things in the proper way.
In difficulties of this sort, it seems,
As always, wiser to avoid extremes.
One shouldn't ape those husbands who permit
Such scandal, and who take a pride in it,
Dropping the names of their wives' latest
 gallants,
Praising their persons, bragging of their
 talents,
Professing warm regard for them, attending
The parties that they give, and so offending
Society, which properly resents
Displays of laxity and impudence.
Needless to say, such conduct will not do;
And yet the other extreme's improper too.
If men do wrong to flatter their wives'
 gallants,
It's no less bad when, lacking tact and
 balance,
They vent their grievances with savage fury,
Calling the whole world to be judge and jury,
And won't be satisfied till they acquaint
All ears whatever with their loud complaint.
Between these two extremes, my friend, there
 lies
A middle way that's favoured by the wise,
And which, if followed, will preserve one's
 face
However much one's wife may court disgrace.
In short, then, cuckoldry need not be dreaded

Like some dire monster, fierce and many-
    headed;
It can be lived with, if one has the wit
To take it calmly, and make the best of it.

ARNOLPHE For that fine speech, the great fraternity
Of cuckolds owes you thanks, your
    Excellency;
And all men, if they heard your wisdom, would
Make joyous haste to join the brotherhood.

CHRYSALDE No, that I shouldn't approve. But since it's
    fate
Whereby we're joined to one or another mate,
One should take marriage as one takes
    picquette,
In which, if one has made a losing bet,
One takes the setback calmly, and takes pains
To do the best one can with what remains.

ARNOLPHE In other words, eat hearty and sleep tight,
And tell yourself that everything's all right.

CHRYSALDE Laugh on, my friend; but I can, in all
    sobriety,
Name fifty things which cause me more
    anxiety,
And would, if they occurred, appal me more
Than this misfortune which you so abhor.
Had I to choose between adversities,
I'd rather be a cuckold, if you please,
Than marry one of those good wives who find
Continual reason to upbraid mankind,
Those virtuous shrews, those fiendish
    paragons,
As violently chaste as Amazons,
Who, having had the goodness not to horn
    us,

Accord themselves the right to nag and scorn
    us,
And make us pay for their fidelity
By being as vexatious as can be.
Do learn, friend, that when all is said and
    done,
Cuckoldry's what you make of it; that one
Might welcome it in certain situations,
And that, like all things, it has compensations.

ARNOLPHE Well, if you want it, may you get your wish;
But, as for me, it's not at all my dish.
Before I'd let my brow be decked with horn –

CHRYSALDE Tut, tut! Don't swear, or you may be
    forsworn.
If fate has willed it, your resolves will fail,
And all your oaths will be of no avail.

ARNOLPHE I! a cuckold?

CHRYSALDE   Don't let it fret you so.
It happens to the best of men, you know.
Cuckolds exist with whom, if I may be frank,
You can't compare for person, wealth, or
    rank.

ARNOLPHE I have no wish to be compared with such.
Enough, now, of your mockery; it's too much.
You try my patience.

CHRYSALDE   So, you're annoyed with me?
Ah, well. Good-bye. But bear in mind that he
Who thumps his chest and swears upon his
    soul
That he will never play the cuckold's role
Is studying for the part, and may well get it.

ARNOLPHE That won't occur, I swear; I shall not let it.
I shall remove that threat this very minute.
(*He knocks at his own gate.*)

SCENE NINE: Alain, Georgette, Arnolphe

ARNOLPHE My friends, the battle's joined, and we must
    win it.
Your love for me, by which I'm touched and
    moved,
Must now, in this emergency, be proved,
And if your deeds repay my confidence,
You may expect a handsome recompense.
This very night – don't tell a soul, my
    friends –
A certain rascal whom you know intends
To scale the wall and see Agnès; but we
Shall lay a little trap for him, we three.
You'll both be armed with clubs, and when
    the young
Villain has almost reached the topmost rung
(I meanwhile shall have flung the shutters
    wide),
You shall lean out and so lambaste his hide,
So bruise his ribs by your combined attack,
That he will never dream of coming back.
Don't speak my name while this is happening,
    mind you,
Or let him know that I am there behind you.
Have you the pluck to serve me in this
    action?

ALAIN If blows are called for, we can give
    satisfaction.
I'll show you that this good right arm's not
    lame.

GEORGETTE Mine looks less strong than his, but all the
        same
        Our foe will know that he's been beaten by it.

ARNOLPHE Go in, then; and, whatever you do, keep quiet.
        (*Alone:*)
        Tonight, I'll give a lesson to mankind.
        If all endangered husbands took a mind
        To greet their wives' intrusive gallants thus,
        Cuckolds, I think, would be less numerous.

Act Five

SCENE ONE: *Alain, Georgette, Arnolphe*

ARNOLPHE You brutes! What made you be so heavy-
      handed?
ALAIN But, Sir, we only did as you commanded.
ARNOLPHE Don't put the blame on me; your guilt is
      plain.
    I wished him beaten; I didn't wish him slain.
    And furthermore, if you'll recall, I said
    To hit him on the ribs, not on the head.
    It's a ghastly situation in which I'm placed;
    How is this young man's murder to be faced?
    Go in, now, and be silent as the grave
    About that innocent command I gave.
    (*Alone:*)
    It's nearly daybreak. I must take thought, and
      see
    How best to cope with this dire tragedy.
    God help me! What will the boy's father say
    When this appalling story comes his way?

SCENE TWO: *Horace, Arnolphe*

HORACE Who's this, I wonder. I'd best approach with
      care.
ARNOLPHE How could I have forseen . . . I say, who's
      there?
HORACE Seigneur Arnolphe?
ARNOLPHE   Yes –

HORACE   It's Horace, once more.
          My, you're up early! I was heading for
          Your house, to ask a favour.
ARNOLPHE   Oh, God, I'm dizzy.
          Is he a vision? Is he a ghost? What is he?
HORACE Sir, I'm in trouble once again, I fear.
          It's providential that you should appear
          Just at the moment when your help was
              needed.
          My plans, I'm happy to tell you, have
              succeeded
          Beyond all expectations, and despite
          An incident which might have spoiled them
              quite.
          I don't know how it happened, but someone
              knew
          About our contemplated rendczvous;
          For, just as I'd almost reached her window
              sill,
          I saw some frightful figures, armed to kill,
          Lean out above me, waving their clubs
              around.
          I lost my footing, tumbled to the ground,
          And thus, though rather scratched and
              bruised, was spared
          The thumping welcome which they had
              prepared.
          Those brutes (of whom Old Jealous, I
              suppose,
          Was one) ascribed my tumble to their blows,
          And since I lay there, motionless, in the dirt
          For several minutes, being stunned and
              hurt,
          They judged that they had killed me, and they
              all

Took fright at that, and so began to brawl.
I lay in silence, hearing their angry cries:
They blamed each other for my sad demise,
Then tiptoed out, in darkness and in dread,
To feel my body, and see if I were dead.
As you can well imagine, I played the part
Of a limp, broken corpse with all my heart.
Quite overcome with terror, they withdrew,
And I was thinking of withdrawing, too,
When young Agnès came hurrying, out of
    breath
And much dismayed by my supposèd death:
She had been able, of course, to overhear
All that my foes had babbled in their fear,
And while they were distracted and unnerved
She'd slipped from the house, entirely
    unobserved.
Ah, how she wept with happiness when she
    found
That I was, after all, both safe and sound!
Well, to be brief: electing to be guided
By her own heart, the charming girl decided
Not to return to her guardian, but to flee,
Entrusting her security to me.
What must his tyranny be, if it can force
So shy a girl to take so bold a course!
And think what peril she might thus incur,
If I were capable of wronging her.
Ah, but my love's too pure for that, too
    strong;
I'd rather die than do her any wrong;
So admirable is she that all I crave
Is to be with her even to the grave.
I know my father: this will much displease
    him,

But we shall manage somehow to appease him.
In any case, she's won my heart, and I
Could not desert her, even if I chose to try.
The favour I ask of you is rather large:
It's that you take my darling in your charge,
And keep her, if you will, for several days
In your own house, concealed from the world's
    gaze.
I ask your help in this because I'm bent
On throwing all pursuers off the scent;
Also because, if she were seen with me,
There might be talk of impropriety.
To you, my loyal friend, I've dared to impart,
Without reserve, the secrets of my heart,
And likewise it's to you I now confide
My dearest treasure and my future bride.

ARNOLPHE   I'm at your service; on that you may depend.

HORACE   You'll grant the favour that I ask, dear friend?

ARNOLPHE   Of course; most willingly. I'm glad indeed
That I can help you in your hour of need.
Thank Heaven that you asked me! There's no
    request
To which I could accede with greater zest.

HORACE   How kind you are! What gratitude I feel!
I feared you might refuse my rash appeal;
But you're a man of the world, urbane and
    wise,
Who looks upon young love with tolerant
    eyes.
My man is guarding her, just down the street.

ARNOLPHE   It's almost daylight. Where had we better
    meet?
Someone might see me, if you brought her
    here,
And should you bring her to my house, I fear

'T would start the servants talking. We must
    look
For some more shadowy and secluded nook.
That garden's handy; I shall await her there.

HORACE You're right, Sir. We must act with the utmost
    care.
I'll go, and quickly bring Agnès to you,
Then seek my lodgings without more ado.

ARNOLPHE (*alone*).
Ah, Fortune! This good turn will compensate
For all the tricks you've played on me of late.
(*He hides his face in his cloak.*)

SCENE THREE: *Agnès, Horace, Arnolphe*

HORACE Just come with me; there's no cause for alarm.
I'm taking you where you'll be safe from
    harm.
To stay together would be suicide:
Go in, and let this gentleman be your guide.
(ARNOLPHE, *whom she does not recognize, takes
    her hand.*)

AGNES Why are you leaving me?

HORACE   Dear Agnès, I must.

AGNES You'll very soon be coming back, I trust?

HORACE I shall; my yearning heart will see to that.

AGNES Without you, life is miserable and flat.

HORACE When I'm away from you, I pine and grieve.

AGNES Alas! If that were so, you wouldn't leave.

HORACE You know how strong my love is, and how
    true.

AGNES Ah, no, you don't love me as I love you.
    (ARNOLPHE *tugs at her hand.*)
    Why does he pull my hand?

HORACE   'T would ruin us,
    My dear, if we were seen together thus,
    And therefore this true friend, who's filled
      with worry
    About our welfare, urges you to hurry.

AGNES But why must I go with him – a perfect
    stranger?

HORACE Don't fret. In his hands you'll be out of
    danger.

AGNES I'd rather be in *your* hands; that was why –
    (*To* ARNOLPHE, *who tugs her hand again:*)
    Wait, wait.

HORACE   It's daybreak. I must go. Good-bye.

AGNES When shall I see you?

HORACE   Very soon, I swear.

AGNES Till that sweet moment, I'll be in despair.

HORACE (*leaving, to himself*).
    My happiness is assured; my fears may cease;
    Praise be to Heaven, I now can sleep in
    peace.

SCENE FOUR: Arnolphe, Agnès

ARNOLPHE (*hiding his face in his cloak, and disguising his
    voice*).
    Come, this is not where you're to stay, my
    child;
    It's elsewhere that you shall be domiciled.
    You're going to a safe, sequestered place.

(*Revealing himself, and using his normal voice:*)
Do you know me?

AGNES (*recognizing him*).

Aagh!

ARNOLPHE   You wicked girl! My face
Would seem, just now, to give you rather a
    fright.
Oh, clearly I'm a most unwelcome sight:
I interfere with your romantic plan.
(AGNES *turns and looks in vain for* HORACE.)
No use to look for help from that young man;
He couldn't hear you now; he's gone too far.
Well, well! For one so young, how sly you
    are!
You ask – most innocently, it would appear –
If children are begotten through the ear,
Yet you know all too well, I now discover,
How to keep trysts – at midnight – with a
    lover!
What honeyed words you spoke to him just
    now!
Who taught you such beguilements? Tell me
    how,
Within so short a time, you've learned so
    much!
You used to be afraid of ghosts and such:
Has your gallant taught you not to fear the
    night?
You ingrate! To deceive me so, despite
The loving care with which you have been
    blessed!
Oh, I have warmed a serpent at my breast
Until, reviving, it unkindly bit
The very hand that was caressing it!

AGNES Why are you cross with me?

ARNOLPHE   Oh! So I'm unfair?

AGNES I've done no wrong of which I am aware.

ARNOLPHE Was it right, then, to run off with that young
              beau?

AGNES He wants me for his wife; he's told me so.
          I've only done as you advised; you said
          That, so as not to sin, one ought to wed.

ARNOLPHE Yes, but I made it perfectly clear that I'd
              Resolved, myself, to take you as my bride.

AGNES Yes; but if I may give my point of view,
          He'd suit me, as a husband, better than you.
          In all your talk of marriage, you depict
          A state that's gloomy, burdensome, and strict;
          But, ah! when *he* describes the married state,
          It sounds so sweet that I can hardly wait.

ARNOLPHE Ah! So you love him, faithless girl!

AGNES   Why, yes.

ARNOLPHE Have you the gall to tell me that, Agnès?

AGNES If it's the truth, what's wrong with telling it?

ARNOLPHE How dared you fall in love with him, you
              chit?

AGNES It was no fault of mine; he made me do it.
          I was in love with him before I knew it.

ARNOLPHE You should have overcome your amorous
              feeling.

AGNES It's hard to overcome what's so appealing.

ARNOLPHE Didn't you know that I would be put out?

AGNES Why, no. What have you to complain about?

ARNOLPHE Nothing, of course! I'm wild with happiness!
              You don't, I take it, love me.

AGNES   Love you?

ARNOLPHE   Yes.

AGNES Alas, I don't.

ARNOLPHE   You *don't?*

AGNES   Would you have me lie?

ARNOLPHE Why don't you love me, hussy? Tell me why!

AGNES Good heavens, it's not I whom you should
blame.

He made me love him; why didn't you do the
same?

I didn't hinder you, as I recall.

ARNOLPHE I tried to make you love me; I gave my all;

Yet all my pains and strivings were in vain.

AGNES He has more aptitude than you, that's
plain;

To win my heart, he scarcely had to try.

ARNOLPHE (*aside*).

This peasant girl can frame a neat reply!

What lady wit could answer with more art?

Either she's bright, or in what concerns the
heart

A foolish girl can best the wisest man.

(*To* AGNES:)

Well, then, Miss Back-Talk, answer this if you
can:

Did I raise you, all these years, at such
expense,

For another's benefit? Does that make sense?

AGNES No. But he'll gladly pay you for your trouble.

ARNOLPHE (*aside*).

Such flippancy! It makes my rage redouble.

(*To* AGNES:)

You minx! How could he possibly discharge

Your obligations to me? They're too large.

AGNES Frankly, they don't seem very large to me.

ARNOLPHE Did I not nurture you from infancy?

AGNES Yes, that you did. I'm deeply obligated.

How wondrously you've had me educated!

Do you fancy that I'm blind to what you've
done,

And cannot see that I'm a simpleton?
Oh, it humiliates me; I revolt
Against the shame of being such a dolt.

ARNOLPHE Do you think you'll gain the knowledge that
you need
Through that young dandy's tutelage?

AGNES   Yes, indeed.
It's thanks to him I know what little I do;
I owe far more to him than I do to you.

ARNOLPHE What holds me back, I ask myself, from
treating
So insolent a girl to a sound beating?
Your coldness irks me to the point of tears,
And it would ease my soul to box your ears.

AGNES Alas, then, beat me, if you so desire.

ARNOLPHE (*aside*).
Those words and that sweet look dissolve my
ire,
Restoring to my heart such tender feeling
As makes me quite forget her double-dealing.
How strange love is! How strange that men,
from such
Perfidious beings, will endure so much!
Women, as all men know, are fraily wrought:
They're foolish and illogical in thought,
Their souls are weak, their characters are
bad,
There's nothing quite so silly, quite so mad,
So faithless; yet, despite these sorry features,
What won't we do to please the wretched
creatures?
(*To* AGNES:)
Come, traitress, let us be at peace once more.
I'll pardon you, and love you as before.
Repay my magnanimity, and learn

From my great love to love me in return.

AGNES Truly, if I were able to, I would.
I'd gladly love you if I only could.

ARNOLPHE You can, my little beauty, if you'll but try.
(*He sighs.*)
Just listen to that deep and yearning sigh!
Look at my haggard face! See how it suffers!
Reject that puppy, and the love he offers:
He must have cast a spell on you; with me,
You'll be far happier, I guarantee.
I know that clothes and jewels are your
passion;
Don't worry: you shall always be in fashion.
I'll pet you night and day; you shall be
showered
With kisses; you'll be hugged, caressed,
devoured.
And you shall have your wish in every way.
I'll say no more; what further could I say?
(*Aside:*)
Lord, what extremes desire will drive us to!
(*To* AGNES:)
In short, no love could match my love for you.
Tell me, ungrateful girl, what proof do you
need?
Shall I weep? Or beat myself until I bleed?
What if I tore my hair out – would that sway
you?
Shall I kill myself? Command, and I'll obey
you.
I'm ready, cruel one, for you to prove me.

AGNES Somehow, your lengthy speeches fail to move
me.
Horace, in two words, could be more
engaging.

ARNOLPHE Enough of this! Your impudence is enraging.
          I have my plans for you, you stubborn dunce,
          And I shall pack you out of town at once.
          You've spurned my love, and baited me as
              well –
          Which you'll repent of in a convent cell.

SCENE FIVE: Alain, Arnolphe, Agnès

ALAIN It's very strange, but Agnès has vanished, Sir.
       I think that corpse has run away with her.
ARNOLPHE She's here. Go shut her in my room, securely.
          That's not where he'd come looking for her,
              surely,
          And she'll be there but half an hour, at most.
          Meanwhile I'll get a carriage, in which we'll
              post
          To a safe retreat. Go now, and lock up tight,
          And see that you don't let her out of sight.
          (*Alone:*)
          Perhaps a change of scene and circumstance
          Will wean her from this infantile romance.

SCENE SIX: Horace, Arnolphe

HORACE Seigneur Arnolphe, I'm overwhelmed with
            grief,
        And Heaven's cruelty is beyond belief;
        It seems now that a brutal stroke of fate

May force my love and me to separate.
My father, just this minute, chanced to
  appear,
Alighting from his coach not far from here,
And what has brought him into town this
  morning
Is a dire errand of which I'd had no warning:
He's made a match for me, and, ready or not,
I am to marry someone on the spot.
Imagine my despair! What blacker curse
Could fall on me, what setback could be
  worse?
I told you, yesterday, of Enrique. It's he
Who's brought about my present misery;
He's come with Father, to lead me to the
  slaughter,
And I am doomed to wed his only daughter.
When they told me that, it almost made me
  swoon;
And, since my father spoke of coming soon
To see you, I excused myself, in fright,
And hastened to forewarn you of my plight.
Take care, Sir, I entreat you, not to let him
Know of Agnès and me; 't would much upset
  him.
And try, since he so trusts your judgment, to
Dissuade him from the match he has in
  view.

ARNOLPHE I shall.

HORACE   That failing, you could be of aid
By urging that the wedding be delayed.

ARNOLPHE Trust me.

HORACE   On you, my dearest hopes repose.

ARNOLPHE Fine, fine.

HORACE   You're a father to me, Heaven knows.

Tell him that young men – Ah! He's coming!
  I spy him.
Here are some arguments with which to ply
  him.
(*They withdraw to a corner of the stage, and
  confer in whispers.*)

SCENE SEVEN: *Enrique, Oronte,
  Chrysalde, Horace, Arnolphe*

ENRIQUE (*to* CHRYSALDE).
  No need for introductions, Sir. I knew
  Your name as soon as I set eyes on you.
  You have the very features of your late
  Sister, who was my well-belovèd mate;
  Oh, how I wish that cruel Destiny
  Had let me bring my helpmeet back with me,
  After such years of hardship as we bore,
  To see her home and family once more.
  But fate has ruled that we shall not again
  Enjoy her charming presence; let us, then,
  Find solace in what joys we may design
  For the sole offspring of her love and
    mine.
  You are concerned in this; let us confer,
  And see if you approve my plans for her.
  Oronte's young son, I think, is a splendid
    choice;
  But in this matter you've an equal voice.
CHRYSALDE I've better judgment, Brother, than to
    question
  So eminently worthy a suggestion.
ARNOLPHE (*to* HORACE).

	Yes, yes, don't worry; I'll represent you well.
HORACE	Once more, don't tell him –
ARNOLPHE	I promise not to tell.

(ARNOLPHE *leaves* HORACE, *and crosses to embrace* ORANTE.)

ORONTE	Ah, my old friend: what a warm, hearty greeting!
ARNOLPHE	Oronte, dear fellow, what a welcome meeting!
ORONTE	I've come to town –
ARNOLPHE	You needn't say a word; I know what brings you.
ORONTE	You've already heard?
ARNOLPHE	Yes.
ORONTE	Good.
ARNOLPHE	Your son regards this match with dread; His heart rebels at being forced to wed, And I've been asked, in fact, to plead his case. Well, do you know what I'd do, in your place? I'd exercise a father's rightful sway And tie the wedding knot without delay. What the young need, my friend, is discipline; We only do them harm by giving in.
HORACE	(*aside*). Traitor!
CHRYSALDE	If the prospect fills him with revulsion, Then surely we should not employ compulsion. My brother-in-law, I trust, would say the same.
ARNOLPHE	Shall a man be governed by his son? For shame! Would you have a father be so meek and mild As not to exact obedience from his child? At his wise age, 't would be grotesque indeed

To see him led by one whom he should lead.
No, no; my dear old friend is honour-bound;
He's given his word, and he must not give
    ground.
Let him be firm, as a father should, and force
His son to take the necessary course.

ORONTE Well said: we shall proceed with this alliance,
And I shall answer for my son's compliance.

CHRYSALDE (*to* ARNOLPHE).
It much surprises me to hear you press
For this betrothal with such eagerness.
What is your motive? I can't make you out.

ARNOLPHE Don't worry, friend; I know what I'm
    about.

ORONTE Indeed, Arnolphe –

CHRYSALDE   He finds that name unpleasant.
Monsieur de la Souche is what he's called at
    present.

ARNOLPHE No matter.

HORACE   What do I hear?

ARNOLPHE (*turning towards* HORACE).
                Well, now you know,
And now you see why I have spoken so.

HORACE Oh, what confusion –

SCENE EIGHT: Georgette, Enrique,
Oronte, Chrysalde, Horace, Arnolphe

GEORGETTE   Sir, please come. Unless
You do, I fear we can't restrain Agnès.

The girl is frantic to escape, I swear,
And might jump out of the window in
    despair.

ARNOLPHE Bring her to me: I'll take her away from here
Posthaste, this very minute.
(*To* HORACE:)
                       Be of good cheer.
Too much good luck could spoil you; and, as
    they say
In the proverb, every dog must have his day.

HORACE What man, O Heaven, was ever betrayed like
    this,
Or hurled into so hopeless an abyss?

ARNOLPHE (*to* ORONTE).
Pray don't delay the nuptials – which, dear
    friend,
I shall be most delighted to attend.

ORONTE I shan't delay.

    SCENE NINE: Agnès, Alain, Georgette,
    Oronte, Enrique, Arnolphe, Horace,
    Chrysalde

ARNOLPHE   Come, come, my pretty child,
You who are so intractable and wild.
Here is your gallant: perhaps he should
    receive
A little curtsey from you, as you leave.
(*To* HORACE:)
Farewell: your sweet hopes seem to have
    turned to gall;
But love, my boy, can't always conquer all.

AGNES Horace! Will you let him take me away from
    you?

HORACE   I'm dazed with grief, and don't know what to do.

ARNOLPHE   Come, chatterbox.

AGNES   No. Here I shall remain.

ORONTE   Now, what's the mystery? Will you please
    explain?

And all this is very odd; we're baffled by it.

ARNOLPHE   When I've more time, I'll gladly clarify it.
Till then, good-bye.

ORONTE   Where is it you mean to go?

And why won't you tell us what we ask to
    know?

ARNOLPHE   I've told you that, despite your stubborn
    son,
You ought to hold the wedding.

ARNOLPHE   It shall be done.

But weren't you told that his intended
    spouse
Is the young woman who's living in your
    house –
The long-lost child of that dear Angélique
Who secretly was married to Enrique?
What, then, did your behaviour mean just
    now?

CHRYSALDE   His words amazed me, too, I must allow.

ARNOLPHE   What? What?

CHRYSALDE   My sister married secretly;
Her daughter's birth was kept from the
    family.

ORONTE   The child was placed with an old country
    dame,
Who reared her under a fictitious name.

CHRYSALDE   My sister's husband, beset by circumstance,
Was soon obliged to take his leave of France,

ORONTE   And undergo great trials and miseries
In a strange, savage land beyond the seas,

CHRYSALDE Where, through his labours, he regained
    abroad
    What here he'd lost through men's deceit and
    fraud.

ORONTE Returning home, he sought at once to find
    The nurse to whom his child had been
    consigned,

CHRYSALDE And the good creature told him, as was true,
    That she'd transferred her little charge to you,

ORONTE Because of your benevolent disposition,
    And the dire poverty of her condition.

CHRYSALDE What's more, Enrique, transported with
    delight,
    Has brought the woman here to set things
    right.

ORONTE She'll join us in a moment, and then we'll see
    A public end to all this mystery.

CHRYSALDE (*to* ARNOLPHE).
    I know that you're in a painful state of mind;
    Yet what the Fates have done is not unkind.
    Since your chief treasure is a hornless head,
    The safest course, for you, is not to wed.

ARNOLPHE (*leaving in a speechless passion*).
    Oof!

ORONTE   Why is he rushing off without a word?

HORACE Father, a great coincidence has occurred.
    What in your wisdom you projected, chance
    Has wondrously accomplished in advance.
    The fact is, Sir, that I am bound already,
    By the sweet ties of love, to this fair lady;
    It's she whom you have come to seek, and she
    For whose sake I opposed your plans for me.

ENRIQUE I recognized her from the very first,
    With such deep joy, I thought my heart would
    burst.

Dear daughter, let me take you in my
    embrace.
(*He does so.*)

CHRYSALDE I have the same urge, Brother, but this place
Will hardly do for private joys like these.
Let us go in, resolve all mysteries,
Commend our friend Arnolphe, and for the
    rest
Thank Heaven, which orders all things for the
    best.

Tartuffe

Comedy in Five Acts

Translated into English verse by Richard Wilbur

CHARACTERS

PERNELLE, Orgon's mother

ORGON, Elmire's husband

ELMIRE, Orgon's wife

DAMIS, Orgon's son, Elmire's stepson

MARIANE, Orgon's daughter, Elmire's stepdaughter, in
in love with Valère

VALERE, in love with Mariane

CLEANTE, Orgon's brother-in-law

TARTUFFE, a hypocrite

DORINE, Mariane's lady's-maid

M. LOYAL, a bailiff

A POLICE OFFICER

FLIPOTE, Mme Pernelle's maid

The scene throughout: Orgon's house in Paris

Act One

SCENE ONE:

*Madame Pernelle and Flipote, her maid, Elmire,
Mariane, Dorine, Damis, Cléante*

PERNELLE Come, come, Flipote; it's time I left this
        place.

ELMIRE I can't keep up, you walk at such a pace.

PERNELLE Don't trouble, child; no need to show me out.
        It's not your manners I'm concerned about.

ELMIRE We merely pay you the respect we owe.
        But, Mother, why this hurry? Must you go?

PERNELLE I must. This house appals me. No one in it
        Will pay attention for a single minute.
        Children, I take my leave much vexed in
           spirit.
        I offer good advice, but you won't hear it.
        You all break in and chatter on and on.
        It's like a madhouse with the keeper gone.

DORINE If . . .

PERNELLE   Girl, you talk too much, and I'm afraid
        You're far too saucy for a lady's-maid.
        You push in everywhere and have your say.

DAMIS But . . .

PERNELLE   You, boy, grow more foolish every
        day.
        To think my grandson should be such a
           dunce!
        I've said a hundred times, if I've said it once,

That if you keep the course on which you've
    started,
You'll leave your worthy father broken-
    hearted.

MARIANE I think . . .

PERNELLE   And you, his sister, seem so pure,
So shy, so innocent, and so demure.
But you know what they say about still waters.
I pity parents with secretive daughters.

ELMIRE Now, Mother . . .

PERNELLE   And as for you, child, let me add
That your behaviour is extremely bad,
And a poor example for these children,
    too.
Their dear, dead mother did far better than
    you.
You're much too free with money, and I'm
    distressed
To see you so elaborately dressed.
When it's one's husband that one aims to
    please,
One has no need of costly fripperies.

CLEANTE Oh, Madame, really . . .

PERNELLE   You are her brother, Sir,
And I respect and love you; yet if I were
My son, this lady's good and pious spouse,
I wouldn't make you welcome in my house.
You're full of worldly counsels which, I
    fear,
Aren't suitable for decent folk to hear.
I've spoken bluntly, Sir; but it behooves
    us
Not to mince words when righteous fervour
    moves us.

DAMIS Your man Tartuffe is full of holy speeches . . .

PERNELLE And practises precisely what he preaches.
          He's a fine man, and should be listened to.
          I will not hear him mocked by fools like you.

DAMIS   Good God! Do you expect me to submit
          To the tyranny of that carping hypocrite?
          Must we forgo all joys and satisfactions
          Because that bigot censures all our actions?

DORINE   To hear him talk – and he talks all the time –
          There's nothing one can do that's not a crime.
          He rails at everything, your dear Tartuffe.

PERNELLE Whatever he reproves deserves reproof.
          He's out to save your souls, and all of you
          Must love him, as my son would have you do.

DAMIS   Ah no, Grandmother, I could never take
          To such a rascal, even for my father's sake.
          That's how I feel, and I shall not dissemble.
          His every action makes me seethe and tremble
          With helpless anger, and I have no doubt
          That he and I will shortly have it out.

DORINE   Surely it is a shame and a disgrace
          To see this man usurp the master's place –
          To see this beggar who, when first he came,
          Had not a shoe or shoestring to his name
          So far forget himself that he behaves
          As if the house were his, and we his slaves.

PERNELLE Well, mark my words, your souls would fare
              far better
          If you obeyed his precepts to the letter.

DORINE   You see him as a saint. I'm far less awed;
          In fact, I see right through him. He's a fraud.

PERNELLE Nonsense!

DORINE   His man Laurent's the same, or worse;
          I'd not trust either with a penny purse.

PERNELLE I can't say what his servant's morals may
              be;

His own great goodness I can guarantee.
You all regard him with distaste and fear
Because he tells you what you're loath to hear,
Condemns your sins, points out your moral
    flaws,
And humbly strives to further Heaven's cause.

DORINE   If sin is all that bothers him, why is it
He's so upset when folk drop in to visit?
Is Heaven so outraged by a social call
That he must prophesy against us all?
I'll tell you what I think: if you ask me,
He's jealous of my mistress' company.

PERNELLE   Rubbish! (*To* ELMIRE:) He's not alone, child,
    in complaining
Of all of your promiscuous entertaining.
Why, the whole neighbourhood's upset, I
    know,
By all these carriages that come and go,
With crowds of guests parading in and out
And noisy servants loitering about.
In all of this, I'm sure there's nothing vicious;
But why give people cause to be suspicious?

CLEANTE   They need no cause; they'll talk in any case.
Madam, this world would be a joyless place
If, fearing what malicious tòngues might say,
We locked our doors and turned our friends
    away.
And even if one did so dreary a thing,
D'you think those tongues would cease their
    chattering?
One can't fight slander; it's a losing battle;
Let us instead ignore their tittle-tattle.
Let's strive to live by conscience' clear
    decrees,
And let the gossips gossip as they please.

DORINE   If there is talk against us, I know the source:
          It's Daphne and her little husband, of course.
          Those who have greatest cause for guilt and
              shame
          Are quickest to besmirch a neighbour's name.
          When there's a chance for libel, they never
              miss it;
          When something can be made to seem illicit
          They're off at once to spread the joyous news,
          Adding to fact what fantasies they choose.
          By talking up their neighbour's indiscretions
          They seek to camouflage their own
              transgressions,
          Hoping that others' innocent affairs
          Will lend a hue of innocence to theirs,
          Or that their own black guilt will come to
              seem
          Part of a general shady colour-scheme.

PERNELLE All that is quite irrelevant. I doubt
          That anyone's more virtuous and devout
          Than dear Orante; and I'm informed that she
          Condemns your mode of life most
              vehemently.

DORINE   Oh, yes, she's strict, devout, and has no taint
          Of worldliness; in short, she seems a saint.
          But it was time which taught her that disguise;
          She's thus because she can't be otherwise.
          So long as her attractions could enthrall,
          She flounced and flirted and enjoyed it all,
          But now that they're no longer what they were
          She quits a world which fast is quitting her,
          And wears a veil of virtue to conceal
          Her bankrupt beauty and her lost appeal.
          That's what becomes of old coquettes today:
          Distressed when all their lovers fall away,

They see no recourse but to play the prude,
And so confer a style on solitude.
Thereafter, they're severe with everyone,
Condemning all our actions, pardoning none,
And claiming to be pure, austere, and zealous
When, if the truth were known, they're merely
    jealous,
And cannot bear to see another know
The pleasures time has forced them to forgo.

PERNELLE (*initially to* ELMIRE:)

That sort of talk is what you like to hear;
Therefore you'd have us all keep still, my
    dear,
While Madam rattles on the livelong day.
Nevertheless, I mean to have my say.
I tell you that you're blest to have Tartuffe
Dwelling, as my son's guest, beneath this
    roof;
That Heaven has sent him to forestall its
    wrath
By leading you, once more, to the true path;
That all he reprehends is reprehensible,
And that you'd better heed him, and be
    sensible.
These visits, balls, and parties in which you
    revel
Are nothing but inventions of the Devil.
One never hears a word that's edifying:
Nothing but chaff and foolishness and lying,
As well as vicious gossip in which one's
    neighbour
Is cut to bits with épée, foil, and sabre.
People of sense are driven half-insane
At such affairs, where noise and folly reign
And reputations perish thick and fast.

As a wise preacher said on Sunday last,
Parties are Towers of Babylon, because
The guests all babble on with never a pause;
And then he told a story which, I think . . .
(*To* CLEANTE:)
I heard that laugh, Sir, and I saw that wink!
Go find your silly friends and laugh some
   more!
Enough; I'm going; don't show me to the
   door.
I leave this household much dismayed and
   vexed;
I cannot say when I shall see you next.
(*slapping* FLIPOTE:)
Wake up, don't stand there gaping into
   space!
I'll slap some sense into that stupid face.
Move, move, you slut.

SCENE TWO : *Cléante, Dorine*

CLEANTE   I think I'll stay behind;
I want no further pieces of her mind.
How that old lady . . .

DORINE   Oh, what wouldn't she say
If she could hear you speak of her that way!
She'd thank you for the *lady*, but I'm sure
She'd find the *old* a little premature.

CLEANTE My, what a scene she made, and what a din!
And how this man Tartuffe has taken her
   in!

DORINE Yes, but her son is even worse deceived;
His folly must be seen to be believed.
In the late troubles, he played an able part

And served his king with wise and loyal heart,
But he's quite lost his senses since he fell
Beneath Tartuffe's infatuating spell.
He calls him brother, and loves him as his life,
Preferring him to mother, child, or wife.
In him and him alone will he confide;
He's made him his confessor and his guide;
He pets and pampers him with love more
    tender
Than any pretty mistress could engender,
Gives him the place of honour when they dine,
Delights to see him gorging like a swine,
Stuffs him with dainties till his guts distend,
And when he belches, cries 'God bless you,
    friend!'
In short, he's mad; he worships him; he
    dotes;
His deeds he marvels at, his words he quotes,
Thinking each act a miracle, each word
Oracular as those that Moses heard.
Tartuffe, much pleased to find so easy a
    victim,
Has in a hundred ways beguiled and tricked
    him,
Milked him of money, and with his
    permission
Established here a sort of Inquisition.
Even Laurent, his lackey, dares to give
Us arrogant advice on how to live;
He sermonizes us in thundering tones
And confiscates our ribbons and colognes.
Last week he tore a kerchief into pièces
Because he found it pressed in a *Life of Jesus:*
He said it was a sin to juxtapose
Unholy vanities and holy prose.

SCENE THREE: *Elmire, Mariane, Damis, Cléante, Dorine*

ELMIRE (*to* CLEANTE:)
    You did well not to follow; she stood in the door
    And said *verbatim* all she'd said before.
    I saw my husband coming. I think I'd best
    Go upstairs now, and take a little rest.

CLEANTE I'll wait and greet him here; then I must go.
    I've really only time to say hello.

DAMIS Sound him about my sister's wedding, please.
    I think Tartuffe's against it, and that he's
    Been urging Father to withdraw his blessing.
    As you well know, I'd find that most distressing.
    Unless my sister and Valère can marry,
    My hopes to wed *his* sister will miscarry,
    And I'm determined . . .

DORINE   He's coming.

SCENE FOUR: *Orgon, Cléante, Dorine*

ORGON   Ah, Brother, good-day.

CLEANTE Well, welcome back. I'm sorry I can't stay.
    How was the country? Blooming, I trust, and green?

ORGON Excuse me, Brother; just one moment.
    (*To* DORINE:)   Dorine . . .

(*To* CLEANTE:)
To put my mind at rest, I always learn
The household news the moment I return.
(*To* DORINE:)
Has all been well, these two days I've been
   gone?
How are the family? What's been going on?

DORINE Your wife, two days ago, had a bad fever,
And a fierce headache which refused to leave
   her.

ORGON Ah. And Tartuffe?

DORINE   Tartuffe? Why, he's round and red,
Bursting with health, and excellently fed.

ORGON Poor fellow!

DORINE   That night, the mistress was unable
To take a single bite at the dinner-table.
Her headache-pains, she said, were simply
   hellish.

ORGON Ah. And Tartuffe?

DORINE   He ate his meal with relish,
And zealously devoured in her presence
A leg of mutton and a brace of pheasants.

ORGON Poor fellow

DORINE   Well, the pains continued strong,
And so she tossed and tossed the whole night
   long,
Now icy-cold, now burning like a flame.
We sat beside her bed till morning came.

ORGON Ah. And Tartuffe?

DORINE   Why, having eaten, he rose
And sought his room, already in a doze,
Got into his warm bed, and snored away
In perfect peace until the break of day.

ORGON Poor fellow!

DORINE After much ado, we talked her

Into dispatching someone for the doctor.
He bled her, and the fever quickly fell.

ORGON Ah. And Tartuffe?

DORINE   He bore it very well.
To keep his cheerfulness at any cost,
And make up for the blood *Madame* had lost,
He drank, at lunch, four beakers full of port.

ORGON Poor fellow!

DORINE   Both are doing well, in short.
I'll go and tell *Madame* that you've expressed
Keen sympathy and anxious interest.

SCENE FIVE: Orgon, Cléante

CLEANTE That girl was laughing in your face, and
       though
I've no wish to offend you, even so
I'm bound to say that she had some excuse.
How can you possibly be such a goose?
Are you so dazed by this man's hocus-pocus
That all the world, save him, is out of focus?
You've given him clothing, shelter, food, and
       care;
Why must you also . . .

ORGON   Brother, stop right there.
You do not know the man of whom you speak.

CLEANTE I grant you that. But my judgment's not so
       weak
That I can't tell, by his effect on others . . .

ORGON Ah, when you meet him, you two will be like
       brothers!
There's been no loftier soul since time began.

He is a man-who . . . a man who . . . an
    excellent man.
To keep his precepts is to be reborn,
And view this dunghill of a world with scorn.
Yes, thanks to him I'm a changed man indeed.
Under his tutelage my soul's been freed
From earthly loves, and every human tie:
My mother, children, brother, and wife could
    die,
And I'd not feel a single moment's pain.

CLEANTE That's a fine sentiment, Brother; most
    humane.

ORGON Oh, had you seen Tartuffe as I first knew him,
Your heart, like mine, would have surrendered
    to him.
He used to come into our church each day
And humbly kneel nearby, and start to pray.
He'd draw the eyes of everybody there
By the deep fervour of his heartfelt prayer;
He'd sigh and weep, and sometimes with a
    sound
Of rapture he would bend and kiss the
    ground;
And when I rose to go, he'd run before
To offer me holy-water at the door.
His serving-man, no less devout than he,
Informed me of his master's poverty;
I gave him gifts, but in his humbleness
He'd beg me every time to give him less.
'Oh, that's too much,' he'd cry, 'too much by
    twice!
I don't deserve it. The half, Sir, would
    suffice.'
And when I wouldn't take it back, he'd share
Half of it with the poor, right then and there.

At length, Heaven prompted me to take
   him in
To dwell with us, and free our souls from sin.
He guides our lives, and to protect my honour
Stays by my wife, and keeps an eye upon her;
He tells me whom she sees, and all she does,
And seems more jealous than I ever was!
And how austere he is! Why, he can detect
A mortal sin where you would least suspect;
In smallest trifles, he's extremely strict.
Last week, his conscience was severely
   pricked
Because, while praying, he had caught a flea
And killed it, so he felt, too wrathfully.

CLEANTE Good God, man! Have you lost your common
   sense –
Or is this all some joke at my expense?
How can you stand there and in all
   sobriety . . .

ORGON Brother, your language savours of impiety.
Too much free-thinking's made your faith
   unsteady,
And as I've warned you many times already,
'Twill get you into trouble before you're
   through.

CLEANTE So I've been told before by dupes like you:
Being blind, you'd have all others blind as
   well;
The clear-eyed man you call an infidel,
And he who sees through humbug and
   pretence
Is charged, by you, with want of reverence.
Spare me your warnings, Brother; I have no
   fear
Of speaking out, for you and Heaven to hear,

Against affected zeal and pious knavery.
There's true and false in piety, as in bravery,
And just as those whose courage shines the
    most
In battle, are the least inclined to boast,
So those whose hearts are truly pure and
    lowly
Don't make a flashy show of being holy.
There's a vast difference, so it seems to me,
Between true piety and hypocrisy:
How do you fail to see it, may I ask?
Is not a face quite different from a mask?
Cannot sincerity and cunning art,
Reality and semblance, be told apart?
Are scarecrows just like men, and do you hold
That a false coin is just as good as gold?
Ah, Brother, man's a strangely fashioned
    creature
Who seldom is content to follow Nature,
But recklessly pursues his inclination
Beyond the narrow bounds of moderation,
And often, by transgressing Reason's laws,
Perverts a loftly aim or noble cause.
A passing observation, but it applies.

ORGON I see, dear Brother, that you're profoundly
    wise;
You harbour all the insight of the age.
You are our one clear mind, our only sage,
The era's oracle, its Cato too,
And all mankind are fools compared to you.

CLEANTE Brother, I don't pretend to be a sage,
Nor have I all the wisdom of the age.
There's just one insight I would dare to claim:
I know that true and false are not the same;
And just as there is nothing I more revere

Than a soul whose faith is steadfast and
    sincere,
Nothing that I more cherish and admire
Than honest zeal and true religious fire,
So there is nothing that I find more base
Than specious piety's dishonest face –
Than these bold mountebanks, these histrios
Whose impious mummeries and hollow shows
Exploit our love of Heaven, and make a jest
Of all that men think holiest and best;
These calculating souls who offer prayers
Not to their Maker, but as public wares,
And seek to buy respect and reputation
With lifted eyes and sighs of exaltation;
These charlatans, I say, whose pilgrim souls
Proceed, by way of Heaven, toward earthly
    goals,
Who weep and pray and swindle and extort,
Who preach the monkish life, but haunt the
    court,
Who make their zeal the partner of their vice –
Such men are vengeful, sly, and cold as ice,
And when there is an enemy to defame
They cloak their spite in fair religion's name,
Their private spleen and malice being made
To seem a high and virtuous crusade,
Until, to mankind's reverent applause,
They crucify their foe in Heaven's cause.
Such knaves are all too common; yet, for the
    wise,
True piety isn't hard to recognize,
And, happily, these present times provide us
With bright examples to instruct and guide
    us.
Consider Ariston and Périandre;

Look at Oronte, Alcidamas, Clitandre;
Their virtue is acknowledged; who could
    doubt it?
But you won't hear them beat the drum about
    it.
They're never ostentatious, never vain,
And their religion's moderate and humane;
It's not their way to criticize and chide:
They think censoriousness a mark of pride,
And therefore, letting others preach and rave,
They show, by deeds, how Christians should
    behave.
They think no evil of their fellow man,
But judge of him as kindly as they can.
They don't intrigue and wangle and conspire;
To lead a good life is their one desire;
The sinner wakes no rancorous hate in them;
It is the sin alone which they condemn;
Nor do they try to show a fiercer zeal
For Heaven's cause than Heaven itself could
    feel.
These men I honour, these men I advocate
As models for us all to emulate.
Your man is not their sort at all, I fear:
And, while your praise of him is quite sincere,
I think that you've been dreadfully deluded.

ORGON   Now then, dear Brother, is your speech
    concluded?
CLEANTE Why, yes.
ORGON   Your servant, Sir. (*He turns to go.*)
CLEANTE   No, Brother; wait.
There's one more matter. You agreed of late
That young Valère might have your daughter's
    hand.
ORGON   I did.

CLEANTE   And set the date, I understand.
ORGON Quite so.
CLEANTE   You've now postponed it; is that true?
ORGON No doubt.
CLEANTE   The match no longer pleases you?
ORGON Who knows?
CLEANTE   D'you mean to go back on your word?
ORGON I won't say that.
CLEANTE   Has anything occurred
Which might entitle you to break your pledge?
ORGON Perhaps.
CLEANTE   Why must you hem, and haw, and hedge?
The boy asked me to sound you in this
         affair . . .
ORGON It's been a pleasure.
CLEANTE   But what shall I tell Valère?
ORGON Whatever you like.
CLEANTE   But what have you decided?
What are your plans?
ORGON   I plan, Sir, to be guided
By Heaven's will.
CLEANTE   Come, Brother, don't talk rot.
You've given Valère your word; will you keep
         it, or not?
ORGON Good day.
CLEANTE This looks like poor Valère's undoing;
I'll go and warn him that there's trouble
         brewing.

Act Two

SCENE ONE: Orgon, Mariane

ORGON Mariane.

MARIANE Yes, Father?

ORGON A word with you; come here.

MARIANE What are you looking for?

ORGON (*peering into a small closet:*)

Eavesdroppers, dear.
I'm making sure we shan't be overheard.
Someone in there could catch our every word.
Ah, good, we're safe. Now, Mariane, my
child,
You're a sweet girl who's tractable and mild,
Whom I hold dear, and think most highly
of.

MARIANE I'm deeply grateful, Father, for your love.

ORGON That's well said, Daughter; and you can repay
me
If, in all things, you'll cheerfully obey me.

MARIANE To please you, Sir, is what delights me best.

ORGON Good, good. Now, what d'you think of
Tartuffe, our guest?

MARIANE I, Sir?

ORGON Yes. Weigh your answer; think it through.

MARIANE Oh, dear. I'll say whatever you wish me to.

ORGON That's wisely said, my Daughter. Say of him,
then,
That he's the very worthiest of men,
And that you're fond of him, and would rejoice

In being his wife, if that should be my choice.
Well?

MARIANE What?

ORGON What's that?

MARIANE I . . .

ORGON Well?

MARIANE Forgive me, pray.

ORGON Did you not hear me?

MARIANE Of *whom*, Sir, must I say
That I am fond of him, and would rejoice
In being his wife, if that should be your
choice?

ORGON Why, of Tartuffe.

MARIANE But, Father, that's false, you
know.
Why would you have me say what isn't so?

ORGON Because I am resolved it shall be true.
That it's my wish should be enough for
you.

MARIANE You can't mean, Father . . .

ORGON Yes, Tartuffe shall be
Allied by marriage to this family,
And he's to be your husband, is that clear?
It's a father's privilege . . .

SCENE TWO : *Dorine, Orgon, Mariane*

ORGON (*to* DORINE:)
What are you doing in here?
Is curiosity so fierce a passion
With you, that you must eavesdrop in this
fashion?

DORINE There's lately been a rumour going about –
        Based on some hunch or chance remark, no
           doubt –
        That you mean Mariane to wed Tartuffe.
        I've laughed it off, of course, as just a spoof.
ORGON You find it so incredible?
DORINE   Yes, I do.
        I won't accept that story, even from you.
ORGON Well, you'll believe it when the thing is done.
DORINE Yes, yes, of course. Go on and have your
           fun.
ORGON I've never been more serious in my life.
DORINE Ha!
ORGON   Daughter, I mean it; you're to be his wife.
DORINE No, don't believe your father; it's all a hoax.
ORGON See here, young woman . . .
DORINE   Come, Sir, no more jokes;
        You can't fool us.
ORGON   How dare you talk that way?
DORINE All right, then: we believe you, sad to say.
        But how a man like you, who looks so wise
        And wears a moustache of such splendid size,
        Can be so foolish as to . . .
ORGON   Silence, please!
        My girl, you take too many liberties.
        I'm master here, as you must not forget.
DORINE Do let's discuss this calmly; don't be upset.
        You can't be serious, Sir, about this plan.
        What should that bigot want with Mariane?
        Praying and fasting ought to keep him busy.
        And then, in terms of wealth and rank, what is
           he?
        Why should a man of property like you
        Pick out a beggar son-in-law?
ORGON   That will do.

Speak of his poverty with reverence.
His is a pure and saintly indigence
Which far transcends all worldly pride and
    pelf.
He lost his fortune, as he says himself,
Because he cared for Heaven alone, and so
Was careless of his interests here below.
I mean to get him out of his present straits
And help him to recover his estates –
Which, in his part of the world, have no small
    fame.
Poor though he is, he's a gentleman just the
    same.

DORINE   Yes, so he tells us; and, Sir, it seems to me
Such pride goes very ill with piety.
A man whose spirit spurns this dungy earth
Ought not to brag of lands and noble birth;
Such worldly arrogance will hardly square
With meek devotion and the life of prayer.
. . . But this approach, I see, has drawn a
    blank;
Let's speak, then, of his person, not his rank.
Doesn't it seem to you a trifle grim
To give a girl like her to a man like him?
When two are so ill-suited, can't you see
What the sad consequence is bound to be?
A young girl's virtue is imperilled, Sir,
When such a marriage is imposed on her;
For if one's bridegroom isn't to one's taste,
It's hardly an inducement to be chaste,
And many a man with horns upon his brow
Has made his wife the thing that she is now.
It's hard to be a faithful wife, in short,
To certain husbands of a certain sort,
And he who gives his daughter to a man she hates

Must answer for her sins at Heaven's gates.
Think, Sir, before you play so risky a role.

ORGON This servant-girl presumes to save my soul!

DORINE You would do well to ponder what I've said.

ORGON Daughter, we'll disregard this dunderhead.
Just trust your father's judgment. Oh, I'm
    aware
That I once promised you to young Valère;
But now I hear he gambles, which greatly
    shocks me;
What's more, I've doubts about his
    orthodoxy.
His visits to church, I note, are very few.

DORINE Would you have him go at the same hours as you,
And kneel nearby, to be sure of being seen?

ORGON I can dispense with such remarks, Dorine.
(*To* MARIANE:)
Tartuffe, however, is sure of Heaven's
    blessing,
And that's the only treasure worth possessing.
This match will bring you joys beyond all
    measure;
Your cup will overflow with every pleasure;
You two will interchange your faithful loves
Like two sweet cherubs, or two turtle-doves.
No harsh word shall be heard, no frown be
    seen,
And he shall make you happy as a queen.

DORINE And she'll make him a cuckold, just wait and
    see.

ORGON What language!

DORINE   Oh, he's a man of destiny;
He's *made* for horns, and what the stars
    demand
Your daughter's virtue surely can't withstand.

ORGON   Don't interrupt me further. Why can't you
       learn
      That certain things are none of your concern?

DORINE   It's for your own sake that I interfere.
      (*She repeatedly interrupts* ORGON *just as he is
        turning to speak to his daughter:*)

ORGON   Most kind of you. Now, hold your tongue,
      d'you hear?

DORINE   If I didn't love you . . .

ORGON   Spare me your affection.

DORINE   I'll love you, Sir, in spite of your objection.

ORGON   Blast!

DORINE   I can't bear, Sir, for your honour's sake,
      To let you make this ludicrous mistake.

ORGON   You mean to go on talking?

DORINE   If I didn't protest
      This sinful marriage, my conscience couldn't
       rest.

ORGON   If you don't hold your tongue, you little
      shrew . . .

DORINE   What, lost your temper? A pious man like
      you?

ORGON   Yes! Yes! You talk and talk. I'm maddened by
      it.
      Once and for all, I tell you to be quiet.

DORINE   Well, I'll be quiet. But I'll be thinking hard.

ORGON   Think all you like, but you had better
      guard
      That saucy tongue of yours, or I'll . . .
      (*Turning back to* MARIAN:)
                     Now, child,
      I've weighed this matter fully.

DORINE   (*aside:*)   It drives me wild
      That I can't speak.
      (ORGON *turns his head, and she is silent.*)

ORGON   Tartuffe is no young dandy,
But, still, his person . . .

DORINE (*aside:*)   Is as sweet as candy.

ORGON Is such that, even if you shouldn't care
For his other merits . . .
    (*He turns and stands facing* DORINE, *arms
       crossed.*)

DORINE (*aside:*)   They'll make a lovely pair.
If I were she, no man would marry me
Against my inclination, and go scot-free.
He'd learn, before the wedding-day was over,
How readily a wife can find a lover.

ORGON (*to* DORINE:)
It seems you treat my orders as a joke.

DORINE Why, what's the matter? 'Twas not to you I
      spoke.

ORGON What *were* you doing?

DORINE   Talking to myself, that's all.

ORGON Ah! (*aside:*) One more bit of impudence and
      gall,
And I shall give her a good slap in the face.
    (*He puts himself in position to slap her;* DORINE,
       *whenever he glances at her, stands immobile
       and silent:*)
Daughter, you shall accept, and with good
      grace,
The husband I've selected . . . Your wedding-
      day . . .
    (*To* DORINE:)
Why don't you talk to yourself?

DORINE   I've nothing to say.

ORGON Come, just one word.

DORINE   No thank you, Sir. I pass.

ORGON Come, speak; I'm waiting.

DORINE   I'd not be such an ass.

ORGON (*turning to* MARIANE:)

> In short, dear Daughter, I mean to be obeyed,
> And you must bow to the sound choice I've made.

DORINE (*moving away:*)

> I'd not wed such a monster, even in jest.
> (ORGON *attempts to slap her, but misses.*)

ORGON Daughter, that maid of yours is a thorough pest;

> She makes me sinfully annoyed and nettled.
> I can't speak further; my nerves are too unsettled.
> She's so upset me by her insolent talk,
> I'll calm myself by going for a walk.

SCENE THREE: *Dorine, Mariane*

DORINE (*returning:*)

> Well, have you lost your tongue, girl? Must I play
> Your part, and say the lines you ought to say?
> Faced with a fate so hideous and absurd,
> Can you not utter one dissenting word?

MARIANE What good would it do? A father's power is great.

DORINE Resist him now, or it will be too late.

MARIANE But . . .

DORINE   Tell him one cannot love at a father's whim;
         That you shall marry for yourself, not him;
         That since it's you who are to be the bride,
         It's you, not he, who must be satisfied;
         And that if his Tartuffe is so sublime,
         He's free to marry him at any time.

MARIANE I've bowed so long to Father's strict control,
         I couldn't oppose him now, to save my
            soul.

DORINE   Come, come, Mariane. Do listen to reason,
            won't you?
         Valère has asked your hand. Do you love him,
            or don't you?

MARIANE Oh, how unjust of you! What can you
            mean
         By asking such a question, dear Dorine?
         You know the depth of my affection for
            him;
         I've told you a hundred times how I adore
            him.

DORINE   I don't believe in everything I hear;
         Who knows if your professions were sincere?

MARIANE There were, Dorine, and you do me wrong to
            doubt it;
         Heaven knows that I've been all too frank
            about it.

DORINE   You love him, then?

MARIANE   Oh, more than I can express.

DORINE   And he, I take it, cares for you no less?

MARIANE I think so.

DORINE   And you both, with equal fire,
         Burn to be married?

MARIANE   That is our one desire.

DORINE   What of Tartuffe, then? What of your father's
            plan?

MARIANE   I'll kill myself, if I'm forced to wed that man.

DORINE   I hadn't thought of that recourse. How splendid!
Just die, and all your troubles will be ended!
A fine solution. Oh, it maddens me
To hear you talk in that self-pitying key.

MARIANE   Dorine, how harsh you are! It's most unfair.
You have no sympathy for my despair.

DORINE   I've none at all for people who talk drivel
And, faced with difficulties, whine and snivel.

MARIANE   No doubt I'm timid, but it would be wrong . . .

DORINE   True love requires a heart that's firm and strong.

MARIANE   I'm strong in my affection for Valère,
But coping with my father is his affair.

DORINE   But if your father's brain has grown so cracked
Over his dear Tartuffe that he can retract
His blessing, though your wedding-day was named,
It's surely not Valère who's to be blamed.

MARIANE   If I defied my father, as you suggest,
Would it not seem unmaidenly, at best?
Shall I defend my love at the expense
Of brazenness and disobedience?
Shall I parade my heart's desires, and flaunt . . .

DORINE   No, I ask nothing of you. Clearly you want
To be Madame Tartuffe, and I feel bound
Not to oppose a wish so very sound.
What right have I to criticize the match?
Indeed, my dear, the man's a brilliant catch.

Monsieur Tartuffe! Now, there's a man of
    weight!
Yes, yes, Monsieur Tartuffe, I'm bound to
    state,
Is quite a person; that's not to be denied;
'Twill be no little thing to be his bride.
The world already rings with his renown;
He's a great noble – in his native town;
His ears are red, he has a pink complexion,
And all in all, he'll suit you to perfection.

MARIANE Dear God!

DORINE   Oh, how triumphant you will feel
At having caught a husband so ideal!

MARIANE Oh, do stop teasing, and use your cleverness
To get me out of this appalling mess.
Advise me, and I'll do whatever you say.

DORINE Ah no, a dutiful daughter must obey
Her father, even if he weds her to an ape.
You've a bright future; why struggle to
    escape?
Tartuffe will take you back where his family
    lives,
To a small town aswarm with relatives –
Uncle and cousins whom you'll be charmed to
    meet.
You'll be received at once by the elite,
Calling upon the bailiff's wife, no less –
Even, perhaps, upon the mayoress,
Who'll sit you down in the *best* kitchen chair.
Then, once a year, you'll dance at the village
    fair
To the drone of bagpipes – two of them, in
    fact –
And see a puppet-show, or an animal act.
Your husband . . .

MARIANE   Oh, you turn my blood to ice!
Stop torturing me, and give me your advice.

DORINE (*threatening to go:*)
Your servant, Madam.

MARIANE   Dorine, I beg of you . . .

DORINE No, you deserve it; this marriage must go
through.

MARIANE Dorine!

DORINE   No.

MARIANE   Not Tartuffe! You know I think him . . .

DORINE Tartuffe's your cup of tea, and you shall drink
him.

MARIANE I've always told you everything, and relied . . .

DORINE No. You deserve to be tartuffified.

MARIANE Well, since you mock me and refuse to care,
I'll henceforth seek my solace in despair:
Despair shall be my counsellor and friend,
And help me bring my sorrows to an end.
(*She starts to leave.*)

DORINE There now, come back; my anger has
subsided.
You do deserve some pity, I've decided.

MARIANE Dorine, if Father makes me undergo
This dreadful martyrdom, I'll die, I know.

DORINE Don't fret; it won't be difficult to discover
Some plan of action . . . But here's Valère,
your lover.

SCENE FOUR: Valère, Mariane, Dorine

VALERE Madam, I've just received some wondrous news
Regarding which I'd like to hear your views.

MARIANE What news?

VALERE You're marrying Tartuffe.

MARIANE I find
That Father does have such a match in mind.

VALERE Your father, Madam . . .

MARIANE . . . has just this minute said
That it's Tartuffe he wishes me to wed.

VALERE Can he be serious?

MARIANE Oh, indeed he can;
He's clearly set his heart upon the plan.

VALERE And what position do you propose to take, Madam?

MARIANE Why – I don't know.

VALERE For heaven's sake –
You don't know?

MARIANE No.

VALERE Well, well!

MARIANE Advise me, do.

VALERE Marry the man. That's my advice to you.

MARIANE That's your advice?

VALERE Yes.

MARIANE Truly?

VALERE Oh, absolutely.
You couldn't choose more wisely, more astutely.

MARIANE Thanks for this counsel; I'll follow it, of
         course.

VALERE Do, do; I'm sure 'twill cost you no remorse.

MARIANE To give it didn't cause your heart to break.

VALERE I gave it, Madam, only for your sake.

MARIANE And it's for your sake that I take it, Sir.

DORINE (*withdrawing to the rear of the stage:*)
        Let's see which fool will prove the stubborner.

VALERE So! I am nothing to you, and it was flat
        Deception when you . . .

MARIANE   Please, enough of that.
        You've told me plainly that I should agree
        To wed the man my father's chosen for me,
        And since you've deigned to counsel me so
           wisely,
        I promise, Sir, to do as you advise me.

VALERE Ah, no, 'twas not by me that you were swayed.
        No, your decision was already made;
        Though now, to save appearances, you
           protest
        That you're betraying me at my behest.

MARIANE Just as you say.

VALERE   Quite so. And I now see
        That you were never truly in love with me.

MARIANE Alas, you're free to think so if you choose.

VALERE I choose to think so, and here's a bit of news:
        You've spurned my hand, but I know where
           to turn
        For kinder treatment, as you shall quickly
           learn.

MARIANE I'm sure you do. Your noble qualities
        Inspire affection . . .

VALERE   Forget my qualities, please.
        They don't inspire you overmuch, I find.
        But there's another lady I have in mind

Whose sweet and generous nature will not
    scorn
To compensate me for the loss I've borne.

MARIANE   I'm no great loss, and I'm sure that you'll
    transfer
Your heart quite painlessly from me to her.

VALERE   I'll do my best to take it in my stride.
The pain I feel at being cast aside
Time and forgetfulness may put an end to.
Or if I can't forget, I shall pretend to.
No self-respecting person is expected
To go on loving once he's been rejected.

MARIANE   Now, that's a fine, high-minded sentiment.

VALERE   One to which any sane man would assent.
Would you prefer it if I pined away
In hopeless passion till my dying day?
Am I to yield you to a rival's arms
And not console myself with other charms?

MARIANE   Go then: console yourself; don't hesitate.
I wish you to; indeed, I cannot wait.

VALERE   You wish me to?

MARIANE   Yes.

VALERE   That's the final straw.
Madam, farewell. Your wish shall be my law.
(*He starts to leave, and then returns: this
    repeatedly:*)

MARIANE   Splendid.

VALERE   (*coming back again:*)
           This breach, remember, is of your making;
It's you who've driven me to the step I'm
    taking.

MARIANE   Of course.

VALERE   (*coming back again:*)
                Remember, too, that I am
merely

Following your example.

MARIANE   I see that clearly.

VALERE   Enough. I'll go and do your bidding,
       then.

MARIANE   Good.

VALERE   (*coming back again:*)
              You shall never see my face again.

MARIANE   Excellent.

VALERE   (*walking to the door, then turning about:*)
             Yes?

MARIANE   What?

VALERE   What's that? What did you say?

MARIANE   Nothing. You're dreaming.

VALERE   Ah. Well, I'm on my way.
      Farewell, *Madame.*
      (*He moves slowly away.*)

MARIANE   Farewell.

DORINE   (*to* MARIANE:)

                  If you ask me,
      Both of you are as mad as mad can be.
      Do stop this nonsense, now. I've only let
       you
      Squabble so long to see where it would get
       you.
      Whoa there, Monsieure Valère!
      (*She goes and seizes* VALERE *by the arm; he
      makes a great show of resistance.*)

VALERE   What's this, Dorine?

DORINE   Come here.

VALERE   No, no, my heart's too full of spleen.
      Don't hold me back; her wish must be
       obeyed.

DORINE   Stop!

VALERE   It's too late now; my decision's made.

DORINE   Oh, pooh!

MARIANE (*aside:*)
> He hates the sight of me, that's plain.
> I'll go, and so deliver him from pain.

DORINE (*leaving* VALERE, *running after* MARIANE:)
And now *you* run away! Come back.

MARIANE
> No, no.
> Nothing you say will keep me here. Let go!

VALERE (*aside:*)
> She cannot bear my presence, I perceive.
> To spare her further torment, I shall leave.

DORINE (*leaving* MARIANE, *running after* VALERE:)
Again! You'll not escape, Sir; don't you try it.
Come here, you two. Stop fussing, and be
> quiet.
(*She takes* VALERE *by the hand, then* MARIANE,
> *and draws them together.*)

VALERE (*to* DORINE:)
What do you want of me?

MARIANE (*to* DORINE:)
> What is the point of this?

DORINE We're going to have a little armistice.
(*To* VALERE:)
Now, weren't you silly to get so overheated?

VALERE Didn't you see how badly I was treated?

DORINE (*to* MARIANE:)
Aren't you a simpleton, to have lost your
> head?

MARIANE Didn't you hear the hateful things he said?

DORINE (*to* VALERE:)
You're both great fools. Her sole desire,
> Valère,
Is to be yours in marriage. To that I'll swear.
(*To* MARIANE:)
He loves you only, and he wants no wife
But you, Mariane. On that I'll stake my life.

MARIANE (*to* VALERE:)
Then why you advised me so, I cannot see.

VALERE (*to* MARIANE:)
On such a question, why ask advice of *me*?

DORINE Oh, you're impossible. Give me your hands,
you two.
(*To* VALERE:)
Yours first.

VALERE (*giving* DORINE *his hand:*)
But why?

DORINE (*to* MARIANE:)
And now a hand from you.

MARIANE (*also giving* DORINE *her hand:*)
What are you doing?

DORINE There: a perfect fit.
You suit each other better than you'll admit.
(VALERE *and* MARIANE *hold hands for some time
without looking at each other.*)

VALERE (*turning towards* MARIANE:)
Ah, come, don't be so haughty. Give a man
A look of kindness, won't you, Mariane?
(MARIANE *turns towards* VALERE *and smiles.*)

DORINE I tell you, lovers are completely mad!

VALERE (*to* MARIANE:)
Now come, confess that you were very bad
To hurt my feelings as you did just now.
I have a just complaint, you must allow.

MARIANE *You* must allow that you were most
unpleasant . . .

DORINE Let's table that discussion for the present;
Your father has a plan which must be stopped.

MARIANE Advise us, then; what means must we adopt?

DORINE We'll use all manner of means, and all at once.
(*To* MARIANE:)
Your father's addled; he's acting like a dunce.

Therefore you'd better humour the old fossil.
Pretend to yield to him, be sweet and docile,
And then postpone, as often as necessary,
The day on which you have agreed to marry.
You'll thus gain time, and time will turn the
    trick.
Sometimes, for instance, you'll be taken sick,
And that will seem good reason for delay;
Or some bad omen will make you change the
    day –
You'll dream of muddy water, or you'll pass
A dead man's hearse, or break a looking-glass.
If all else fails, no man can marry you
Unless you take his ring and say 'I do.'
But now, let's separate. If they should find
Us talking here, our plot might be divined.
(*To* VALERE:)
Go to your friends, and tell them what's
    occurred,
And have them urge her father to keep his
    word.
Meanwhile, we'll stir her brother into action,
And get Elmire, as well, to join our faction.
Good-bye.

VALERE (*to* MARIANE:)
                Though each of us will do his best,
It's your true heart on which my hopes shall
    rest.

MARIANE (*to* VALERE:)
Regardless of what Father may decide,
None but Valère shall claim me as his bride.

VALERE Oh, how those words content me! Come what
    will . . .

DORINE Oh, lovers, lovers! Their tongues are never
    still.

Be off, now.

VALERE (*turning to go, then turning back:*)
One last word . . .

DORINE   No time to chat:
You leave by this door; and *you* leave by that.
(DORINE *pushes them, by the shoulders, towards
opposing doors.*)

Act Three

SCENE ONE: Damis, Dorine

DAMIS   May lightning strike me even as I speak,
        May all men call me cowardly and weak,
        If any fear or scruple holds me back
        From settling things, at once, with that great
        quack!

DORINE Now, don't give way to violent emotion.
        Your father's merely talked about this notion,
        And words and deeds are far from being one.
        Much that is talked about is left undone.

DAMIS   No, I must stop that scoundrel's
        machinations;
        I'll go and tell him off; I'm out of patience.

DORINE Do calm down and be practical. I had rather
        My mistress dealt with him – and with your
        father.
        She has some influence with Tartuffe, I've
        noted.
        He hangs upon her words, seems most
        devoted,
        And may, indeed, be smitten by her charm.
        Pray Heaven it's true! 'Twould do our cause
        no harm.
        She sent for him, just now, to sound him out
        On this affair you're so incensed about;
        She'll find out where he stands, and tell him,
        too,
        What dreadful strife and trouble will ensue
        If he lends countenance to your father's plan.

I couldn't get in to see him, but his man
Says that he's almost finished with his prayers.
Go, now. I'll catch him when he comes
    downstairs.

DAMIS I want to hear this conference, and I will.

DORINE No, they must be alone.

DAMIS   Oh, I'll keep still.

DORINE Not you. I know your temper. You'd start a
    brawl,
And shout and stamp your foot and spoil it all.
Go on.

DAMIS   I won't; I have a perfect right . . .

DORINE Lord, you're a nuisance! He's coming; get out
    of sight.

(DAMIS *conceals himself in a closet at the rear of
the stage.*)

SCENE TWO: *Tartuffe, Dorine*

TARTUFFE (*observing* DORINE, *and calling to his
    manservant offstage:*)
Hang up my hair-shirt, put my scourge in
    place,
And pray, Laurent, for Heaven's perpetual
    grace.
I'm going to the prison now, to share
My last few coins with the poor wretches
    there.

DORINE (*aside:*)
Dear God, what affectation! What a fake!

TARTUFFE You wished to see me?

DORINE   Yes . . .

TARTUFFE (*taking a handkerchief from his pocket:*)

                  For mercy's sake,
Please take this handkerchief, before you
    speak.

DORINE What?

TARTUFFE   Cover that bosom, girl. The flesh is weak,
And unclean thoughts are difficult to control.
Such sights as that can undermine the soul.

DORINE Your soul, it seems, has very poor defences,
And flesh makes quite an impact on your
    senses.
It's strange that you're so easily excited;
My own desires are not so soon ignited,
And if I saw you naked as a beast,
Not all your hide would tempt me in the least.

TARTUFFE Girl, speak more modestly; unless you do,
I shall be forced to take my leave of you.

DORINE Oh, no, it's I who must be on my way;
I've just one little message to convey.
Madame is coming down, and begs you, Sir,
To wait and have a word or two with her.

TARTUFFE Gladly.

DORINE (*aside:*)

         That had a softening effect!
I think my guess about him was correct.

TARTUFFE Will she be long?

DORINE   No: that's her step I hear.
Ah, here she is, and I shall disappear.

SCENE THREE: Elmire, Tartuffe

TARTUFFE   May Heaven, whose infinite goodness we
        adore,
    Preserve your body and soul forevermore,
    And bless your days, and answer thus the plea
    Of one who is its humblest votary.

ELMIRE   I thank you for that pious wish. But please,
    Do take a chair and let's be more at ease.
    (*They sit down.*)

TARTUFFE   I trust that you are once more well and
        strong?

ELMIRE   Oh, yes: the fever didn't last for long.

TARTUFFE   My prayers are too unworthy, I am sure,
    To have gained from Heaven this most
        gracious cure;
    But lately, Madam, my every supplication
    Has had for object your recuperation.

ELMIRE   You shouldn't have troubled so. I don't
        deserve it.

TARTUFFE   Your health is priceless, Madam, and to
        preserve it
    I'd gladly give my own, in all sincerity.

ELMIRE   Sir, you outdo us all in Christian charity.
    You've been most kind. I count myself your
        debtor.

TARTUFFE   'Twas nothing, Madam. I long to serve you
        better.

ELMIRE   There's a private matter I'm anxious to
        discuss.
    I'm glad there's no one here to hinder us.

TARTUFFE I too am glad; it floods my heart with bliss
To find myself alone with you like this.
For just this chance I've prayed with all my
power –
But prayed in vain, until this happy hour.

ELMIRE This won't take long, Sir, and I hope you'll
be
Entirely frank and unconstrained with me.

TARTUFFE Indeed, there's nothing I had rather do
Than bare my inmost heart and soul to you.
First, let me say that what remarks I've made
About the constant visits you are paid
Were prompted not by any mean emotion,
But rather by a pure and deep devotion,
A fervent zeal . . .

ELMIRE   No need for explanation.
Your sole concern, I'm sure, was my salvation.

TARTUFFE (*taking* ELMIRE'*s hand and pressing her
fingertips:*)
Quite so; and such great fervour do I feel . . .

ELMIRE Ooh! Please! You're pinching.

TARTUFFE   'Twas from excess of zeal.
I never meant to cause you pain, I swear.
I'd rather . . .
(*He places his hand on* ELMIRE'*s knee.*)

ELMIRE   What can your hand be doing there?

TARTUFFE Feeling your gown; what soft, fine-woven
stuff!

ELMIRE Please, I'm extremely ticklish. That's enough.
(*She draws her chair away;* TARTUFFE *pulls his
after her.*)

TARTUFFE (*fondling the lace collar of her gown:*)
My, my, what lovely lacework on your dress!
The workmanship's miraculous, no less.
I've not seen anything to equal it.

ELMIRE   Yes, quite. But let's talk business for a bit.
         They say my husband means to break his
            word
         And give his daughter to you, Sir. Had you
            heard?

TARTUFFE He did once mention it. But I confess
         I dream of quite a different happiness.
         It's elsewhere, Madam, that my eyes discern
         The promise of that bliss for which I yearn.

ELMIRE   I see: you care for nothing here below.

TARTUFFE Ah, well – my heart's not made of stone, you
            know.

ELMIRE   All your desires mount heavenward, I'm sure,
         In scorn of all that's earthly and impure.

TARTUFFE A love of heavenly beauty does not preclude
         A proper love for earthly pulchritude;
         Our senses are quite rightly captivated
         By perfect works our Maker has created.
         Some glory clings to all that Heaven has
            made;
         In you, all Heaven's marvels are displayed.
         On that fair face, such beauties have been
            lavished,
         The eyes are dazzled and the heart is ravished;
         How could I look on you, O flawless creature,
         And not adore the Author of all Nature,
         Feeling a love both passionate and pure
         For you, his triumph of self-portraiture?
         At first, I trembled lest that love should be
         A subtle snare that Hell had laid for me;
         I vowed to flee the sight of you, eschewing
         A rapture that might prove my soul's
            undoing;
         But soon, fair being, I became aware
         That my deep passion could be made to square

With rectitude, and with my bounden duty.
I thereupon surrendered to your beauty.
It is, I know, presumptuous on my part
To bring you this poor offering of my heart,
And it is not my merit, Heaven knows,
But your compassion on which my hopes
    repose.
You are my peace, my solace, my salvation;
On you depends my bliss – or desolation;
I bide your judgment and, as you think best,
I shall be either miserable or blest.

ELMIRE Your declaration is most gallant, Sir,
But don't you think it's out of character?
You'd have done better to restrain your
    passion
And think before you spoke in such a fashion.
It ill becomes a pious man like you . . .

TARTUFFE I may be pious, but I'm human too:
With your celestial charms before his eyes,
A man has not the power to be wise.
I know such words sound strangely, coming
    from me,
But I'm no angel, nor was meant to be,
And if you blame my passion, you must needs
Reproach as well the charms on which it
    feeds.
Your loveliness I had no sooner seen
Than you became my soul's unrivalled queen;
Before your seraph glance, divinely sweet,
My heart's defences crumbled in defeat,
And nothing fasting, prayer, or tears might do
Could stay my spirit from adoring you.
My eyes, my sighs have told you in the past
What now my lips make bold to say at last,
And if, in your great goodness, you will deign

To look upon your slave, and ease his pain, –
If, in compassion for my soul's distress,
You'll stoop to comfort my unworthiness,
I'll raise to you, in thanks for that sweet
    manna,
An endless hymn, an infinite hosanna.
With me, of course, there need be no anxiety,
No fear of scandal or of notoriety.
These young court gallants, whom all the
    ladies fancy,
Are vain in speech, in action rash and chancy;
When they succeed in love, the world soon
    knows it;
No favour's granted them but they disclose it
And by the looseness of their tongues profane
The very altar where their hearts have lain.
Men of my sort, however, love discreetly,
And one may trust our reticence completely.
My keen concern for my good name insures
The absolute security of yours;
In short, I offer you, my dear Elmire,
Love without scandal, pleasure without fear.

ELMIRE I've heard your well-turned speeches to the
    end,
And what you urge·I clearly apprehend.
Aren't you afraid that I may take a notion
To tell my husband of your warm devotion,
And that, supposing he were duly told,
His feelings toward you might grow rather
    cold?

TARTUFFE I know, dear lady, that your exceeding charity
Will lead your heart to pardon my temerity;
That you'll excuse my violent affection
As human weakness, human imperfection;
And that – O fairest – you will bear in mind

That I'm but flesh and blood, and am not
    blind.

ELMIRE Some women might do otherwise, perhaps,
But I shall be discreet about your lapse;
I'll tell my husband nothing of what's
    occurred
If, in return, you'll give your solemn word
To advocate as forcefully as you can
The marriage of Valère and Mariane,
Renouncing all desire to dispossess
Another of his rightful happiness,
And . . .

SCENE FOUR: *Damis, Elmire, Tartuffe*

DAMIS (*emerging from the closet where he has been
    hiding:*)
        No! We'll not hush up this vile affair;
I heard it all inside that closet there,
Where Heaven, in order to confound the pride
Of this great rascal, prompted me to hide.
Ah, now I have my long-awaited chance
To punish his deceit and arrogance,
And give my father clear and shocking proof
Of the black character of his dear Tartuffe.

ELMIRE Ah no, Damis; I'll be content if he
Will study to deserve my leniency.
I've promised silence – don't make me break
    my word;
To make a scandal would be too absurd.
Good wives laugh off such trifles, and forget
    them;

Why should they tell their husbands, and
upset them?

DAMIS You have your reasons for taking such a
course,
And I have reasons, too, of equal force.
To spare him now would be insanely wrong.
I've swallowed my just wrath for far too long
And watched this insolent bigot bringing
strife
And bitterness into our family life.
Too long he's meddled in my father's affairs,
Thwarting my marriage-hopes, and poor
Valère's.
It's high time that my father was undeceived,
And now I've proof that can't be disbelieved —
Proof that was furnished me by Heaven above.
It's too good not to take advantage of.
This is my chance, and I deserve to lose it
If, for one moment, I hesitate to use it.

ELMIRE Damis . . .

DAMIS No, I must do what I think right.
Madam, my heart is bursting with delight,
And, say whatever you will, I'll not consent
To lose the sweet revenge on which I'm bent.
I'll settle matters without more ado;
And here, most opportunely, is my cue.

*SCENE FIVE: Orgon, Damis, Tartuffe,
Elmire*

DAMIS Father, I'm glad you've joined us. Let us
advise you
Of some fresh news which doubtless will
surprise you.

You've just now been repaid with interest
For all your loving-kindness to our guest.
He's proved his warm and grateful feelings
    toward you;
It's with a pair of horns he would reward you.
Yes, I surprised him with your wife, and
    heard
His whole adulterous offer, every word.
She, with her all too gentle disposition,
Would not have told you of his proposition;
But I shall not make terms with brazen
    lechery,
And feel that not to tell you would be
    treachery.

ELMIRE And I hold that one's husband's peace of
    mind
Should not be spoilt by tattle of this kind.
One's honour doesn't require it: to be
    proficient
In keeping men at bay is quite sufficient.
These are my sentiments, and I wish, Damis,
That you had heeded me and held your peace.

SCENE SIX: Orgon, Damis, Tartuffe

ORGON Can it be true, this dreadful thing I hear?
TARTUFFE Yes, Brother, I'm a wicked man, I fear:
A wretched sinner, all depraved and twisted,
The greatest villain that has ever existed.
My life's one heap of crimes, which grows each
    minute;
There's naught but foulness and corruption in
    it;
And I perceive that Heaven, outraged by me,

Has chosen this occasion to mortify me.
Charge me with any deed you wish to name;
I'll not defend myself, but take the blame.
Believe what you are told, and drive Tartuffe
Like some base criminal from beneath your
    roof;
Yes, drive me hence, and with a parting curse:
I shan't protest, for I deserve far worse.

ORGON (*to* DAMIS:)

Ah, you deceitful boy, how dare you try
To stain his purity with so foul a lie?

DAMIS What! Are you taken in by such a bluff?
Did you not hear . . . ?

ORGON   Enough, you rogue, enough!

TARTUFFE Ah, Brother, let him speak: you're being
    unjust.

Believe his story; the boy deserves your trust.
Why, after all, should you have faith in me?
How can yóu know what I might do, or be?
Is it on my good actions that you base
Your favour? Do you trust my pious facę?
Ah, no, don't be deceived by hollow shows;
I'm far, alas, from being what men suppose,
Though the world takes me for a man of
    worth,
I'm truly the most worthless man on earth.
(*To* DAMIS:)
Yes, my dear son, speak out now: call me the
    chief
Of sinners, a wretch, a murderer, a thief;
Load me with all the names men most abhor;
I'll not complain; I've earned them all, and
    more;
I'll kneel here while you pour them on my head
As a just punishment for the life I've led.

ORGON (*to* TARTUFFE:)
This is too much, dear Brother.
(*To* DAMIS:)
                          Have you no heart?

DAMIS Are you so hoodwinked by this rascal's art . . . ?

ORGON Be still, you monster.
(*To* TARTUFFE:)
                    Brother, I pray you, rise.
(*To* DAMIS:)
Villain!

DAMIS   But . . .

ORGON   Silence!

DAMIS   Can't you realize . . . ?

ORGON Just one word more, and I'll tear you limb
            from limb.

TARTUFFE In God's name, Brother, don't be harsh with
            him.
            I'd rather far be tortured at the stake
            Than see him bear one scratch for my poor
            sake.

ORGON (*To* DAMIS:)
Ingrate!

TARTUFFE   If I must beg you, on bended knee,
            To pardon him . . .

ORGON (*falling to his knees, addressing* TARTUFFE:)
                          Such goodness cannot be!
(*To* DAMIS:)
Now, *there's* true charity!

DAMIS   What, you . . . ?

ORGON   Villain, be still!
            I know your motives; I know you wish him
            ill:
            Yes, all of you – wife, children, servants, all –
            Conspire against him and desire his fall,
            Employing every shameful trick you can

To alienate me from this saintly man.
Ah, but the more you seek to drive him away,
The more I'll do to keep him. Without delay,
I'll spite this household and confound its pride
By giving him my daughter as his bride.

DAMIS You're going to force her to accept his hand?

ORGON Yes, and this very night, d'you understand?
I shall defy you all, and make it clear
That I'm the one who gives the orders here.
Come, wretch, kneel down and clasp his
   blessed feet,
And ask his pardon for your black deceit.

DAMIS I ask that swindler's pardon? Why, I'd
   rather . . .

ORGON So! You insult him, and defy your father!
A stick! A stick! (*To* TARTUFFE:) No, no –
   release me, do.
(*To* DAMIS:)
Out of my house this minute! Be off with you,
And never dare set foot in it again.

DAMIS Well, I shall go, but . . .

ORGON   Well, go quickly, then.
I disinherit you; an empty purse
Is all you'll get from me – except my curse!

SCENE SEVEN: *Orgon, Tartuffe*

ORGON How he blasphemed your goodness! What a
   son!

TARTUFFE Forgive him, Lord, as I've already done.
(*To* ORGON:)
You can't know how it hurts when someone
   tries
To blacken me in my dear Brother's eyes.

ORGON Ahh!

TARTUFFE The mere thought of such ingratitude
Plunges my soul into so dark a mood . . .
Such horror grips my heart . . . I gasp for
breath,
And cannot speak, and feel myself near death.

ORGON (*he runs, in tears, to the door through which he
has just driven his son.*)
You blackguard! Why did I spare you? Why
did I not
Break you in little pieces on the spot?
Compose yourself, and don't be hurt, dear
friend.

TARTUFFE These scenes, these dreadful quarrels, have got
to end.
I've much upset your household, and I
perceive
That the best thing will be for me to leave.

ORGON What are you saying!

TARTUFFE They're all against me here;
They'd have you think me false and insincere.

ORGON Ah, what of that? Have I ceased believing in
you?

TARTUFFE Their adverse talk will certainly continue,
And charges which you now repudiate
You may find credible at a later date.

ORGON No, Brother, never.

TARTUFFE Brother, a wife can sway
Her husband's mind in many a subtle way.

ORGON No, no.

TARTUFFE To leave at once is the solution;
Thus only can I end their persecution.

ORGON No, no, I'll not allow it; you shall remain.

TARTUFFE Ah, well; 'twill mean much martyrdom and
pain,

But if you wish it . . .

ORGON   Ah!

TARTUFFE   Enough; so be it.
But one thing must be settled, as I see it.
For your dear honour, and for our friendship's
    sake,
There's one precaution I feel bound to take.
I shall avoid your wife, and keep away . . .

ORGON No, you shall not, whatever they may say.
It pleases me to vex them, and for spite
I'd have them see you with her day and night.
What's more, I'm going to drive them to
    despair
By making you my only son and heir;
This very day, I'll give to you alone
Clear deed and title to everything I own.
A dear, good friend and son-in-law-to-be
Is more than wife, or child, or kin to me.
Will you accept my offer, dearest son?

TARTUFFE In all things, let the will of Heaven be done.

ORGON Poor fellow! Come, we'll go draw up the deed.
Then let them burst with disappointed greed!

Act Four

SCENE ONE: *Cléante, Tartuffe*

CLEANTE Yes, all the town's discussing it, and truly,
Their comments do not flatter you unduly.
I'm glad we've met, Sir, and I'll give my view
Of this sad matter in a word or two.
As for who's guilty, that I shan't discuss;
Let's say it was Damis who caused the fuss;
Assuming, then, that you have been ill-used
By young Damis, and groundlessly accused,
Ought not a Christian to forgive, and ought
He not to stifle every vengeful thought?
Should you stand by and watch a father make
His only son an exile for your sake?
Again I tell you frankly, be advised:
The whole town, high and low, is scandalized;
This quarrel must be mended, and my
   advice is
Not to push matters to a further crisis.
No, sacrifice your wrath to God above,
And help Damis regain his father's love.

TARTUFFE Alas, for my part I should take great
   joy
In doing so. I've nothing against the boy.
I pardon all, I harbour no resentment;
To serve him would afford me much
   contentment.
But Heaven's interest will not have it so:
If he comes back, then I shall have to go.
After his conduct – so extreme, so vicious –

Our further intercourse would look
    suspicious.
God knows what people would think! Why,
    they'd describe
My goodness to him as a sort of bribe;
They'd say that out of guilt I made pretence
Of loving-kindness and benevolence –
That, fearing my accuser's tongue, I strove
To buy his silence with a show of love.

CLEANTE Your reasoning is badly warped and stretched,
And these excuses, Sir, are most far-fetched.
Why put yourself in charge of Heaven's
    cause?
Does Heaven need our help to enforce its
    laws?
Leave vengeance to the Lord, Sir; while we
    live,
Our duty's not to punish, but forgive;
And what the Lord commands, we should
    obey
Without regard to what the world may say.
What! Shall the fear of being misunderstood
Prevent our doing what is right and good?
No, no; let's simply do what Heaven ordains,
And let no other thoughts perplex our brains.

TARTUFFE Again, Sir, let me say that I've forgiven
Damis, and thus obeyed the laws of Heaven;
But I am not commanded by the Bible
To live with one who smears my name with
    libel.

CLEANTE Were you commanded, Sir, to indulge the
    whim
Of poor Orgon, and to encourage him
In suddenly transferring to your name
A large estate to which you have no claim?

TARTUFFE 'Twould never occur to those who know me
best
To think I acted from self-interest.
The treasures of this world I quite despise;
Their specious glitter does not charm my
eyes;
And if I have resigned myself to taking
The gift which my dear Brother insists on
making,
I do so only, as he well understands,
Lest so much wealth fall into wicked hands,
Lest those to whom it might descend in time
Turn it to purposes of sin and crime,
And not, as I shall do, make use of it
For Heaven's glory and mankind's benefit.

CLEANTE Forget these trumped-up fears. Your
argument
Is one the rightful heir might well resent;
It *is* a moral burden to inherit
Such a wealth, but give Damis a chance to
bear it.
And would it not be worse to be accused
Of swindling, than to see that wealth misused?
I'm shocked that you allowed Orgon to broach
This matter, and that you feel no self-
reproach;
Does true religion teach that lawful heirs
May freely be deprived of what is theirs?
And if the Lord has told you in your heart
That you and young Damis must dwell apart
Would it not be the decent thing to beat
A generous and honourable retreat,
Rather than let the son of the house be
sent,
For your convenience, into banishment?

Sir, if you wish to prove the honesty
Of your intentions . . .

TARTUFFE   Sir, it is half-past three.
I've certain pious duties to attend to,
And hope my prompt departure won't offend
     you.

CLEANTE (*alone:*)
Damn.

*SCENE TWO: Elmire, Mariane, Cléante,
     Dorine*

DORINE   Stay, Sir, and help Mariane, for
     Heaven's sake!
She's suffering so, I fear her heart will break.
Her father's plan to marry her off tonight
Has put the poor child in a desperate plight.
I hear him coming. Let's stand together, now,
And see if we can't change his mind,
     somehow,
About this match we all deplore and fear.

*SCENE THREE: Orgon, Elmire, Mariane,
     Cléante, Dorine*

ORGON Hah! Glad to find you all assembled here.
(*To* MARIANE:)
This contract, child, contains your happiness,
And what it says I think your heart can guess.

MARIANE (*falling to her knees:*)

Sir, by that Heaven which sees me here
distressed,
And by whatever else can move your breast,
Do not employ a father's power, I pray you,
To crush my heart and force it to obey you,
Nor by your harsh commands oppress me
so
That I'll begrudge the duty which I owe –
And do not so embitter and enslave me
That I shall hate the very life you gave me.
If my sweet hopes must perish, if you refuse
To give me to the one I've dared to choose,
Spare me at least – I beg you, I implore –
The pain of wedding one whom I abhor;
And do not, by a heartless use of force,
Drive me to contemplate some desperate
course.

ORGON (*feeling himself touched by her:*)

Be firm, my soul. No human weakness, now.

MARIANE I don't resent your love for him. Allow
Your heart free rein, Sir; give him your
property,
And if that's not enough, take mine from me;
He's welcome to my money; take it, do,
But don't, I pray, include my person too.
Spare me, I beg you; and let me end the tale
Of my sad days behind a convent veil.

ORGON A convent! Hah! When crossed in their
amours,
All lovesick girls have the same thought as
yours.
Get up! The more you loathe the man, and
dread him,
The more ennobling it will be to wed him.

Marry Tartuffe, and mortify your flesh!
Enough; don't start that whimpering afresh.

DORINE But why . . . ?

ORGON   Be still, there. Speak when you're spoken to.
Not one more bit of impudence out of you.

CLEANTE If I may offer a word of counsel here . . .

ORGON Brother, in counselling you have no peer;
All your advice is forceful, sound, and clever;
I don't propose to follow it, however.

ELMIRE (*to* ORGON:)
I am amazed, and don't know what to say;
Your blindness simply takes my breath away.
You are indeed bewitched, to take no warning
From our account of what occurred this
    morning.

ORGON Madam, I know a few plain facts, and one
Is that you're partial to my rascal son;
Hence, when he sought to make Tartuffe the
    victim
Of a base lie, you dared not contradict him.
Ah, but you underplayed your part, my pet;
You should have looked more angry, more
    upset.

ELMIRE When men make overtures, must we reply
With righteous anger and a battle-cry?
Must we turn back their amorous advances
With sharp reproaches and with fiery glances?
Myself, I find such offers merely amusing,
And make no scenes and fusses in refusing;
My taste is for good-natured rectitude,
And I dislike the savage sort of prude
Who guards her virtue with her teeth and
    claws,
And tears men's eyes out for the slightest
    cause:

The Lord preserve me from such honour as
    that,
Which bites and scratches like an alley-cat!
I've found that a polite and cool rebuff
Discourages a lover quite enough.

ORGON   I know the facts, and I shall not be shaken.

ELMIRE   I marvel at your power to be mistaken.
Would it, I wonder, carry weight with you
If I could *show* you that our tale was true?

ORGON   Show me?

ELMIRE   Yes.

ORGON   Rot.

ELMIRE   Come, what if I found a way
To make you see the facts as plain as day?

ORGON   Nonsense.

ELMIRE   Do answer me; don't be absurd.
I'm not now asking you to trust our word.
Suppose that from some hiding-place in here
You learned the whole sad truth by eye and
    ear –
What would you say of your good friend, after
    that?

ORGON   Why, I'd say . . . nothing, by Jehoshaphat!
It can't be true.

ELMIRE   You've been too long deceived,
And I'm quite tired of being disbelieved.
Come now: let's put my statements to the test,
And you shall see the truth made manifest.

ORGON   I'll take that challenge. Now do your
    uttermost.
We'll see how you make good your empty
    boast.

ELMIRE   (*to* DORINE:)
Send him to me.

DORINE   He's crafty; it may be hard

To catch the cunning scoundrel off his guard.

ELMIRE No, amorous men are gullible. Their conceit
So blinds them that they're never hard to
cheat.
Have him come down. (*To* CLEANTE *and*
MARIANE:) Please leave us, for a bit.

SCENE FOUR: Elmire, Orgon

ELMIRE Pull up this table, and get under it.
ORGON What?
ELMIRE   It's essential that you be well-hidden.
ORGON Why there?
ELMIRE   Oh, Heavens! Just do as you are bidden.
I have my plans; we'll soon see how they fare.
Under the table, now; and once you're there,
Take care that you are neither seen nor heard.
ORGON Well, I'll indulge you, since I gave my word
To see you through this infantile charade.
ELMIRE Once it is over, you'll be glad we played.
(*To her husband, who is now under the table:*)
I'm going to act quite strangely, now, and you
Must not be shocked at anything I do.
Whatever I may say, you must excuse
As part of that deceit I'm forced to use.
I shall employ sweet speeches in the task
Of making that imposter drop his mask;
I'll give encouragement to his bold desires,
And furnish fuel to his amorous fires.
Since it's for your sake, and for his
destruction,
That I shall seem to yield to his seduction,

I'll gladly stop whenever you decide
That all your doubts are fully satisfied.
I'll count on you, as soon as you have seen
What sort of man he is, to intervene,
And not expose me to his odious lust
One moment longer than you feel you must.
Remember: you're to save me from my plight
Whenever . . . He's coming! Hush! Keep out
    of sight!

SCENE FIVE: Tartuffe, Elmire, Orgon

TARTUFFE You wish to have a word with me, I'm told.
ELMIRE Yes. I've a little secret to unfold.
Before I speak, however, it would be wise
To close that door, and look about for spies.
(TARTUFFE *goes to the door, closes it, and*
    returns.)
The very last thing that must happen now
Is a repetition of this morning's row.
I've never been so badly caught off guard.
Oh, how I feared for you! You saw how hard
I tried to make that troublesome Damis
Control his dreadful temper, and hold his
    peace.
In my confusion, I didn't have the sense
Simply to contradict his evidence;
But as it happened, that was for the best,
And all has worked out in our interest.
This storm has only bettered your position;
My husband doesn't have the least suspicion,
And now, in mockery of those who do,
He bids me be continually with you.

And that is why, quite fearless of reproof,
I now can be alone with my Tartuffe,
And why my heart – perhaps too quick to
    yield –
Feels free to let its passion be revealed.

TARTUFFE Madam, your words confuse me. Not long
    ago,
You spoke in quite a different style, you
    know.

ELMIRE Ah, Sir, if that refusal made you smart,
It's little that you know of woman's heart,
Or what that heart is trying to convey
When it resists in such a feeble way!
Always, at first, our modesty prevents
The frank avowal of tender sentiments;
However high the passion which inflames us,
Still, to confess its power somehow shames
    us.
Thus we reluct, at first, yet in a tone
Which tells you that our heart is overthrown,
That what our lips deny, our pulse confesses,
And that, in time, all noes will turn to yesses.
I fear my words are all too frank and free.
And a poor proof of woman's modesty;
But since I'm started, tell me, if you will –
Would I have tried to make Damis be still,
Would I have listened, calm and unoffended,
Until your lengthy offer of love was ended,
And been so very mild in my reaction,
Had your sweet words not given me
    satisfaction?
And when I tried to force you to undo
The marriage-plans my husband has in view,
What did my urgent pleading signify
If not that I admired you, and that I

Deplored the thought that someone else might
own
Part of a heart I wished for mine alone?

TARTUFFE Madam, no happiness is so complete
As when, from lips we love, come words so
sweet;
Their nectar floods my every sense, and drains
In honeyed rivulets through all my veins.
To please you is my joy, my only goal;
Your love is the restorer of my soul;
And yet I must beg leave, now, to confess
Some lingering doubts as to my happiness.
Might this not be a trick? Might not the catch
Be that you wish me to break off the match
With Mariane, and so have feigned to love
me?
I shan't quite trust your fond opinion of me
Until the feelings you've expressed so sweetly
Are demonstrated somewhat more concretely,
And you have shown, by certain kind
concessions,
That I may put my faith in your professions.

ELMIRE (*she coughs, to warn her husband.*)
Why be in such a hurry? Must my heart
Exhaust its bounty at the very start?
To make that sweet admission cost me dear,
But you'll not be content, it would appear,
Unless my store of favours is disbursed
To the last farthing, and at the very first.

TARTUFFE The less we merit, the less we dare to hope,
And with our doubts, mere words can never
cope.
We trust no promised bliss till we receive it;
Not till a joy is ours can we believe it.
I, who so little merit your esteem,

Can't credit this fulfilment of my dream,
And shan't believe it, Madam, until I savour
Some palpable assurance of your favour.

ELMIRE My, how tyrannical your love can be,
And how it flusters and perplexes me!
How furiously you take one's heart in hand,
And make your every wish a fierce command!
Come, must you hound and harry me to
    death?
Will you not give me time to catch my breath?
Can it be right to press me with such force,
Give me no quarter, show me no remorse,
And take advantage, by your stern insistence,
Of the fond feelings which weaken my
    resistance?

TARTUFFE Well, if you look with favour upon my love,
Why, then, begrudge me some clear proof
    thereof?

ELMIRE But how can I consent without offence
To Heaven, toward which you feel such
    reverence?

TARTUFFE If Heaven is all that holds you back, don't
    worry.
I can remove that hindrance in a hurry.
Nothing of that sort need obstruct our path.

ELMIRE Must one not be afraid of Heaven's wrath?

TARTUFFE Madam, forget such fears, and be my pupil,
And I shall teach you how to conquer scruple.
Some joys, it's true, are wrong in Heaven's
    eyes;
Yet Heaven is not averse to compromise;
There is a science, lately formulated,
Whereby one's conscience may be liberated,
And any wrongful act you care to mention
May be redeemed by purity of intention.

I'll teach you, Madam, the secrets of that
   science;
Meanwhile, just place on me your full reliance.
Assuage my keen desires, and feel no dread:
The sin, if any, shall be on my head.
(ELMIRE *coughs, this time more loudly.*)
You've a bad cough.

ELMIRE   Yes, yes. It's bad indeed.

TARTUFFE (*producing a little paper bag:*)
A bit of liquorice may be what you need.

ELMIRE No, I've a stubborn cold, it seems. I'm sure it
Will take much more than liquorice to cure it.

TARTUFFE How aggravating.

ELMIRE   Oh, more than I can say.

TARTUFFE If you're still troubled, think of things this
   way:
No one shall know our joys, save us alone,
And there's no evil till the act is known;
It's scandal, Madam, which makes it an
   offence,
And it's no sin to sin in confidence.

ELMIRE (*having coughed once more:*)
Well, clearly I must do as you require,
And yield to your importunate desire.
It is apparent, now, that nothing less
Will satisfy you, and so I acquiesce.
To go so far is much against my will;
I'm vexed that it should come to this; but
   still,
Since you are so determined on it, since you
Will not allow mere language to convince
   you,
And since you ask for concrete evidence, I
See nothing for it, now, but to comply.
If this is sinful, if I'm wrong to do it,

So much the worse for him who drove me to
    it.
The fault can surely not be charged to me.

TARTUFFE Madam, the fault is mine, if fault there be,
And . . .

ELMIRE   Open the door a little, and peek out;
I wouldn't want my husband poking about.

TARTUFFE Why worry about the man? Each day he grows
More gullible; one can lead him by the nose.
To find us here would fill him with delight,
And if he saw the worst, he'd doubt his sight.

ELMIRE Nevertheless, do step out for a minute
Into the hall, and see that no one's in it.

SCENE SIX : Orgon, Elmire

ORGON   (*coming out from under the table:*)
That man's a perfect monster, I must admit!
I'm simply stunned. I can't get over it.

ELMIRE What, coming out so soon? How premature!
Get back in hiding, and wait until you're sure.
Stay till the end, and be convinced
    completely;
We mustn't stop till things are proved
    concretely.

ORGON Hell never harboured anything so vicious!

ELMIRE Tut, don't be hasty. Try to be judicious.
Wait, and be certain that there's no mistake.
No jumping to conclusions, for Heaven's sake!
(*She places* ORGON *behind her, as* TARTUFFE *re-
enters.*)

SCENE SEVEN: Tartuffe, Elmire, Orgon

TARTUFFE (*not seeing* ORGON*:*)
Madam, all things have worked out to
    perfection;
I've given the neighbouring rooms a full
    inspection;
No one's about; and now I may at last . . .

ORGON (*intercepting him:*)
Hold on, my passionate fellow, not so fast!
I should advise a little more restraint.
Well, so you thought you'd fool me, my dear
    saint!
How soon you wearied of the saintly life –
Wedding my daughter, and coveting my wife!
I've long suspected you, and had a feeling
That soon I'd catch you at your double-
    dealing.
Just now, you've given me evidence galore;
It's quite enough; I have no wish for more.

ELMIRE (*to* TARTUFFE*:*)
I'm sorry to have treated you so slyly,
But circumstances forced me to be wily.

TARTUFFE Brother, you can't think . . .

ORGON   No more talk from you;
Just leave this household, without more ado.

TARTUFFE What I intended . . .

ORGON   That seems fairly clear.
Spare me your falsehoods and get out of here.

TARTUFFE No, I'm the master, and you're the one to go!
This house belongs to me, I'll have you know,
And I shall show you that you can't hurt *me*

By this contemptible conspiracy,
That those who cross me know not what they
    do,
And that I've means to expose and punish
    you,
Avenge offended Heaven, and make you
    grieve
That ever you dared order me to leave.

SCENE EIGHT: Elmire, Orgon

ELMIRE What was the point of all that angry chatter?
ORGON Dear God, I'm worried. This is no laughing
       matter.
ELMIRE How so?
ORGON   I fear I understood his drift.
I'm much disturbed about that deed of gift.
ELMIRE You gave him . . . ?
ORGON   Yes, it's all been drawn and signed.
But one thing more is weighing on my mind.
ELMIRE What's that?
ORGON   I'll tell you; first let's see if there's
A certain strong-box in his room upstairs.

Act Five

SCENE ONE: *Orgon, Cléante*

CLEANTE Where are you going so fast?
ORGON   God knows!
CLEANTE   Then wait;
         Let's have a conference, and deliberate
         On how this situation's to be met.
ORGON   That strong-box has me utterly upset;
         This is the worst of many, many shocks.
CLEANTE Is there some fearful mystery in that box?
ORGON   My poor friend Argas brought that box to me
         With his own hands, in utmost secrecy;
         'Twas on the very morning of his flight.
         It's full of papers which, if they came to light,
         Would ruin him – or such is my impression.
CLEANTE Then why did you let it out of your
            possession?
ORGON   Those papers vexed my conscience, and it
            seemed best
         To ask the counsel of my pious guest.
         The cunning scoundrel got me to agree
         To leave the strong-box in his custody,
         So that, in case of an investigation,
         I could employ a slight equivocation
         And swear I didn't have it, and thereby,
         At no expense to conscience, tell a lie.
CLEANTE It looks to me as if you're out on a limb.
         Trusting him with that box, and offering him
         That deed of gift, were actions of a kind
         Which scarcely indicate a prudent mind.

With two such weapons, he has the upper
   hand,
And since you're vulnerable, as matters stand,
You erred once more in bringing him to bay.
You should have acted in some subtler way.

ORGON Just think of it: behind that fervent face,
A heart so wicked, and a soul so base!
I took him in, a hungry beggar, and then . . .
Enough, by God! I'm through with pious men:
Henceforth I'll hate the whole false
   brotherhood,
And persecute them worse than Satan could

CLEANTE Ah, there you go – extravagant as ever!
Why can you not be rational? You never
Manage to take the middle course, it seems,
But jump, instead, between absurd extremes.
You've recognized your recent grave mistake
In falling victim to a pious fake;
Now, to correct that error, must you embrace
An even greater error in its place,
And judge our worthy neighbours as a whole
By what you've learned of one corrupted soul?
Come, just because one rascal made you
   swallow
A show of zeal which turned out to be hollow,
Shall you conclude that all men are deceivers,
And that, today, there are no true believers?
Let atheists make that foolish inference;
Learn to distinguish virtue from pretence,
Be cautious in bestowing admiration,
And cultivate a sober moderation.
Don't humour fraud, but also don't asperse
True piety; the latter fault is worse,
And it is best to err, if err one must,
As you have done, upon the side of trust.

SCENE TWO: Damis, Orgon, Cléante

DAMIS Father, I hear that scoundrel's uttered threats
    Against you; that he pridefully forgets
    How, in his need, he was befriended by you,
    And means to use your gifts to crucify you.

ORGON It's true, my boy. I'm too distressed for tears.

DAMIS Leave it to me, Sir; let me trim his ears.
    Faced with such insolence, we must not waver.
    I shall rejoice in doing you the favour
    Of cutting short his life, and your distress.

CLEANTE What a display of young hotheadedness!
    Do learn to moderate your fits of rage.
    In this just kingdom, this enlightened age,
    One does not settle things by violence.

SCENE THREE: Madame Pernelle,
    Mariane, Elmire, Dorine, Damis, Orgon,
    Cléante

PERNELLE I hear strange tales of very strange events.

ORGON Yes, strange events which these two eyes
    beheld.
    The man's ingratitude is unparalleled.
    I save a wretched pauper from starvation,
    House him, and treat him like a blood relation,
    Shower him every day with my largesse,
    Give him my daughter, and all that I possess;

And meanwhile the unconscionable knave
Tries to induce my wife to misbehave;
And not content with such extreme rascality,
Now threatens me with my own liberality,
And aims, by taking base advantage of
The gifts I gave him out of Christian love,
To drive me from my house, a ruined man,
And make me end a pauper, as he began.

DORINE   Poor fellow!

PERNELLE   No, my son, I'll never bring
Myself to think him guilty of such a thing.

ORGON   How's that?

PERNELLE   The righteous always were maligned.

ORGON   Speak clearly, Mother. Say what's on your
mind.

PERNELLE   I mean that I can smell a rat, my dear.
You know how everybody hates him, here.

ORGON   That has no bearing on the case at all.

PERNELLE   I told you a hundred times, when you were
small,
That virtue in this world is hated ever;
Malicious men may die, but malice never.

ORGON   No doubt that's true, but how does it apply?

PERNELLE   They've turned you against him by a clever lie.

ORGON   I've told you, I was there and saw it done.

PERNELLE   Ah, slanderers will stop at nothing, Son.

ORGON   Mother, I'll lose my temper . . . For the last
time,
I tell you I was witness to the crime.

PERNELLE   The tongues of spite are busy night and noon,
And to their venom no man is immune.

ORGON   You're talking nonsense. Can't you realize
I saw it; saw it; saw it with my eyes?
Saw, do you understand me? Must I shout it
Into your ears before you'll cease to doubt it?

PERNELLE Appearances can deceive, my son. Dear me,
We cannot always judge by what we see.

ORGON Drat! Drat!

PERNELLE One often interprets things awry;
Good can seem evil to a suspicious eye.

ORGON Was I to see his pawing at Elmire
As an act of charity?

PERNELLE Till his guilt is clear,
A man deserves the benefit of the doubt.
You should have waited, to see how things
turned out.

ORGON Great God in Heaven, what more proof did I
need?
Was I to sit there, watching, until he'd . . .
You drive me to the brink of impropriety.

PERNELLE No, no, a man of such surpassing piety
Could not do such a thing. You cannot shake
me.
I don't believe it, and you shall not make me.

ORGON You vex me so that, if you weren't my mother,
I'd say to you . . . some dreadful thing or
other.

DORINE It's your turn now, Sir, not to be listened to;
You'd not trust us, and now she won't trust
you.

CLEANTE My friends, we're wasting time which should
be spent
In facing up to our predicament.
I fear that scoundrel's threats weren't made in
sport.

DAMIS Do you think he'd have the nerve to go to
court?

ELMIRE I'm sure he won't; they'd find it all too crude
A case of swindling and ingratitude.

CLEANTE Don't be too sure. He won't be at a loss

To give his claims a high and righteous gloss;
And clever rogues with far less valid cause.
Have trapped their victims in a web of laws.
I say again that to antagonize
A man so strongly armed was most unwise.

ORGON I know it; but the man's appalling cheek
Outraged me so, I couldn't control my pique.

CLEANTE I wish to Heaven that we could devise
Some truce between you, or some
    compromise.

ELMIRE If I had known what cards he held, I'd not
Have roused his anger by my little plot.

ORGON (*to* DORINE, *as* M. LOYAL *enters:*)
What is that fellow looking for? Who is he?
Go talk to him – and tell him that I'm busy.

*SCENE FOUR: Monsieur Loyal, Madame
Pernelle, Orgon, Damis, Mariane, Dorine,
Elmire, Cléante*

M. LOYAL Good day, dear sister. Kindly let me see
Your master.

DORINE   He's involved with company,
And cannot be disturbed just now, I fear.

M. LOYAL I hate to intrude; but what has brought me
    here
Will not disturb your master, in any event.
Indeed, my news will make him most content.

DORINE Your name?

M. LOYAL   Just say that I bring greetings from
Monsieur Tartuffe, on whose behalf I've
    come.

DORINE (*to* ORGON:)

Sir, he's a very gracious man, and bears
A message from Tartuffe, which, he declares,
Will make you most content.

CLEANTE   Upon my word,
I think this man had best be seen, and heard.

ORGON Perhaps he has some settlement to suggest.
How shall I treat him? What manner would be
best?

CLEANTE Control your anger, and if he should mention
Some fair adjustment, give him your full
attention.

M. LOYAL Good health to you, good Sir. May Heaven
confound
Your enemies, and may your joys abound.

ORGON (*aside, to* CLEANTE:)
A gentle salutation: it confirms
My guess that he is here to offer terms.

M. LOYAL I've always held your family most dear;
I served your father, Sir, for many a year.

ORGON Sir, I must ask your pardon; to my shame,
I cannot now recall your face or name.

M. LOYAL Loyal's my name; I come from Normandy,
And I'm a bailiff, in all modesty.
For forty years, praise God, it's been my
boast
To serve with honour in that vital post,
And I am here, Sir, if you will permit
The liberty, to serve you with this writ . . .

ORGON To – *what?*

M. LOYAL   Now, please, Sir, let us have no friction:
It's nothing but an order of eviction.
You are to move your goods and family
out
And make way for new occupants, without
Deferment or delay, and give the keys . . .

ORGON I? Leave this house?

M. LOYAL   Why yes, Sir, if you please.
This house, Sir, from the cellar to the roof,
Belongs now to the good Monsieur Tartuffe,
And he is lord and master of your estate
By virtue of a deed of present date,
Drawn in due form, with clearest legal
    phrasing . . .

DAMIS Your insolence is utterly amazing!

M. LOYAL Young man, my business here is not with
    you,
But with your wise and temperate father,
    who,
Like every worthy citizen, stands in awe
Of justice, and would never obstruct the law.

ORGON But . . .

M. LOYAL   Not for a million, Sir, would you rebel
Against authority; I know that well.
You'll not make trouble, Sir, or interfere
With the execution of my duties here.

DAMIS Someone may execute a smart tattoo
On that black jacket of yours, before you're
    through.

M. LOYAL Sir, bid your son be silent. I'd much regret
Having to mention such a nasty threat
Of violence, in writing my report.

DORINE (*aside:*)
This man Loyal's a most disloyal sort!

M. LOYAL I love all men of upright character,
And when I agreed to serve these papers,
    Sir,
It was your feelings that I had in mind.
I couldn't bear to see the case assigned
To someone else, who might esteem you less
And so subject you to unpleasantness.

ORGON What's more unpleasant than telling a man to leave
His house and home?

M. LOYAL You'd like a short reprieve?
If you desire it, Sir, I shall not press you,
But wait until tomorrow to dispossess you.
Splendid. I'll come and spend the night here, then,
Most quietly, with half a score of men.
For form's sake, you might bring me, just before
You go to bed, the keys to the front door.
My men, I promise, will be on their best
Behaviour, and will not disturb your rest.
But bright and early, Sir, you must be quick
And move out all your furniture, every stick:
The men I've chosen are both young and strong,
And with their help it shouldn't take you long.
In short, I'll make things pleasant and convenient,
And since I'm being so extremely lenient,
Please show me, Sir, a like consideration,
And give me your entire cooperation.

ORGON (*aside:*)
I may be all but bankrupt, but I vow
I'd give a hundred louis, here and now,
Just for the pleasure of landing one good clout
Right on the end of that complacent snout.

CLEANTE Careful; don't make things worse.

DAMIS My bootsole itches
To give that beggar a good kick in the breeches.

DORINE Monsieur Loyal, I'd love to hear the whack
Of a stout stick across your fine broad back.

M. LOYAL Take care: a woman too may go to jail if
         She uses threatening language to a bailiff.
CLEANTE Enough, enough, Sir. This must not go on.
         Give me that paper, please, and then begone.
M. LOYAL Well, *au revoir*. God give you all good cheer!
ORGON May God confound you, and him who sent
         you here!

SCENE FIVE: Orgon, Cléante, Mariane,
Elmire, Madame Pernelle, Dorine, Damis

ORGON Now, Mother, was I right or not? This writ
         Should change your notion of Tartuffe a bit.
         Do you perceive his villainy at last?
PERNELLE I'm thunderstruck. I'm utterly aghast.
DORINE Oh, come, be fair. You mustn't take offence
         At this new proof of his benevolence.
         He's acting out of selfless love, I know.
         Material things enslave the soul, and so
         He kindly has arranged your liberation
         From all that might endanger your salvation.
ORGON Will you not ever hold your tongue, you
         dunce?
CLEANTE Come, you must take some action, and at
         once.
ELMIRE Go tell the world of the low trick he's tried.
         The deed of gift is surely nullified
         By such behaviour, and public rage will not
         Permit the wretch to carry out his plot.

SCENE SIX: Valère, Orgon, Cléante,
Elmire, Mariane, Madame Pernelle, Damis,
Dorine

VALERE   Sir, though I hate to bring you more bad
     news,
   Such is the danger that I cannot choose.
   A friend who is extremely close to me
   And knows my interest in your family
   Has, for my sake, presumed to violate
   The secrecy that's due to things of state,
   And sends me word that you are in a plight
   From which your one salvation lies in flight.
   That scoundrel who's imposed upon you so
   Denounced you to the King an hour ago
   And, as supporting evidence, displayed
   The strong-box of a certain renegade
   Whose secret papers, so he testified,
   You had disloyally agreed to hide.
   I don't know just what charges may be
     pressed,
   But there's a warrant out for your arrest;
   Tartuffe has been instructed, furthermore,
   To guide the arresting officer to your door.

CLEANTE   He's clearly done this to facilitate
   His seizure of your house and your estate.

ORGON   That man, I must say, is a vicious beast!

VALERE   Quick, Sir; you mustn't tarry in the least.
   My carriage is outside, to take you hence;
   This thousand louis should cover all expense.
   Let's lose no time, or you shall be undone;

The sole defence, in this case, is to run.
I shall go with you all the way, and place you
In a safe refuge to which they'll never trace
   you.

ORGON Alas, dear boy, I wish that I could show you
My gratitude for everything I owe you..
But now is not the time; I pray the Lord
That I may live to give you your reward.
Farewell, my dears; be careful . . .

CLEANTE   Brother, hurry.
We shall take care of things; you needn't
   worry.

*SCENE SEVEN:The Officer, Tartuffe,
Valère, Orgon, Elmire, Mariane, Madame
Pernelle, Dorine, Cléante, Damis*

TARTUFFE Gently, Sir, gently; stay right where you are.
No need for haste; your lodging isn't far.
You're off to prison, by order of the Prince.

ORGON This is the crowning blow, you wretch; and
   since
It means my total ruin and defeat,
Your villainy is now at last complete.

TARTUFFE You needn't try to provoke me; it's no use.
Those who serve Heaven must expect abuse.

CLEANTE You are indeed most patient, sweet, and
   blameless.

DORINE How he exploits the name of Heaven! It's
   shameless.

TARTUFFE Your taunts and mockeries are all for naught;
To do my duty is my only thought.

MARIANE Your love of duty is most meritorious,

           And what you've done is little short of glorious.

TARTUFFE All deeds are glorious, Madam, which obey
           The sovereign prince who sent me here today.

ORGON I rescued you when you were destitute;
           Have you forgotten that, you thankless brute?

TARTUFFE No, no, I well remember everything;
           But my first duty is to serve my King.
           That obligation is so paramount
           That other claims, beside it, do not count;
           And for it I would sacrifice my wife,
           My family, my friend, or my own life.

ELMIRE Hypocrite!

DORINE   All that we most revere, he uses
           To cloak his plots and camouflage his ruses.

CLEANTE If it is true that you are animated
           By pure and loyal zeal, as you have stated,
           Why was this zeal not roused until you'd sought
           To make Orgon a cuckold, and been caught?
           Why weren't you moved to give your evidence
           Until your outraged host had driven you hence?
           I shan't say that the gift of all his treasure
           Ought to have damped your zeal in any
               measure;
           But if he is a traitor, as you declare,
           How could you condescend to be his heir?

TARTUFFE (*to the* OFFICER:)
           Sir, spare me all this clamour; it's growing
               shrill.
           Please carry out your orders, if you will.

OFFICER Yes, I've delayed too long, Sir. Thank you
               kindly.
           You're just the proper person to remind me.
           Come, you are off to join the other boarders
           In the King's prison, according to his orders.

TARTUFFE Who? I, Sir?

OFFICER   Yes.

TARTUFFE   To prison? This can't be true!

OFFICER   I owe an explanation, but not to you.
(*To* ORGON:)
Sir, all is well; rest easy, and be grateful.
We serve a Prince to whom all sham is hateful,
A Prince who sees into our inmost hearts,
And can't be fooled by any trickster's arts.
His royal soul, though generous and human,
Views all things with discernment and acumen;
His sovereign reason is not lightly swayed,
And all his judgments are discreetly weighed.
He honours righteous men of every kind,
And yet his zeal for virtue is not blind,
Nor does his love of piety numb his wits
And make him tolerant of hypocrites.
'Twas hardly likely that this man could cozen
A King who's foiled such liars by the dozen.
With one keen glance, the King perceived the
    whole
Perverseness and corruption of his soul,
And thus high Heaven's justice was displayed:
Betraying you, the rogue stood self-betrayed.
The King soon recognized Tartuffe as one
Notorious by another name, who'd done
So many vicious crimes that one could fill
Ten volumes with them, and be writing still.
But to be brief: our sovereign was appalled
By this man's treachery toward you, which he
    called
The last, worst villainy of a vile career,
And bade me follow the impostor here
To see how gross his impudence could be,
And force him to restore your property.
Your private papers, by the King's command,

I hereby seize and give into your hand.
The King, by royal order, invalidates
The deed which gave this rascal your estates,
And pardons, furthermore, your grave offence
In harbouring an exile's documents.
By these decrees, our Prince rewards you for
Your loyal deeds in the late civil war,
And shows how heartfelt is his satisfaction
In recompensing any worthy action,
How much he prizes merit, and how he makes
More of men's virtues than of their mistakes.

DORINE   Heaven be praised!

PERNELLE   I breathe again, at last.

ELMIRE   We're safe.

MARIANE   I can't believe the danger's past.

ORGON   (*to* TARTUFFE:)

Well, traitor, now you see . . .

CLEANTE   Ah, Brother, please,
Let's not descend to such indignities.
Leave the poor wretch to his unhappy fate,
And don't say anything to aggravate
His present woes; but rather hope that he
Will soon embrace an honest piety,
And mend his ways, and by a true repentance
Move our just King to moderate his sentence.
Meanwhile, go kneel before your sovereign's
    throne
And thank him for the mercies he has shown.

ORGON   Well said: let's to at once and, gladly kneeling,
Express the gratitude which we all are feeling.
Then, when that first great duty has been done,
We'll turn with pleasure to a second one,
And give Valère, whose love has proven so true,
The wedded happiness which is his due.

The Misanthrope

Comedy in Five Acts

Translated into English Verse by Richard Wilbur

CHARACTERS

ALCESTE, in love with Célimène
PHILINTE, Alceste's friend
ORONTE, in love with Célimène
CELIMENE, Alceste's beloved
ELIANTE, Célimène's cousin
ARSINOE, a friend of Célimène's
ACASTE
CLITANDRE } marquesses
BASQUE, Célimène's servant
A GUARD of the Marshalsea
DUBOIS, Alceste's valet

The scene throughout is in Célimène's house at Paris.

This translation was first produced by The Poets' Theatre, *Cambridge, Massachusetts, on October 25th, 1955*

Act One

SCENE ONE: *Philinte, Alceste*

PHILINTE	Now, what's got into you ?
ALCESTE	*(seated).*
	Kindly leave me alone.
PHILINTE	Come, come, what is it ? This lugubrious tone . . .
ALCESTE	Leave me, I said; you spoil my solitude.
PHILINTE	Oh, listen to me, now, and don't be rude.
ALCESTE	I choose to be rude, Sir, and to be hard of hearing.
PHILINTE	These ugly moods of yours are not endearing;
	Friends though we are, I really must insist . . .
ALCESTE	*(abruptly rising).*
	Friends ? Friends, you say ? Well, cross me off your list.
	I've been your friend till now, as you well know;
	But after what I saw a moment ago
	I tell you flatly that our ways must part.
	I wish no place in a dishonest heart.
PHILINTE	Why, what have I done, Alceste ? Is this quite just ?
ALCESTE	My God, you ought to die of self-disgust.
	I call your conduct inexcusable, Sir,
	And every man of honour will concur.
	I see you almost hug a man to death,
	Exclaim for joy until you're out of breath,
	And supplement these loving demonstrations
	With endless offers, vows, and protestations;
	Then when I ask you 'Who was that ?', I find
	That you can barely bring his name to mind!
	Once the man's back is turned, you cease to love him,
	And speak with absolute indifference of him!

By God, I say it's base and scandalous
To falsify the heart's affections thus;
If I caught myself behaving in such a way,
I'd hang myself for shame, without delay.

PHILINTE It hardly seems a hanging matter to me;
I hope that you will take it graciously
If I extend myself a slight reprieve,
And live a little longer, by your leave.

ALCESTE How dare you joke about a crime so grave?

PHILINTE What crime? How else are people to behave?

ALCESTE I'd have them be sincere, and never part
With any word that isn't from the heart.

PHILINTE When someone greets us with a show of pleasure,
It's but polite to give him equal measure,
Return his love the best that we know how,
And trade him offer for offer, vow for vow.

ALCESTE No, no, this formula you'd have me follow,
However fashionable, is false and hollow,
And I despise the frenzied operations
Of all these barterers of protestations,
These lavishers of meaningless embraces,
These utterers of obliging commonplaces,
Who court and flatter everyone on earth
And praise the fool no less than the man of worth.
Should you rejoice that someone fondles you,
Offers his love and service, swears to be true,
And fills your ears with praises of your name,
When to the first damned fop he'll say the same?
No, no: no self-respecting heart would dream
Of prizing so promiscuous an esteem;
However high the praise, there's nothing worse
Than sharing honours with the universe.
Esteem is founded on comparison:
To honour all men is to honour none.
Since you embrace this indiscriminate vice,

Your friendship comes at far too cheap a price;
I spurn the easy tribute of a heart
Which will not set the worthy man apart:
I choose, Sir, to be chosen; and in fine,
The friend of mankind is no friend of mine.

PHILINTE But in polite society, custom decrees
That we show certain outward courtesies. . . .

ALCESTE Ah, no! we should condemn with all our force
Such false and artificial intercourse.
Let men behave like men; let them display
Their inmost hearts in everything they say;
Let the heart speak, and let our sentiments
Not mask themselves in silly compliments.

PHILINTE In certain cases it would be uncouth
And most absurd to speak the naked truth;
With all respect for your exalted notions,
It's often best to veil one's true emotions.
Wouldn't the social fabric come undone
If we were wholly frank with everyone?
Suppose you met with someone you couldn't bear;
Would you inform him of it then and there?

ALCESTE Yes.

PHILINTE   Then you'd tell old Emilie it's pathetic
The way she daubs her features with cosmetic
And plays the gay coquette at sixty-four?

ALCESTE I would.

PHILINTE   And you'd call Dorilas a bore,
And tell him every ear at court is lame
From hearing him brag about his noble name?

ALCESTE Precisely.

PHILINTE   Ah, you're joking.

ALCESTE   *Au contraire:*
In this regard there's none I'd choose to spare.
All are corrupt; there's nothing to be seen
In court or town but aggravates my spleen.

I fall into deep gloom and melancholy
When I survey the scene of human folly,
Finding on every hand base flattery,
Injustice, fraud, self-interest, treachery. . . .
Ah, it's too much; mankind has grown so base,
I mean to break with the whole human race.

PHILINTE This philosophic rage is a bit extreme;
You've no idea how comical you seem;
Indeed, we're like those brothers in the play
Called *School for Husbands*, one of whom was prey . . .

ALCESTE Enough, now! None of your stupid similes.

PHILINTE Then let's have no more tirades, if you please.
The world won't change, whatever you say or do;
And since plain speaking means so much to you,
I'll tell you plainly that by being frank
You've earned the reputation of a crank,
And that you're thought ridiculous when you rage
And rant against the manners of the age.

ALCESTE So much the better; just what I wish to hear.
No news could be more grateful to my ear.
All men are so detestable in my eyes,
I should be sorry if they thought me wise.

PHILINTE Your hatred's very sweeping, is it not?

ALCESTE Quite right: I hate the whole degraded lot.

PHILINTE Must all poor human creatures be embraced,
Without distinction, by your vast distaste?
Even in these bad times, there are surely a few . . .

ALCESTE No, I include all men in one dim view:
Some men I hate for being rogues; the others
I hate because they treat the rogues like brothers,
And, lacking a virtuous scorn for what is vile,
Receive the villain with a complaisant smile.
Notice how tolerant people choose to be
Toward that bold rascal who's at law with me.
His social polish can't conceal his nature;

One sees at once that he's a treacherous creature;
No one could possibly be taken in
By those soft speeches and that sugary grin.
The whole world knows the shady means by which
The low-brow's grown so powerful and rich,
And risen to a rank so bright and high
That virtue can but blush, and merit sigh.
Whenever his name comes up in conversation,
None will defend his wretched reputation;
Call him knave, liar, scoundrel, and all the rest,
Each head will nod, and no one will protest.
And yet his smirk is seen in every house,
He's greeted everywhere with smiles and bows,
And when there's any honour that can be got
By pulling strings, he'll get it, like as not.
My God! It chills my heart to see the ways
Men come to terms with evil nowadays;
Sometimes, I swear, I'm moved to flee and find
Some desert land unfouled by humankind.

PHILINTE Come, let's forget the follies of the times
And pardon mankind for its petty crimes;
Let's have an end of rantings and of railings,
And show some leniency toward human failings.
This world requires a pliant rectitude;
Too stern a virtue makes one stiff and rude;
Good sense views all extremes with detestation,
And bids us to be noble in moderation.
The rigid virtues of the ancient days
Are not for us; they jar with all our ways
And ask of us too lofty a perfection.
Wise men accept their times without objection,
And there's no greater folly, if you ask me,
Than trying to reform society.
Like you, I see each day a hundred and one
Unhandsome deeds that might be better done,

But still, for all the faults that meet my view,
I'm never known to storm and rave like you.
I take men as they are, or let them be,
And teach my soul to bear their frailty;
And whether in court or town, whatever the
    scene,
My phlegm's as philosophic as your spleen.

ALCESTE This phlegm which you so eloquently commend,
Does nothing ever rile it up, my friend?
Suppose some man you trust should treacherously
Conspire to rob you of your property,
And do his best to wreck your reputation?
Wouldn't you feel a certain indignation?

PHILINTE Why, no. These faults of which you so complain
Are part of human nature, I maintain,
And it's no more a matter for disgust
That men are knavish, selfish and unjust,
Than that the vulture dines upon the dead,
And wolves are furious, and apes ill-bred.

ALCESTE Shall I see myself betrayed, robbed, torn to bits,
And not . . . Oh, let's be still and rest our wits.
Enough of reasoning, now. I've had my fill.

PHILINTE Indeed, you would do well, Sir, to be still.
Rage less at your opponent, and give some thought
To how you'll win this lawsuit that he's brought.

ALCESTE I assure you I'll do nothing of the sort.

PHILINTE Then who will plead your case before the court?

ALCESTE Reason and right and justice will plead for me.

PHILINTE Oh, Lord. What judges do you plan to see?

ALCESTE Why, none. The justice of my cause is clear.

PHILINTE Of course, man; but there's politics to fear. . . .

ALCESTE No, I refuse to lift a hand. That's flat.
I'm either right, or wrong.

PHILINTE   Don't count on that.

ALCESTE No, I'll do nothing.

PHILINTE   Your enemy's influence
Is great, you know . . .

ALCESTE   That makes no difference.

PHILINTE It will; you'll see.

ALCESTE   Must honour bow to guile?
If so, I shall be proud to lose the trial.

PHILINTE Oh, really . . .

ALCESTE   I'll discover by this case
Whether or not men are sufficiently base
And impudent and villainous and perverse
To do me wrong before the universe.

PHILINTE What a man!

ALCESTE   Oh, I could wish, whatever the cost,
Just for the beauty of it, that my trial were lost.

PHILINTE If people heard you talking so, Alceste,
They'd split their sides. Your name would be a jest.

ALCESTE So much the worse for jesters.

PHILINTE   May I enquire
Whether this rectitude you so admire,
And these hard virtues you're enamoured of
Are qualities of the lady whom you love?
It much surprises me that you, who seem
To view mankind with furious disesteem,
Have yet found something to enchant your eyes
Amidst a species which you so despise.
And what is more amazing, I'm afraid,
Is the most curious choice your heart has made.
The honest Eliante is fond of you,
Arsinoé, the prude, admires you too;
And yet your spirit's been perversely led
To choose the flighty Célimène instead,
Whose brittle malice and coquettish ways
So typify the manners of our days.
How is it that the traits you most abhor
Are bearable in this lady you adore?

Are you so blind with love that you can't find them?
Or do you contrive, in her case, not to mind them?

ALCESTE My love for that young widow's not the kind
That can't perceive defects; no, I'm not blind.
I see her faults, despite my ardent love,
And all I see I fervently reprove.
And yet I'm weak; for all her falsity,
That woman knows the art of pleasing me,
And though I never cease complaining of her,
I swear I cannot manage not to love her.
Her charm outweighs her faults; I can but aim
To cleanse her spirit in my love's pure flame.

PHILINTE That's no small task; I wish you all success.
You think then that she loves you?

ALCESTE   Heavens, yes!
I wouldn't love her did she not love me.

PHILINTE Well, if her taste for you is plain to see,
Why do these rivals cause you such despair?

ALCESTE True love, Sir, is possessive, and cannot bear
To share with all the world. I'm here today
To tell her she must send that mob away.

PHILINTE If I were you, and had your choice to make,
Eliante, her cousin, would be the one I'd take;
That honest heart, which cares for you alone,
Would harmonize far better with your own.

ALCESTE True, true: each day my reason tells me so;
But reason doesn't rule in love, you know.

PHILINTE I fear some bitter sorrow is in store;
This love . . .

SCENE TWO: *Oronte, Alceste, Philinte*

ORONTE (*to Alceste*). The servants told me at the door
    That Eliante and Célimène were out,
    But when I heard, dear Sir, that you were about,
    I came to say, without exaggeration,
    That I hold you in the vastest admiration,
    And that it's always been my dearest desire
    To be the friend of one I so admire.
    I hope to see my love of merit requited,
    And you and me in friendship's bond united.
    I'm sure you won't refuse – if I may be frank –
    A friend of my devotedness – and rank.
    (*During this speech of Oronte's,* ALCESTE *is abstracted,
    and seems unaware that he is being spoken to. He only
    breaks off his reverie when* ORONTE *says:*)
    It was for you, if you please, that my words were
     intended.
ALCESTE For me, Sir?
ORONTE   Yes, for you. You're not offended?
ALCESTE By no means. But this much surprises me. . . .
    The honour comes most unexpectedly. . . .
ORONTE My high regard should not astonish you;
    The whole world feels the same. It is your due.
ALCESTE Sir . . .
ORONTE   Why, in all the State there isn't one
    Can match your merits; they shine, Sir, like the sun.
ALCESTE Sir . . .
ORONTE   You are higher in my estimation
    Than all that's most illustrious in the nation.
ALCESTE Sir . . .
ORONTE   If I lie, may heaven strike me dead!
    To show you that I mean what I have said,

Permit me, Sir, to embrace you most sincerely,
And swear that I will prize our friendship dearly.
Give me your hand. And now, Sir, if you choose,
We'll make our vows.

ALCESTE   Sir . . .

ORONTE   What! You refuse?

ALCESTE Sir, it's a very great honour you extend:
But friendship is a sacred thing, my friend;
It would be profanation to bestow
The name of friend on one you hardly know.
All parts are better played when well-rehearsed;
Let's put off friendship, and get acquainted first.
We may discover it would be unwise
To try to make our natures harmonize.

ORONTE By heaven! You're sagacious to the core;
This speech has made me admire you even more.
Let time, then, bring us closer day by day;
Meanwhile, I shall be yours in every way.
If, for example, there should be anything
You wish at court, I'll mention it to the King.
I have his ear, of course; it's quite well known
That I am much in favour with the throne.
In short, I am your servant. And now, dear friend,
Since you have such fine judgment, I intend
To please you, if I can, with a small sonnet
I wrote not long ago. Please comment on it,
And tell me whether I ought to publish it.

ALCESTE You must excuse me, Sir; I'm hardly fit
To judge such matters.

ORONTE   Why not?

ALCESTE   I am, I fear,
Inclined to be unfashionably sincere.

ORONTE Just what I ask; I'd take no satisfaction
In anything but your sincere reaction.
I beg you not to dream of being kind.

ALCESTE Since you desire it, Sir, I'll speak my mind.

ORONTE *Sonnet*. It's a sonnet. . . . *Hope* . . . The poem's addressed

To a lady who wakened hopes within my breast.
Hope . . . this is not the pompous sort of thing,
Just modest little verses, with a tender ring.

ALCESTE Well, we shall see.

ORONTE   *Hope* . . . I'm anxious to hear

Whether the style seems properly smooth and clear,
And whether the choice of words is good or bad.

ALCESTE We'll see, we'll see.

ORONTE   Perhaps I ought to add

That it took me only a quarter-hour to write it.

ALCESTE The time's irrelevant, Sir: kindly recite it.

ORONTE *(reading)*.

    Hope comforts us awhile, 'tis true,
    Lulling our cares with careless laughter,
    And yet such joy is full of rue,
    My Phyllis, if nothing follows after.

PHILINTE I'm charmed by this already; the style's delightful.

ALCESTE *(sotto voce, to* PHILINTE*)*.

How can you say that? Why, the thing is frightful.

ORONTE *Your fair face smiled on me awhile,*
    But was it kindness so to enchant me?
    'Twould have been fairer not to smile,
    If hope was all you meant to grant me.

PHILINTE What a clever thought! How handsomely you phrase it!

ALCESTE *(sotto voce, to* PHILINTE*)*.

You know the thing is trash. How dare you praise it?

ORONTE *If it's to be my passion's fate*
    Thus everlastingly to wait,
    Then death will come to set me free:
    For death is fairer than the fair;
    Phyllis, to hope is to despair

When one must hope eternally.

PHILINTE The close is exquisite – full of feeling and grace.

ALCESTE (*sotto voce, aside*).

Oh, blast the close; you'd better close your face
Before you send your lying soul to hell.

PHILINTE I can't remember a poem I've liked so well.

ALCESTE (*sotto voce, aside*).

Good Lord!

ORONTE (*to* PHILINTE).

I fear you're flattering me a bit.

PHILINTE Oh, no!

ALCESTE (*sotto voce, aside*).

What else d'you call it, you hypocrite?

ORONTE (*to* ALCESTE).

But you, Sir, keep your promise now: don't shrink
From telling me sincerely what you think.

ALCESTE Sir, these are delicate matters; we all desire
To be told that we've the true poetic fire.
But once, to one whose name I shall not mention,
I said, regarding some verse of his invention,
That gentlemen should rigorously control
That itch to write which often afflicts the soul;
That one should curb the heady inclination
To publicize one's little avocation;
And that in showing off one's works of art
One often plays a very clownish part.

ORONTE Are you suggesting in a devious way
That I ought not . . .

ALCESTE   Oh, that I do not say.
Further, I told him that no fault is worse
Than that of writing frigid, lifeless verse,
And that the merest whisper of such a shame
Suffices to destroy a man's good name.

ORONTE D'you mean to say my sonnet's dull and trite?

ALCESTE I don't say that. But I went on to cite

          Numerous cases of once-respected men
          Who came to grief by taking up the pen.

ORONTE And am I like them? Do I write so poorly?

ALCESTE I don't say that. But I told this person, 'Surely
          You're under no necessity to compose;
          Why you should wish to publish, heaven knows.
          There's no excuse for printing tedious rot
          Unless one writes for bread, as you do not.
          Resist temptation, then, I beg of you;
          Conceal your pastimes from the public view;
          And don't give up, on any provocation,
          Your present high and courtly reputation,
          To purchase at a greedy printer's shop
          The name of silly author and scribbling fop.'
          These were the points I tried to make him see.

ORONTE I sense that they are also aimed at me;
          But now – about my sonnet – I'd like to be told . . .

ALCESTE Frankly, that sonnet should be pigeonholed.
          You've chosen the worst models to imitate.
          The style's unnatural. Let me illustrate:

> For example, *Your fair face smiled on me awhile*,
> Followed by, *'Twould have been fairer not to smile!*
> Or this: *such joy is full of rue;*
> Or this: *For death is fairer than the fair;*
> Or, *Phyllis, to hope is to despair*
>   *When one must hope eternally!*

          This artificial style, that's all the fashion,
          Has neither taste, nor honesty, nor passion;
          It's nothing but a sort of wordy play,
          And nature never spoke in such a way.
          What, in this shallow age, is not debased?
          Our fathers, though less refined, had better taste;
          I'd barter all that men admire today
          For one old love-song I shall try to say:

If the King had given me for my own
Paris, his citadel,
And I for that must leave alone
Her whom I love so well,
I'd say then to the Crown,
Take back your glittering town;
My darling is more fair, I swear,
My darling is more fair.

The rhyme's not rich, the style is rough and old,
But don't you see that it's the purest gold
Beside the tinsel nonsense now preferred,
And that there's passion in its every word?

If the King had given me for my own
Paris, his citadel,
And I for that must leave alone
Her whom I love so well,
I'd say then to the Crown,
Take back your glittering town;
My darling is more fair, I swear,
My darling is more fair.

There speaks a loving heart. (*To* PHILINTE.)
    You're laughing, eh?
Laugh on, my precious wit. Whatever you say,
I hold that song's worth all the bibelots
That people hail today with ah's and oh's.

ORONTE And I maintain my sonnet's very good.

ALCESTE It's not at all surprising that you should.
You have your reasons; permit me to have mine
For thinking that you cannot write a line.

ORONTE Others have praised my sonnet to the skies.

ALCESTE I lack their art of telling pleasant lies.

ORONTE You seem to think you've got no end of wit.

ALCESTE   To praise your verse, I'd need still more of it.

ORONTE   I'm not in need of your approval, Sir.

ALCESTE   That's good; you couldn't have it if you were.

ORONTE   Come now, I'll lend you the subject of my sonnet;
　　　　　I'd like to see you try to improve upon it.

ALCESTE   I might, by chance, write something just as shoddy;
　　　　　But then I wouldn't show it to everybody.

ORONTE   You're most opinionated and conceited.

ALCESTE   Go find your flatterers, and be better treated.

ORONTE   Look here, my little fellow, pray watch your tone.

ALCESTE   My great big fellow, you'd better watch your own.

PHILINTE   (*stepping between them*).
　　　　　Oh, please, please, gentlemen! This will never do.

ORONTE   The fault is mine, and I leave the field to you.
　　　　　I am your servant, Sir, in every way.

ALCESTE   And I, Sir, am your most abject valet.

SCENE THREE: Philinte, *Alceste*

PHILINTE   Well, as you see, sincerity in excess
　　　　　Can get you into a very pretty mess;
　　　　　Oronte was hungry for appreciation. . . .

ALCESTE   Don't speak to me.

PHILINTE   　　　　　What?

ALCESTE   　　　　　　　　No more conversation.

PHILINTE   Really, now . . .

ALCESTE   　　　　Leave me alone.

PHILINTE   　　　　　　　　If I . . .

ALCESTE   　　　　　　　　　　Out of my sight!

PHILINTE   But what . . .

ALCESTE   　　　　I won't listen.

PHILINTE   　　　　　　　　But . . .

ALCESTE   Silence!
PHILINTE   Now, is it polite . . .
ALCESTE By heaven, I've had enough. Don't follow me.
PHILINTE Ah, you're just joking. I'll keep you company.

Act Two

SCENE ONE: Alceste, Célimène

ALCESTE   Shall I speak plainly, Madam? I confess
                Your conduct gives me infinite distress,
                And my resentment's grown too hot to smother.
                Soon, I foresee, we'll break with one another.
                If I said otherwise, I should deceive you;
                Sooner or later, I shall be forced to leave you,
                And if I swore that we shall never part,
                I should misread the omens of my heart.

CELIMENE   You kindly saw me home, it would appear,
                So as to pour invectives in my ear.

ALCESTE   I've no desire to quarrel. But I deplore
                Your inability to shut the door
                On all these suitors who beset you so.
                There's what annoys me, if you care to know.

CELIMENE   Is it my fault that all these men pursue me?
                Am I to blame if they're attracted to me?
                And when they gently beg an audience,
                Ought I to take a stick and drive them hence?

ALCESTE   Madam, there's no necessity for a stick;
                A less responsive heart would do the trick.
                Of your attractiveness I don't complain;
                But those your charms attract, you then detain
                By a most melting and receptive manner,
                And so enlist their hearts beneath your banner.
                It's the agreeable hopes which you excite
                That keep these lovers round you day and night;
                Were they less liberally smiled upon,
                That sighing troop would very soon be gone.

But, tell me, Madam, why it is that lately
This man Clitandre interests you so greatly?
Because of what high merits do you deem
Him worthy of the honour of your esteem?
Is it that your admiring glances linger
On the splendidly long nail of his little finger?
Or do you share the general deep respect
For the blond wig he chooses to affect?
Are you in love with his embroidered hose?
Do you adore his ribbons and his bows?
Or is it that this paragon bewitches
Your tasteful eye with his vast German breeches?
Perhaps his giggle, or his falsetto voice,
Makes him the latest gallant of your choice?

CELIMENE You're much mistaken to resent him so.
Why I put up with him you surely know:
My lawsuit's very shortly to be tried,
And I must have his influence on my side.

ALCESTE Then lose your lawsuit, Madam, or let it drop;
Don't torture me by humouring such a fop.

CELIMENE You're jealous of the whole world, Sir.

ALCESTE   That's true,
Since the whole world is well-received by you.

CELIMENE That my good nature is so unconfined
Should serve to pacify your jealous mind;
Were I to smile on one, and scorn the rest,
Then you might have some cause to be distressed.

ALCESTE Well, if I mustn't be jealous, tell me, then,
Just how I'm better treated than other men.

CELIMENE You know you have my love. Will that not do?

ALCESTE What proof have I that what you say is true?

CELIMENE I would expect, Sir, that my having said it
Might give the statement a sufficient credit.

ALCESTE But how can I be sure that you don't tell
The selfsame thing to other men as well?

CELIMENE   What a gallant speech! How flattering to me!
           What a sweet creature you make me out to be!
           Well then, to save you from the pangs of doubt,
           All that I've said I hereby cancel out;
           Now, none but yourself shall make a monkey of you:
           Are you content?

ALCESTE   Why, why am I doomed to love you?
           I swear that I shall bless the blissful hour
           When this poor heart's no longer in your power!
           I make no secret of it: I've done my best
           To exorcize this passion from my breast;
           But thus far all in vain; it will not go;
           It's for my sins that I must love you so.

CELIMENE   Your love for me is matchless, Sir; that's clear.

ALCESTE   Indeed, in all the world it has no peer;
           Words can't describe the nature of my passion,
           And no man ever loved in such a fashion.

CELIMENE   Yes, it's a brand-new fashion, I agree:
           You show your love by castigating me,
           And all your speeches are enraged and rude.
           I've never been so furiously wooed.

ALCESTE   Yet you could calm that fury, if you chose.
           Come, shall we bring our quarrels to a close?
           Let's speak with open hearts, then, and begin . . .

SCENE TWO: Célimène, Alceste, Basque

CELIMENE   What is it?

BASQUE   Acaste is here.

CELIMENE   Well, send him in.

SCENE THREE: *Célimène, Alceste*

ALCESTE   What! Shall we never be alone at all?
           You're always ready to receive a call,
           And you can't bear, for ten ticks of the clock,
           Not to keep open house for all who knock.

CELIMENE   I couldn't refuse him: he'd be most put out.

ALCESTE   Surely that's not worth worrying about.

CELIMENE   Acaste would never forgive me if he guessed
           That I consider him a dreadful pest.

ALCESTE   If he's a pest, why bother with him then?

CELIMENE   Heavens! One can't antagonize such men;
           Why, they're the chartered gossips of the court,
           And have a say in things of every sort.
           One must receive them, and be full of charm;
           They're no great help, but they can do you harm,
           And though your influence be ever so great,
           They're hardly the best people to alienate.

ALCESTE   I see, dear lady, that you could make a case
           For putting up with the whole human race;
           These friendships that you calculate so nicely . . .

SCENE FOUR: *Alceste, Célimène, Basque*

BASQUE   Madam, Clitandre is here as well.

ALCESTE   Precisely.

CELIMENE   Where are you going?

ALCESTE   Elsewhere.

CELIMENE   Stay.

ALCESTE   No, no.

CELIMENE Stay, Sir.

ALCESTE   I can't.

CELIMENE   I wish it.

ALCESTE   No, I must go.
          I beg you, Madam, not to press the matter;
          You know I have no taste for idle chatter.

CELIMENE Stay: I command you.

ALCESTE   No, I cannot stay.

CELIMENE Very well; you have my leave to go away.

SCENE FIVE: Eliante, Philinte, Acaste,
Clitandre, Alceste, Célimène, Basque

ELIANTE (*to* CELIMENE).
          The Marquesses have kindly come to call.
          Were they announced?

CELIMENE   Yes. Basque, bring chairs for
                              all.
          (BASQUE *provides the chairs, and goes out*).
          (*To* ALCESTE).
          You haven't gone?

ALCESTE   No; and I shan't depart
          Till you decide who's foremost in your heart.

CELIMENE Oh, hush.

ALCESTE   It's time to choose; take them, or me.

CELIMENE You're mad.

ALCESTE   I'm not, as you shall shortly see.

CELIMENE Oh?

ALCESTE   You'll decide.

CELIMENE   You're joking now, dear friend.

ALCESTE No, no; you'll choose; my patience is at an end.

CLITANDRE   Madam, I come from court, where poor Cléonte
            Behaved like a perfect fool, as is his wont.
            Has he no friend to counsel him, I wonder,
            And teach him less unerringly to blunder?

CELIMENE   It's true, the man's a most accomplished dunce;
            His gauche behaviour strikes the eye at once;
            And every time one sees him, on my word,
            His manner's grown a trifle more absurd.

ACASTE   Speaking of dunces, I've just now conversed
            With old Damon, who's one of the very worst;
            I stood a lifetime in the broiling sun
            Before his dreary monologue was done.

CELIMENE   Oh, he's a wondrous talker, and has the power
            To tell you nothing hour after hour:
            If, by mistake, he ever came to the point,
            The shock would put his jawbone out of joint.

ELIANTE (*to* PHILINTE).
            The conversation takes its usual turn,
            And all our dear friends' ears will shortly burn.

CLITANDRE   Timante's a character, Madam.

CELIMENE   Isn't he, though?
            A man of mystery from top to toe,
            Who moves about in a romantic mist
            On secret missions which do not exist.
            His talk is full of eyebrows and grimaces;
            How tired one gets of his momentous faces;
            He's always whispering something confidential
            Which turns out to be quite inconsequential;
            Nothing's too slight for him to mystify;
            He even whispers when he says 'good-bye.'

ACASTE   Tell us about Géralde.

CELIMENE   That tiresome ass.
            He mixes only with the titled class,
            And fawns on dukes and princes, and is bored
            With anyone who's not at least a lord.

          The man's obsessed with rank, and his discourses
          Are all of hounds and carriages and horses;
          He uses Christian names with all the great,
          And the word Milord, with him, is out of date.

CLITANDRE He's very taken with Bélise, I hear.

CELIMENE She is the dreariest company, poor dear.
          Whenever she comes to call, I grope about
          To find some topic which will draw her out,
          But, owing to her dry and faint replies,
          The conversation wilts, and droops, and dies.
          In vain one hopes to animate her face
          By mentioning the ultimate commonplace;
          But sun or shower, even hail or frost
          Are matters she can instantly exhaust.
          Meanwhile her visit, painful though it is,
          Drags on and on through mute eternities,
          And though you ask the time, and yawn, and yawn,
          She sits there like a stone and won't be gone.

ACASTE Now for Adraste.

CELIMENE   Oh, that conceited elf
          Has a gigantic passion for himself;
          He rails against the court, and cannot bear it
          That none will recognize his hidden merit;
          All honours given to others give offence
          To his imaginary excellence.

CLITANDRE What about young Cléon ? His house, they say,
          Is full of the best society, night and day.

CELIMENE His cook has made him popular, not he:
          It's Cléon's table that people come to see.

ELIANTE He gives a splendid dinner, you must admit.

CELIMENE But must he serve himself along with it ?
          For my taste, he's a most insipid dish
          Whose presence sours the wine and spoils the fish.

PHILINTE Damis, his uncle, is admired no end.
          What's your opinion, Madam ?

CELIMENE   Why, he's my friend.

PHILINTE He seems a decent fellow, and rather clever.

CELIMENE He works too hard at cleverness, however.
I hate to see him sweat and struggle so
To fill his conversation with *bons mots*.
Since he's decided to become a wit
His taste's so pure that nothing pleases it;
He scolds at all the latest books and plays,
Thinking that wit must never stoop to praise,
That finding fault's a sign of intellect,
That all appreciation is abject,
And that by damning everything in sight
One shows oneself in a distinguished light.
He's scornful even of our conversations:
Their trivial nature sorely tries his patience;
He folds his arms, and stands above the battle,
And listens sadly to our childish prattle.

ACASTE Wonderful, Madam! You've hit him off precisely.

CLITANDRE No one can sketch a character so nicely.

ALCESTE How bravely, Sirs, you cut and thrust at all
These absent fools, till one by one they fall:
But let one come in sight, and you'll at once
Embrace the man you lately called a dunce,
Telling him in a tone sincere and fervent
How proud you are to be his humble servant.

CLITANDRE Why pick on us? Madame's been speaking, Sir,
And you should quarrel, if you must, with her.

ALCESTE No, no, by God the fault is yours, because
You lead her on with laughter and applause,
And make her think that she's the more delightful
The more her talk is scandalous and spiteful.
Oh, she would stoop to malice far, far less
If no such claque approved her cleverness.
It's flatterers like you whose foolish praise
Nourishes all the vices of these days.

PHILINTE   But why protest when someone ridicules
         Those you'd condemn, yourself, as knaves or fools ?

CELIMENE   Why, Sir ? Because he loves to make a fuss.
         You don't expect him to agree with us,
         When there's an opportunity to express
         His heaven-sent spirit of contrariness ?
         What other people think, he can't abide;
         Whatever they say, he's on the other side;
         He lives in deadly terror of agreeing;
         'Twould make him seem an ordinary being.
         Indeed, he's so in love with contradiction,
         He'll turn against his most profound conviction
         And with a furious eloquence deplore it,
         If only someone else is speaking for it.

ALCESTE   Go on, dear lady, mock me as you please;
         You have your audience in ecstasies.

PHILINTE   But what she says is true: you have a way
         Of bridling at whatever people say;
         Whether they praise or blame, your angry spirit
         Is equally unsatisfied to hear it.

ALCESTE   Men, Sir, are always wrong, and that's the reason
         That righteous anger's never out of season;
         All that I hear in all their conversation
         Is flattering praise or reckless condemnation.

CELIMENE   But . . .

ALCESTE   No, no, Madam, I am forced to state
         That you have pleasures which I deprecate,
         And that these others, here, are much to blame
         For nourishing the faults which are your shame.

CLITANDRE   I shan't defend myself, Sir; but I vow
         I'd thought this lady faultless until now.

ACASTE   I see her charms and graces, which are many;
         But as for faults, I've never noticed any.

ALCESTE   I see them, Sir; and rather than ignore them,
         I strenuously criticize her for them.

The more one loves, the more one should object
To every blemish, every least defect.
Were I this lady, I would soon get rid
Of lovers who approved of all I did,
And by their slack indulgence and applause
Endorsed my follies and excused my flaws.

CELIMENE If all hearts beat according to your measure,
The dawn of love would be the end of pleasure;
And love would find its perfect consummation
In ecstasies of rage and reprobation.

ELIANTE Love, as a rule, affects men otherwise,
And lovers rarely love to criticize.
They see their lady as a charming blur,
And find all things commendable in her.
If she has any blemish, fault, or shame,
They will redeem it by a pleasing name.
The pale-faced lady's lily-white, perforce;
The swarthy one's a sweet brunette, of course;
The spindly lady has a slender grace;
The fat one has a most majestic pace;
The plain one, with her dress in disarray,
They classify as *beauté négligée;*
The hulking one's a goddess in their eyes,
The dwarf, a concentrate of Paradise;
The haughty lady has a noble mind;
The mean one's witty, and the dull one's kind;
The chatterbox has liveliness and verve,
The mute one has a virtuous reserve.
So lovers manage, in their passion's cause,
To love their ladies even for their flaws.

ALCESTE But I still say . . .

CELIMENE   I think it would be nice
To stroll around the gallery once or twice.
What! You're not going, Sirs?

CLITANDRE and ACASTE No, Madam, no.

ALCESTE You seem to be in terror lest they go.
Do what you will, Sirs; leave, or linger on,
But I shan't go till after you are gone.

ACASTE I'm free to linger, unless I should perceive
Madame is tired, and wishes me to leave.

CLITANDRE And as for me, I needn't go today
Until the hour of the King's *coucher.*

CELIMENE (*to* ALCESTE).
You're joking, surely?

ALCESTE Not in the least; we'll see
Whether you'd rather part with them, or me.

*SCENE SIX: Alceste, Célimène, Eliante, Acaste
Philinte, Clitandre, Basque*

BASQUE (*to* ALCESTE).
Sir, there's a fellow here who bids me state
That he must see you, and that it can't wait.

ALCESTE Tell him that I have no such pressing affairs.

BASQUE It's a long tailcoat that this fellow wears,
With gold all over.

CELIMENE (*to* ALCESTE). You'd best go down and see.
Or – have him enter.

*SCENE SEVEN: Alceste, Célimène, Eliante,
Acaste, Philinte, Clitandre, A Guard of the
Marshalsea*

ALCESTE (*confronting the* GUARD).
Well, what do you want with me?

Come in, Sir.

GUARD I've a word, Sir, for your ear.

ALCESTE Speak it aloud, Sir; I shall strive to hear.

GUARD The Marshals have instructed me to say
You must report to them without delay.

ALCESTE Who? Me, Sir?

GUARD   Yes, Sir; you.

ALCESTE   But what do they want?

PHILINTE (*to* ALCESTE).
To scotch your silly quarrel with Oronte.

CELIMENE (*to* PHILINTE).
What quarrel?

PHILINTE   Oronte and he have fallen out
Over some verse he spoke his mind about;
The Marshals wish to arbitrate the matter.

ALCESTE Never shall I equivocate or flatter!

PHILINTE You'd best obey their summons; come, let's go.

ALCESTE How can they mend our quarrel, I'd like to know?
Am I to make a cowardly retraction,
And praise those jingles to his satisfaction?
I'll not recant; I've judged that sonnet rightly.
It's bad.

PHILINTE   But you might say so more politely. . . .

ALCESTE I'll not back down; his verses make me sick.

PHILINTE If only you could be more politic!
But come, let's go.

ALCESTE   I'll go, but I won't unsay
A single word.

PHILINTE   Well, let's be on our way.

ALCESTE Till I am ordered by my lord the King
To praise that poem, I shall say the thing
Is scandalous, by God, and that the poet
Ought to be hanged for having the nerve to show it:
(*To* CLITANDRE *and* ACASTE, *who are laughing*).
By heaven, Sirs, I really didn't know

That I was being humorous.

CELIMENE   Go, Sir, go;
Settle your business.

ALCESTE   I shall, and when I'm through,
I shall return to settle things with you.

Act Three

SCENE ONE: Clitandre, Acaste

CLITANDRE Dear Marquess, how contented you appear;
All things delight you, nothing mars your cheer.
Can you, in perfect honesty, declare
That you've a right to be so debonair?
ACASTE By Jove, when I survey myself, I find
No cause whatever for distress of mind.
I'm young and rich; I can in modesty
Lay claim to an exalted pedigree;
And owing to my name and my condition
I shall not want for honours and position.
Then as to courage, that most precious trait,
I seem to have it, as was proved of late
Upon the field of honour, where my bearing,
They say, was very cool and rather daring.
I've wit, of course; and taste in such perfection
That I can judge without the least reflection,
And at the theatre, which is my delight,
Can make or break a play on opening night,
And lead the crowd in hisses or bravos,
And generally be known as one who knows.
I'm clever, handsome, gracefully polite;
My waist is small, my teeth are strong and white;
As for my dress, the world's astonished eyes
Assure me that I bear away the prize.
I find myself in favour everywhere,
Honoured by men, and worshipped by the fair;
And since these things are so, it seems to me
I'm justified in my complacency.

CLITANDRE Well, if so many ladies hold you dear,
     Why do you press a hopeless courtship here?
ACASTE Hopeless, you say? I'm not the sort of fool
     That likes his ladies difficult and cool.
     Men who are awkward, shy, and peasantish
     May pine for heartless beauties, if they wish,
     Grovel before them, bear their cruelties,
     Woo them with tears and sighs and bended knees,
     And hope by dogged faithfulness to gain
     What their poor merits never could obtain.
     For men like me, however, it makes no sense
     To love on trust, and foot the whole expense.
     Whatever any lady's merits be,
     I think, thank God, that I'm as choice as she;
     That if my heart is kind enough to burn
     For her, she owes me something in return;
     And that in any proper love affair
     The partners must invest an equal share.
CLITANDRE You think, then, that our hostess favours you?
ACASTE I've reason to believe that that is true.
CLITANDRE How did you come to such a mad conclusion?
     You're blind, dear fellow. This is sheer delusion.
ACASTE All right, then: I'm deluded and I'm blind.
CLITANDRE Whatever put the notion in your mind?
ACASTE Delusion.
CLITANDRE   What persuades you that you're right?
ACASTE I'm blind.
CLITANDRE   But have you any proofs to cite?
ACASTE I tell you I'm deluded.
CLITANDRE   Have you, then,
     Received some secret pledge from Célimène?
ACASTE Oh, no: she scorns me.
CLITANDRE   Tell me the truth, I beg.
ACASTE She just can't bear me.
CLITANDRE   Ah, don't pull my leg.

Tell me what hope she's given you, I pray.

ACASTE I'm hopeless, and it's you who win the day.
She hates me thoroughly, and I'm so vexed
I mean to hang myself on Tuesday next.

CLITANDRE Dear Marquess, let us have an armistice
And make a treaty. What do you say to this?
If ever one of us can plainly prove
That Célimène encourages his love,
The other must abandon hope, and yield,
And leave him in possession of the field.

ACASTE Now, there's a bargain that appeals to me;
With all my heart, dear Marquess, I agree.
But hush.

SCENE TWO: *Célimène, Acaste, Clitandre*

CELIMENE Still here?
CLITANDRE 'Twas love that stayed our feet.
CELIMENE I think I heard a carriage in the street.
Whose is it? D'you know?

SCENE THREE: *Célimène, Acaste, Clitandre, Basque*

BASQUE Arsinoé is here,
Madame.
CELIMENE Arsinoé, you say? Oh, dear.
BASQUE Eliante is entertaining her below.
CELIMENE What brings the creature here, I'd like to know?

ACASTE They say she's dreadfully prudish, but in fact
          I think her piety . . .

CELIMENE   It's all an act.
          At heart she's worldly, and her poor success
          In snaring men explains her prudishness.
          It breaks her heart to see the beaux and gallants
          Engrossed by other women's charms and talents,
          And so she's always in a jealous rage
          Against the faulty standards of the age.
          She lets the world believe that she's a prude
          To justify her loveless solitude,
          And strives to put a brand of moral shame
          On all the graces that she cannot claim.
          But still she'd love a lover; and Alceste
          Appears to be the one she'd love the best.
          His visits here are poison to her pride;
          She seems to think I've lured him from her side;
          And everywhere, at court or in the town,
          The spiteful, envious woman runs me down.
          In short, she's just as stupid as can be,
          Vicious and arrogant in the last degree,
          And . . .

*SCENE FOUR: Arsinoé, Célimène, Clitandre,
Acaste*

CELIMENE   Ah! What happy chance has brought you
          here?
          I've thought about you ever so much, my dear.

ARSINOE I've come to tell you something you should know.

CELIMENE How good of you to think of doing so!

        CLITANDRE *and* ACASTE *go out, laughing.*

SCENE FIVE: Arsinoé, Célimène

ARSINOE It's just as well those gentlemen didn't tarry.

CELIMENE Shall we sit down?

ARSINOE   That won't be necessary.
Madam, the flame of friendship ought to burn
Brightest in matters of the most concern,
And as there's nothing which concerns us more
Than honour, I have hastened to your door
To bring you, as your friend, some information
About the status of your reputation.
I visited, last night, some virtuous folk,
And, quite by chance, it was of you they spoke;
There was, I fear, no tendency to praise
Your light behaviour and your dashing ways.
The quantity of gentlemen you see
And your by now notorious coquetry
Were both so vehemently criticized
By everyone, that I was much surprised.
Of course, I needn't tell you where I stood;
I came to your defence as best I could,
Assured them you were harmless, and declared
Your soul was absolutely unimpaired.
But there are some things, you must realize,
One can't excuse, however hard one tries,
And I was forced at last into conceding
That your behaviour, Madam, is misleading,
That it makes a bad impression, giving rise
To ugly gossip and obscene surmise,
And that if you were more *overtly* good,
You wouldn't be so much misunderstood.
Not that I think you've been unchaste – no! no!
The saints preserve me from a thought so low!

But mere good conscience never did suffice:
One must avoid the outward show of vice.
Madam, you're too intelligent, I'm sure,
To think my motives anything but pure
In offering you this counsel – which I do
Out of a zealous interest in you.

CELIMENE Madam, I haven't taken you amiss;
I'm very much obliged to you for this;
And I'll at once discharge the obligation
By telling you about *your* reputation.
You've been so friendly as to let me know
What certain people say of me, and so
I mean to follow your benign example
By offering you a somewhat similar sample.
The other day, I went to an affair
And found some most distinguished people there
Discussing piety, both false and true.
The conversation soon came round to you.
Alas! Your prudery and bustling zeal
Appeared to have a very slight appeal.
Your affectation of a grave demeanour,
Your endless talk of virtue and of honour,
The aptitude of your suspicious mind
For finding sin where there is none to find,
Your towering self-esteem, that pitying face
With which you contemplate the human race,
Your sermonizings and your sharp aspersions
On people's pure and innocent diversions –
All these were mentioned, Madam, and, in fact,
Were roundly and concertedly attacked.
'What good,' they said, 'are all these outward shows,
When everything belies her pious pose?
She prays incessantly; but then, they say,
She beats her maids and cheats them of their pay;
She shows her zeal in every holy place,

But still she's vain enough to paint her face;
She holds that naked statues are immoral,
But with a naked *man* she'd have no quarrel.'
Of course, I said to everybody there
That they were being viciously unfair;
But still they were disposed to criticize you,
And all agreed that someone should advise you
To leave the morals of the world alone,
And worry rather more about your own.
They felt that one's self-knowledge should be great
Before one thinks of setting others straight;
That one should learn the art of living well
Before one threatens other men with hell,
And that the Church is best equipped, no doubt,
To guide our souls and root our vices out.
Madam, you're too intelligent, I'm sure,
To think my motives anything but pure
In offering you this counsel – which I do
Out of a zealous interest in you.

ARSINOE I dared not hope for gratitude, but I
Did not expect so acid a reply;
I judge, since you've been so extremely tart,
That my good counsel pierced you to the heart.

CELIMENE Far from it, Madam. Indeed, it seems to me
We ought to trade advice more frequently.
One's vision of oneself is so defective
That it would be an excellent corrective.
If you are willing, Madam, let's arrange
Shortly to have another frank exchange
In which we'll tell each other, *entre nous*,
What you've heard tell of me, and I of you.

ARSINOE Oh, people never censure you, my dear;
It's me they criticize. Or so I hear.

CELIMENE Madam, I think we either blame or praise
According to our taste and length of days.

There is a time of life for coquetry,
And there's a season, too, for prudery.
When all one's charms are gone, it is, I'm sure,
Good strategy to be devout and pure:
It makes one seem a little less forsaken.
Some day, perhaps, I'll take the road you've taken:
Time brings all things. But I have time aplenty,
And see no cause to be a prude at twenty.

ARSINOE You give your age in such a gloating tone
That one would think I was an ancient crone;
We're not so far apart, in sober truth,
That you can mock me with a boast of youth!
Madam, you baffle me. I wish I knew
What moves you to provoke me as you do.

CELIMENE For my part, Madam, I should like to know
Why you abuse me everywhere you go.
Is it my fault, dear lady, that your hand
Is not, alas, in very great demand?
If men admire me, if they pay me court
And daily make me offers of the sort
You'd dearly love to have them make to you,
How can I help it? What would you have me do?
If what you want is lovers, please feel free
To take as many as you can from me.

ARSINOE Oh, come. D'you think the world is losing sleep
Over that flock of lovers which you keep,
Or that we find it difficult to guess
What price you pay for their devotedness?
Surely you don't expect us to suppose
Mere merit could attract so many beaux?
It's not your virtue that they're dazzled by;
Nor is it virtuous love for which they sigh.
You're fooling no one, Madam; the world's not blind;
There's many a lady heaven has designed
To call men's noblest, tenderest feelings out,

> Who has no lovers dogging her about;
> From which it's plain that lovers nowadays
> Must be acquired in bold and shameless ways,
> And only pay one court for such reward
> As modesty and virtue can't afford.
> Then don't be quite so puffed up, if you please,
> About your tawdry little victories;
> Try, if you can, to be a shade less vain,
> And treat the world with somewhat less disdain.
> If one were envious of your amours,
> One soon could have a following like yours;
> Lovers are no great trouble to collect
> If one prefers them to one's self-respect.

CELIMENE Collect them then, my dear; I'd love to see
> You demonstrate that charming theory;
> Who knows, you might . . .

ARSINOE   Now, Madam, that will do;
> It's time to end this trying interview.
> My coach is late in coming to your door,
> Or I'd have taken leave of you before.

CELIMENE Oh, please don't feel that you must rush away;
> I'd be delighted, Madam, if you'd stay.
> However, lest my conversation bore you,
> Let me provide some better company for you;
> This gentleman, who comes most apropos,
> Will please you more than I could do, I know.

SCENE SIX: *Alceste, Célimène, Arsinoé*

CELIMENE Alceste, I have a little note to write
> Which simply must go out before tonight;
> Please entertain *Madame*; I'm sure that she
> Will overlook my incivility.

SCENE SEVEN: *Alceste, Arsinoé*

ARSINOE Well, Sir, our hostess graciously contrives
For us to chat until my coach arrives;
And I shall be forever in her debt
For granting me this little tête-à-tête.
We women very rightly give our hearts
To men of noble character and parts,
And your especial merits, dear Alceste,
Have roused the deepest sympathy in my breast.
Oh, how I wish they had sufficient sense
At court, to recognize your excellence!
They wrong you greatly, Sir. How it must hurt you
Never to be rewarded for your virtue!

ALCESTE Why, Madam, what cause have I to feel aggrieved?
What great and brilliant thing have I achieved?
What service have I rendered to the King
That I should look to him for anything?

ARSINOE Not everyone who's honoured by the State
Has done great services. A man must wait
Till time and fortune offer him the chance.
Your merit, Sir, is obvious at a glance,
And . . .

ALCESTE   Ah, forget my merit; I'm not neglected.
The court, I think, can hardly be expected
To mine men's souls for merit, and unearth
Our hidden virtues and our secret worth.

ARSINOE *Some* virtues, though, are far too bright to hide;
Yours are acknowledged, Sir, on every side.
Indeed, I've heard you warmly praised of late
By persons of considerable weight.

ALCESTE This fawning age has praise for everyone,
And all distinctions, Madam, are undone.

All things have equal honour nowadays,
And no one should be gratified by praise.
To be admired, one only need exist,
And every lackey's on the honours list.

ARSINOE I only wish, Sir, that you had your eye
On some position at court, however high;
You'd only have to hint at such a notion
For me to set the proper wheels in motion;
I've certain friendships I'd be glad to use
To get you any office you might choose.

ALCESTE Madam, I fear that any such ambition
Is wholly foreign to my disposition.
The soul God gave me isn't of the sort
That prospers in the weather of a court.
It's all too obvious that I don't possess
The virtues necessary for success.
My one great talent is for speaking plain;
I've never learned to flatter or to feign;
And anyone so stupidly sincere
Had best not seek a courtier's career.
Outside the court, I know, one must dispense
With honours, privilege, and influence;
But still one gains the right, forgoing these,
Not to be tortured by the wish to please.
One needn't live in dread of snubs and slights,
Nor praise the verse that every idiot writes,
Nor humour silly Marquesses, nor bestow
Politic sighs on Madam So-and-So.

ARSINOE Forget the court, then; let the matter rest.
But I've another cause to be distressed
About your present situation, Sir.
It's to your love affair that I refer.
She whom you love, and who pretends to love you,
Is, I regret to say, unworthy of you.

ALCESTE Why, Madam! Can you seriously intend

     To make so grave a charge against your friend?

ARSINOE Alas, I must. I've stood aside too long
     And let that lady do you grievous wrong;
     But now my debt to conscience shall be paid:
     I tell you that your love has been betrayed.

ALCESTE I thank you, Madam; you're extremely kind.
     Such words are soothing to a lover's mind.

ARSINOE Yes, though she *is* my friend, I say again
     You're very much too good for Célimène.
     She's wantonly misled you from the start.

ALCESTE You may be right; who knows another's heart?
     But ask yourself if it's the part of charity
     To shake my soul with doubts of her sincerity.

ARSINOE Well, if you'd rather be a dupe than doubt her,
     That's your affair. I'll say no more about her.

ALCESTE Madam, you know that doubt and vague suspicion
     Are painful to a man in my position;
     It's most unkind to worry me this way
     Unless you've some real proof of what you say.

ARSINOE Sir, say no more: all doubt shall be removed,
     And all that I've been saying shall be proved.
     You've only to escort me home, and there
     We'll look into the heart of this affair.
     I've ocular evidence which will persuade you
     Beyond a doubt, that Célimène's betrayed you.
     Then, if you're saddened by that revelation,
     Perhaps I can provide some consolation.

Act Four

SCENE ONE: Eliante, Philinte

PHILINTE Madam, he acted like a stubborn child;
I thought they never would be reconciled;
In vain we reasoned, threatened, and appealed;
He stood his ground and simply would not yield.
The Marshals, I feel sure, have never heard
An argument so splendidly absurd.
'No, gentlemen,' said he, 'I'll not retract.
His verse is bad: extremely bad, in fact.
Surely it does the man no harm to know it.
Does it disgrace him, not to be a poet?
A gentleman may be respected still,
Whether he writes a sonnet well or ill.
That I dislike his verse should not offend him;
In all that touches honour, I commend him;
He's noble, brave, and virtuous – but I fear
He can't in truth be called a sonneteer.
I'll gladly praise his wardrobe; I'll endorse
His dancing, or the way he sits a horse;
But, gentlemen, I cannot praise his rhyme.
In fact, it ought to be a capital crime
For anyone so sadly unendowed
To write a sonnet, and read the thing aloud.'
At length he fell into a gentler mood
And, striking a concessive attitude,
He paid Oronte the following courtesies:
'Sir, I regret that I'm so hard to please,
And I'm profoundly sorry that your lyric
Failed to provoke me to a panegyric.'

After these curious words, the two embraced,
And then the hearing was adjourned – in haste.

ELIANTE His conduct has been very singular lately;
Still, I confess that I respect him greatly.
The honesty in which he takes such pride
Has – to my mind – it's noble, heroic side.
In this false age, such candour seems outrageous;
But I could wish that it were more contagious.

PHILINTE What most intrigues me in our friend Alceste
Is the grand passion that rages in his breast.
The sullen humours he's compounded of
Should not, I think, dispose his heart to love;
But since they do, it puzzles me still more
That he should choose your cousin to adore.

ELIANTE It does, indeed, belie the theory
That love is born of gentle sympathy,
And that the tender passion must be based
On sweet accords of temper and of taste.

PHILINTE Does she return his love, do you suppose?

ELIANTE Ah, that's a difficult question, Sir. Who knows?
How can we judge the truth of her devotion?
Her heart's a stranger to its own emotion.
Sometimes it thinks it loves, when no love's there;
At other times it loves quite unaware.

PHILINTE I rather think Alceste is in for more
Distress and sorrow than he's bargained for;
Were he of my mind, Madam, his affection
Would turn in quite a different direction,
And we would see him more responsive to
The kind regard which he receives from you.

ELIANTE Sir, I believe in frankness, and I'm inclined,
In matters of the heart, to speak my mind.
I don't oppose his love for her; indeed,
I hope with all my heart that he'll succeed,
And were it in my power, I'd rejoice

      In giving him the lady of his choice.
      But if, as happens frequently enough
      In love affairs, he meets with a rebuff –
      If Célimène should grant some rival's suit –
      I'd gladly play the role of substitute;
      Nor would his tender speeches please me less
      Because they'd once been made without success.

PHILINTE Well, Madam, as for me, I don't oppose
      Your hopes in this affair; and heaven knows
      That in my conversations with the man
      I plead your cause as often as I can.
      But if those two should marry, and so remove
      All chance that he will offer you his love,
      Then I'll declare my own, and hope to see
      Your gracious favour pass from him to me.
      In short, should you be cheated of Alceste,
      I'd be most happy to be second best.

ELIANTE Philinte, you're teasing.

PHILINTE   Ah, Madam, never fear;
      No words of mine were ever so sincere,
      And I shall live in fretful expectation
      Till I can make a fuller declaration.

SCENE TWO: Alceste, Eliante, Philinte

ALCESTE Avenge me, Madam! I must have satisfaction,
      Or this great wrong will drive me to distraction!

ELIANTE Why, what's the matter? What's upset you so?

ALCESTE Madam, I've had a mortal, mortal blow.
      If Chaos repossessed the universe,
      I swear I'd not be shaken any worse.
      I'm ruined. . . . I can say no more. . . . My soul . . .

ELIANTE Do try, Sir, to regain your self-control.

ALCESTE Just heaven! Why were so much beauty and grace
Bestowed on one so vicious and so base?

ELIANTE Once more, Sir, tell us. . . .

ALCESTE   My world has gone to wrack;
I'm – I'm betrayed; she's stabbed me in the back:
Yes, Célimène (who would have thought it of her?)
Is false to me, and has another lover.

ELIANTE Are you quite certain? Can you prove these things?

PHILINTE Lovers are prey to wild imaginings
And jealous fancies. No doubt there's some
      mistake. . . .

ALCESTE Mind your own business, Sir, for heaven's sake.
(*To* ELIANTE).
Madam, I have the proof that you demand
Here in my pocket, penned by her own hand.
Yes, all the shameful evidence one could want
Lies in this letter written to Oronte –
Oronte! whom I felt sure she couldn't love,
And hardly bothered to be jealous of.

PHILINTE Still, in a letter, appearances may deceive;
This may not be so bad as you believe.

ALCESTE Once more I beg you, Sir, to let me be;
Tend to your own affairs; leave mine to me.

ELIANTE Compose yourself; this anguish that you feel . . .

ALCESTE Is something, Madam, you alone can heal.
My outraged heart, beside itself with grief,
Appeals to you for comfort and relief.
Avenge me on your cousin, whose unjust
And faithless nature has deceived my trust;
Avenge a crime your pure soul must detest.

ELIANTE But how, Sir?

ALCESTE   Madam, this heart within my breast
Is yours; pray take it; redeem my heart from her,
And so avenge me on my torturer.

Let her be punished by the fond emotion,
The ardent love, the bottomless devotion,
The faithful worship which this heart of mine
Will offer up to yours as to a shrine.

ELIANTE You have my sympathy, Sir, in all you suffer;
Nor do I scorn the noble heart you offer;
But I suspect you'll soon be mollified,
And this desire for vengeance will subside.
When some beloved hand has done us wrong
We thirst for retribution – but not for long;
However dark the deed that she's committed,
A lovely culprit's very soon acquitted.
Nothing's so stormy as an injured lover,
And yet no storm so quickly passes over.

ALCESTE No, Madam, no – this is no lovers' spat;
I'll not forgive her; it's gone too far for that;
My mind's made up; I'll kill myself before
I waste my hopes upon her any more.
Ah, here she is. My wrath intensifies.
I shall confront her with her tricks and lies,
And crush her utterly, and bring you then
A heart no longer slave to Célimène.

SCENE THREE: *Célimène, Alceste*

ALCESTE (*aside*).
Sweet heaven, help me to control my passion.

CELIMENE (*to* ALCESTE).
Oh, Lord. Why stand there staring in that fashion?
And what d'you mean by those dramatic sighs,
And that malignant glitter in your eyes?

ALCESTE I mean that sins which cause the blood to freeze

Look innocent beside your treacheries;
That nothing Hell's or Heaven's wrath could do
Ever produced so bad a thing as you.

CELIMENE Your compliments were always sweet and pretty.

ALCESTE Madam, it's not the moment to be witty.
No, blush and hang your head; you've ample reason,
Since I've the fullest evidence of your treason.
Ah, this is what my sad heart prophesied;
Now all my anxious fears are verified;
My dark suspicion and my gloomy doubt
Divined the truth, and now the truth is out.
For all your trickery, I was not deceived;
It was my bitter stars that I believed.
But don't imagine that you'll go scot-free;
You shan't misuse me with impunity.
I know that love's irrational and blind;
I know the heart's not subject to the mind,
And can't be reasoned into beating faster;
I know each soul is free to choose its master;
Therefore had you but spoken from the heart,
Rejecting my attentions from the start,
I'd have no grievance, or at any rate
I could complain of nothing but my fate.
Ah, but so falsely to encourage me –
That was a treason and a treachery
For which you cannot suffer too severely,
And you shall pay for that behaviour dearly.
Yes, now I have no pity, not a shred;
My temper's out of hand; I've lost my head;
Shocked by the knowledge of your double-dealings,
My reason can't restrain my savage feelings;
A righteous wrath deprives me of my senses,
And I won't answer for the consequences.

CELIMENE What does this outburst mean? Will you please
explain?

Have you, by any chance, gone quite insane?

ALCESTE Yes, yes, I went insane the day I fell
A victim to your black and fatal spell,
Thinking to meet with some sincerity
Among the treacherous charms that beckoned me.

CELIMENE Pooh. Of what treachery can you complain?

ALCESTE How sly you are, how cleverly you feign!
But you'll not victimize me any more.
Look: here's a document you've seen before.
This evidence, which I acquired today,
Leaves you, I think, without a thing to say.

CELIMENE Is this what sent you into such a fit?

ALCESTE You should be blushing at the sight of it.

CELIMENE Ought I to blush? I truly don't see why.

ALCESTE Ah, now you're being bold as well as sly;
Since there's no signature, perhaps you'll claim . . .

CELIMENE I wrote it, whether or not it bears my name.

ALCESTE And you can view with equanimity
This proof of your disloyalty to me!

CELIMENE Oh, don't be so outrageous and extreme.

ALCESTE You take this matter lightly, it would seem.
Was it no wrong to me, no shame to you,
That you should send Oronte this billet-doux?

CELIMENE Oronte! Who said it was for him?

ALCESTE   Why, those
Who brought me this example of your prose.
But what's the difference? If you wrote the letter
To someone else, it pleases me no better.
My grievance and your guilt remain the same.

CELIMENE But need you rage, and need I blush for shame,
If this was written to a *woman* friend?

ALCESTE Ah! Most ingenious. I'm impressed no end;
And after that incredible evasion
Your guilt is clear. I need no more persuasion.
How dare you try so clumsy a deception?

D'you think I'm wholly wanting in perception?
Come, come, let's see how brazenly you'll try
To bolster up so palpable a lie:
Kindly construe this ardent closing section
As nothing more than sisterly affection!
Here, let me read it. Tell me, if you dare to,
That this is for a woman . . .

CELIMENE   I don't care to.
What right have you to badger and berate me,
And so highhandedly interrogate me?

ALCESTE Now, don't be angry; all I ask of you
Is that you justify a phrase or two . . .

CELIMENE No, I shall not. I utterly refuse,
And you may take those phrases as you choose.

ALCESTE Just show me how this letter could be meant
For a woman's eyes, and I shall be content.

CELIMENE No, no, it's for Oronte; you're perfectly right.
I welcome his attentions with delight,
I prize his character and his intellect,
And everything is just as you suspect.
Come, do your worst now; give your rage free rein;
But kindly cease to bicker and complain.

ALCESTE (*aside*).
Good God! Could anything be more inhuman?
Was ever a heart so mangled by a woman?
When I complain of how she has betrayed me,
She bridles, and commences to upbraid me!
She tries my tortured patience to the limit;
She won't deny her guilt; she glories in it!
And yet my heart's too faint and cowardly
To break these chains of passion, and be free,
To scorn her as it should, and rise above
This unrewarded, mad, and bitter love.
(*To* CELIMENE).
Ah, traitress, in how confident a fashion

You take advantage of my helpless passion,
And use my weakness for your faithless charms
To make me once again throw down my arms!
But do at least deny this black transgression;
Take back that mocking and perverse confession;
Defend this letter and your innocence,
And I, poor fool, will aid in your defence.
Pretend, pretend, that you are just and true,
And I shall make myself believe in you.

CELIMENE Oh, stop it. Don't be such a jealous dunce,
Or I shall leave off loving you at once.
Just why should I *pretend?* What could impel me
To stoop so low as that? And kindly tell me
Why, if I loved another, I shouldn't merely
Inform you of it, simply and sincerely!
I've told you where you stand, and that admission
Should altogether clear me of suspicion;
After so generous a guarantee,
What right have you to harbour doubts of me?
Since women are (from natural reticence)
Reluctant to declare their sentiments,
And since the honour of our sex requires
That we conceal our amorous desires,
Ought any man for whom such laws are broken
To question what the oracle has spoken?
Should he not rather feel an obligation
To trust that most obliging declaration?
Enough, now. Your suspicions quite disgust me;
Why should I love a man who doesn't trust me?
I cannot understand why I continue,
Fool that I am, to take an interest in you.
I ought to choose a man less prone to doubt,
And give you something to be vexed about.

ALCESTE Ah, what a poor enchanted fool I am;
These gentle words, no doubt, were all a sham;

But destiny requires me to entrust
My happiness to you, and so I must.
I'll love you to the bitter end, and see
How false and treacherous you dare to be.

CELIMENE No, you don't really love me as you ought.

ALCESTE I love you more than can be said or thought;
Indeed, I wish you were in such distress
That I might show my deep devotedness.
Yes, I could wish that you were wretchedly poor,
Unloved, uncherished, utterly obscure;
That fate had set you down upon the earth
Without possessions, rank, or gentle birth;
Then, by the offer of my heart, I might
Repair the great injustice of your plight;
I'd raise you from the dust, and proudly prove
The purity and vastness of my love.

CELIMENE This is a strange benevolence indeed!
God grant that I may never be in need. . . .
Ah, here's Monsieur Dubois, in quaint disguise.

SCENE FOUR: *Célimène, Alceste, Dubois*

ALCESTE Well, why this costume? Why those frightened eyes?
What ails you?

DUBOIS   Well, Sir, things are most mysterious.

ALCESTE What do you mean?

DUBOIS   I fear they're very serious.

ALCESTE What?

DUBOIS   Shall I speak more loudly?

ALCESTE   Yes; speak out.

DUBOIS Isn't there someone here, Sir?

ALCESTE   Speak, you lout!

Stop wasting time.

DUBOIS   Sir, we must slip away.

ALCESTE How's that?

DUBOIS   We must decamp without delay.

ALCESTE Explain yourself.

DUBOIS   I tell you we must fly.

ALCESTE What for?

DUBOIS   We mustn't pause to say good-bye.

ALCESTE Now what d'you mean by all of this, you clown?

DUBOIS I mean, Sir, that we've got to leave this town.

ALCESTE I'll tear you limb from limb and joint from joint
        If you don't come more quickly to the point.

DUBOIS Well, Sir, today a man in a black suit,
       Who wore a black and ugly scowl to boot,
       Left us a document scrawled in such a hand
       As even Satan couldn't understand.
       It bears upon your lawsuit, I don't doubt;
       But all hell's devils couldn't make it out.

ALCESTE Well, well, go on. What then? I fail to see
        How this event obliges us to flee.

DUBOIS Well, Sir: an hour later, hardly more,
       A gentleman who's often called before
       Came looking for you in an anxious way.
       Not finding you, he asked me to convey
       (Knowing I could be trusted with the same)
       The following message.... Now, what *was* his name?

ALCESTE Forget his name, you idiot. What did he say?

DUBOIS Well, it was one of your friends, Sir, anyway.
       He warned you to begone, and he suggested
       That if you stay, you may well be arrested.

ALCESTE What? Nothing more specific? Think, man, think!

DUBOIS No, Sir. He had me bring him pen and ink,
       And dashed you off a letter which, I'm sure,
       Will render things distinctly less obscure.

ALCESTE Well – let me have it!

CELIMENE   What *is* this all about?

ALCESTE   God knows; but I have hopes of finding out.
          How long am I to wait, you blitherer?

DUBOIS   (*after a protracted search for the letter*).
          I must have left it on your table, Sir.

ALCESTE   I ought to . . .

CELIMENE   No, no, keep your self-control
          Go find out what's behind his rigmarole.

ALCESTE   It seems that fate, no matter what I do,
          Has sworn that I may not converse with you
          But, Madam, pray permit your faithful lover
          To try once more before the day is over.

Act Five

SCENE ONE: Alceste, Philinte

ALCESTE   No, it's too much. My mind's made up, I tell you.

PHILINTE   Why should this blow, however hard, compel you . . .

ALCESTE   No, no, don't waste your breath in argument;
Nothing you say will alter my intent;
This age is vile, and I've made up my mind
To have no further commerce with mankind.
Did not truth, honour, decency, and the laws
Oppose my enemy and approve my cause?
My claims were justified in all men's sight;
I put my trust in equity and right;
Yet, to my horror and the world's disgrace,
Justice is mocked, and I have lost my case!
A scoundrel whose dishonesty is notorious
Emerges from another lie victorious!
Honour and right condone his brazen fraud,
While rectitude and decency applaud!
Before his smirking face, the truth stands charmed,
And virtue conquered, and the law disarmed!
His crime is sanctioned by a court decree!
And not content with what he's done to me,
The dog now seeks to ruin me by stating
That I composed a book now circulating,
A book so wholly criminal and vicious
That even to speak its title is seditious!
Meanwhile Oronte, my rival, lends his credit
To the same libellous tale, and helps to spread it!
Oronte! a man of honour and of rank,
With whom I've been entirely fair and frank;

Who sought me out and forced me, willy-nilly,
To judge some verse I found extremely silly;
And who, because I properly refused
To flatter him, or see the truth abused,
Abets my enemy in a rotten slander!
There's the reward of honesty and candour!
The man will hate me to the end of time
For failing to commend his wretched rhyme!
And not this man alone, but all humanity
Do what they do from interest and vanity;
They prate of honour, truth, and righteousness,
But lie, betray, and swindle nonetheless.
Come then: man's villainy is too much to bear;
Let's leave this jungle and this jackal's lair.
Yes! treacherous and savage race of men,
You shall not look upon my face again.

PHILINTE   Oh, don't rush into exile prematurely;
Things aren't as dreadful as you make them, surely.
It's rather obvious, since you're still at large,
That people don't believe your enemy's charge.
Indeed, his tale's so patently untrue
That it may do more harm to him than you.

ALCESTE   Nothing could do that scoundrel any harm:
His frank corruption is his greatest charm,
And, far from hurting him, a further shame
Would only serve to magnify his name.

PHILINTE   In any case, his bald prevarication
Has done no injury to your reputation,
And you may feel secure in that regard.
As for your lawsuit, it should not be hard
To have the case reopened, and contest
This judgment . . .

ALCESTE   No, no, let the verdict rest.
Whatever cruel penalty it may bring,
I wouldn't have it changed for anything.

It shows the times' injustice with such clarity
That I shall pass it down to our posterity
As a great proof and signal demonstration
Of the black wickedness of this generation.
It may cost twenty thousand francs; but I
Shall pay their twenty thousand, and gain thereby
The right to storm and rage at human evil,
And send the race of mankind to the devil.

PHILINTE Listen to me. . . .

ALCESTE   Why ? What can you possibly say ?
Don't argue, Sir; your labour's thrown away.
Do you propose to offer lame excuses
For men's behaviour and the times' abuses ?

PHILINTE No, all you say I'll readily concede:
This is a low, conniving age indeed;
Nothing but trickery prospers nowadays,
And people ought to mend their shabby ways.
Yes, man's a beastly creature; but must we then
Abandon the society of men ?
Here in the world, each human frailty
Provides occasion for philosophy,
And that is virtue's noblest exercise;
If honesty shone forth from all men's eyes,
If every heart were frank and kind and just,
What could our virtues do but gather dust
(Since their employment is to help us bear
The villainies of men without despair) ?
A heart well-armed with virtue can endure. . . .

ALCESTE Sir, you're a matchless reasoner, to be sure;
Your words are fine and full of cogency;
But don't waste time and eloquence on me.
My reason bids me go, for my own good.
My tongue won't lie and flatter as it should;
God knows what frankness it might next commit,
And what I'd suffer on account of it.

Pray let me wait for Célimène's return
In peace and quiet. I shall shortly learn,
By her response to what I have in view,
Whether her love for me is feigned or true.

PHILINTE Till then, let's visit Eliante upstairs.

ALCESTE No, I am too weighed down with sombre cares.
Go to her, do; and leave me with my gloom
Here in the darkened corner of this room.

PHILINTE Why, that's no sort of company, my friend;
I'll see if Eliante will not descend.

SCENE TWO: Célimène, Oronte, Alceste

ORONTE Yes, Madam, if you wish me to remain
Your true and ardent lover, you must deign
To give me some more positive assurance.
All this suspense is quite beyond endurance.
If your heart shares the sweet desires of mine,
Show me as much by some convincing sign;
And here's the sign I urgently suggest:
That you no longer tolerate Alceste,
But sacrifice him to my love, and sever
All your relations with the man forever.

CELIMENE Why do you suddenly dislike him so?
You praised him to the skies not long ago.

ORONTE Madam, that's not the point. I'm here to find
Which way your tender feelings are inclined.
Choose, if you please, between Alceste and me,
And I shall stay or go accordingly.

ALCESTE (*emerging from the corner*).
Yes, Madam, choose; this gentleman's demand
Is wholly just, and I support his stand.

I too am true and ardent; I too am here
To ask you that you make your feelings clear.
No more delays, now; no equivocation;
The time has come to make your declaration.

ORONTE Sir, I've no wish in any way to be
An obstacle to your felicity.

ALCESTE Sir, I've no wish to share her heart with you;
That may sound jealous, but at least it's true.

ORONTE If, weighing us, she leans in your direction . . .

ALCESTE If she regards you with the least affection . . .

ORONTE I swear I'll yield her to you there and then.

ALCESTE I swear I'll never see her face again.

ORONTE Now, Madam, tell us what we've come to hear.

ALCESTE Madam, speak openly and have no fear.

ORONTE Just say which one is to remain your lover.

ALCESTE Just name one name, and it will all be over.

ORONTE What! Is it possible that you're undecided?

ALCESTE What! Can your feelings possibly be divided?

CELIMENE Enough: this inquisition's gone too far:
How utterly unreasonable you are!
Not that I couldn't make the choice with ease;
My heart has no conflicting sympathies;
I know full well which one of you I favour,
And you'd not see me hesitate or waver.
But how can you expect me to reveal
So cruelly and bluntly what I feel?
I think it altogether too unpleasant
To choose between two men when both are present;
One's heart has means more subtle and more kind
Of letting its affections be divined,
Nor need one be uncharitably plain
To let a lover know he loves in vain.

ORONTE No, no, speak plainly; I for one can stand it.
I beg you to be frank.

ALCESTE   And I demand it.

The simple truth is what I wish to know,
And there's no need for softening the blow.
You've made an art of pleasing everyone,
But now your days of coquetry are done:
You have no choice now, Madam, but to choose,
For I'll know what to think if you refuse;
I'll take your silence for a clear admission
That I'm entitled to my worst suspicion.

ORONTE   I thank you for this ultimatum, Sir,
And I may say I heartily concur.

CELIMENE   Really, this foolishness is very wearing:
Must you be so unjust and overbearing?
Haven't I told you why I must demur?
Ah, here's Eliante; I'll put the case to her.

SCENE THREE: Eliante, Philinte, Célimène,
Oronte, Alceste

CELIMENE   Cousin, I'm being persecuted here
By these two persons, who, it would appear,
Will not be satisfied till I confess
Which one I love the more, and which the less,
And tell the latter to his face that he
Is henceforth banished from my company.
Tell me, has ever such a thing been done?

ELIANTE   You'd best not turn to me; I'm not the one
To back you in a matter of this kind:
I'm all for those who frankly speak their mind.

ORONTE   Madam, you'll search in vain for a defender.

ALCESTE   You're beaten, Madam, and may as well surrender.

ORONTE   Speak, speak, you must; and end this awful strain.

ALCESTE   Or don't, and your position will be plain.

ORONTE A single word will close this painful scene.
ALCESTE But if you're silent, I'll know what you mean.

SCENE FOUR: *Arsinoé, Célimène, Eliante,* *Alceste, Philinte, Acaste, Clitandre, Oronte*

ACASTE (*to* CELIMENE).
    Madam, with all due deference, we two
    Have come to pick a little bone with you.
CLITANDRE (*to* ORONTE *and* ALCESTE).
    I'm glad you're present, Sirs; as you'll soon learn,
    Our business here is also your concern.
ARSINOE (*to* CELIMENE).
    Madam, I visit you so soon again
    Only because of these two gentlemen,
    Who came to me indignant and aggrieved
    About a crime too base to be believed.
    Knowing your virtue, having such confidence in it,
    I couldn't think you guilty for a minute,
    In spite of all their telling evidence;
    And, rising above our little difference,
    I've hastened here in friendship's name to see
    You clear yourself of this great calumny.
ACASTE Yes, Madam, let us see with what composure
    You'll manage to respond to this disclosure.
    You lately sent Clitandre this tender note.
CLITANDRE And this one, for Acaste, you also wrote.
ACASTE (*to* ORONTE *and* ALCESTE).
    You'll recognize this writing, Sirs, I think;
    The lady is so free with pen and ink
    That you must know it all too well, I fear.
    But listen: this is something you should hear.

'How absurd you are to condemn my lightheartedness in society, and to accuse me of being happiest in the company of others. Nothing could be more unjust; and if you do not come to me instantly and beg pardon for saying such a thing, I shall never forgive as long as I live. Our big bumbling friend the Viscount . . .'

What a shame that he's not here.

'Our big bumbling friend the Viscount, whose name stands first in your complaint, is hardly a man to my taste; and ever since the day I watched him spend three-quarters of an hour spitting into a well, so as to make circles in the water, I have been unable to think highly of him. As for the little Marquess . . .'

In all modesty, gentlemen, that is I.

'As for the little Marquess, who sat squeezing my hand for such a long while yesterday, I find him in all respects the most trifling creature alive; and the only things of value about him are his cape and his sword. As for the man with the green ribbons . . .'

(*To* ALCESTE).
It's your turn now, Sir.

'As for the man with the green ribbons, he amuses me now and then with his bluntness and his bearish ill-humour; but there are many times indeed when I think him the greatest bore in the world. And as for the sonneteer . . .'

(*To* ORONTE).
Here's your helping.

'And as for the sonneteer, who has taken it into his head to be witty, and insists on being an author in the

teeth of opinion, I simply cannot be bothered to
listen to him, and his prose wearies me quite as much
as his poetry. Be assured that I am not always so
well-entertained as you suppose; that I long for your
company, more than I dare to say, at all these entertainments to which people drag me; and that the
presence of those one loves is the true and perfect
seasoning to all one's pleasures.'

CLITANDRE And now for me.

'Clitandre, whom you mention, and who so pesters
me with his saccharine speeches, is the last man on
earth for whom I could feel any affection. He is quite
mad to suppose that I love him, and so are you, to
doubt that you are loved. Do come to your senses;
exchange your suppositions for his; and visit me as
often as possible, to help me bear the annoyance of
his unwelcome attentions.'

It's a sweet character that these letters show,
And what to call it, Madam, you well know.
Enough. We're off to make the world acquainted
With this sublime self-portrait that you've painted.

ACASTE Madam, I'll make you no farewell oration;
No, you're not worthy of my indignation.
Far choicer hearts than yours, as you'll discover,
Would like this little Marquess for a lover.

*SCENE FIVE: Célimène, Eliante, Arsinoé,
Alceste, Oronte, Philinte*

ORONTE So! After all those loving letters you wrote,
You turn on me like this, and cut my throat!

And your dissembling, faithless heart, I find,
Has pledged itself by turns to all mankind!
How blind I've been! But now I clearly see;
I thank you, Madam, for enlightening me.
My heart is mine once more, and I'm content;
The loss of it shall be your punishment.
(*To* ALCESTE).
Sir, she is yours; I'll seek no more to stand
Between your wishes and this lady's hand.

*SCENE SIX : Célimène, Eliante, Arsinoé,
Alceste, Philinte*

ARSINOE (*to* CELIMENE).
    Madam, I'm forced to speak. I'm far too stirred
    To keep my counsel, after what I've heard.
    I'm shocked and staggered by your want of morals.
    It's not my way to mix in others' quarrels;
    But really, when this fine and noble spirit,
    This man of honour and surpassing merit,
    Laid down the offering of his heart before you,
    How *could* you . . .
ALCESTE   Madam, permit me, I implore you,
    To represent myself in this debate.
    Don't bother, please, to be my advocate.
    My heart, in any case, could not afford
    To give your services their due reward;
    And if I chose, for consolation's sake,
    Some other lady, 'twould not be you I'd take.
ARSINOE What makes you think you could, Sir ? And how dare
    you
    Imply that I've been trying to ensnare you ?

If you can for a moment entertain
Such flattering fancies, you're extremely vain.
I'm not so interested as you suppose
In Célimène's discarded gigolos.
Get rid of that absurd illusion, do.
Women like me are not for such as you.
Stay with this creature, to whom you're so attached;
I've never seen two people better matched.

SCENE SEVEN: Célimène, Eliante, Alceste, Philinte

ALCESTE (*to* CELIMENE).
        Well, I've been still throughout this exposé,
Till everyone but me has said his say.
Come, have I shown sufficient self-restraint?
And may I now . . .

CELIMENE   Yes, make your just complaint.
Reproach me freely, call me what you will;
You've every right to say I've used you ill.
I've wronged you, I confess it; and in my shame
I'll make no effort to escape the blame.
The anger of those others I could despise;
My guilt toward you I sadly recognize.
Your wrath is wholly justified, I fear;
I know how culpable I must appear,
I know all things bespeak my treachery,
And that, in short, you've grounds for hating me.
Do so; I give you leave.

ALCESTE   Ah, traitress – how,
How should I cease to love you, even now?
Though mind and will were passionately bent

On hating you, my heart would not consent.
(*To* ELIANTE *and* PHILINTE).
Be witness to my madness, both of you;
See what infatuation drives one to;
But wait; my folly's only just begun,
And I shall prove to you before I'm done
How strange the human heart is, and how far
From rational we sorry creatures are.
(*To* CELIMENE).
Woman, I'm willing to forget your shame,
And clothe your treacheries in a sweeter name;
I'll call them youthful errors, instead of crimes,
And lay the blame on these corrupting times.
My one condition is that you agree
To share my chosen fate, and fly with me
To that wild, trackless, solitary place
In which I shall forget the human race.
Only by such a course can you atone
For those atrocious letters; by that alone
Can you remove my present horror of you,
And make it possible for me to love you.

CELIMENE What! *I* renounce the world at my young age,
And die of boredom in some hermitage?

ALCESTE Ah, if you really loved me as you ought,
You wouldn't give the world a moment's thought;
Must you have me, and all the world beside?

CELIMENE Alas, at twenty one is terrified
Of solitude. I fear I lack the force
And depth of soul to take so stern a course.
But if my hand in marriage will content you,
Why, there's a plan which I might well consent to,
And . . .

ALCESTE   No, I detest you now. I could excuse
Everything else, but since you thus refuse
To love me wholly, as a wife should do,

And see the world in me, as I in you,
Go! I reject your hand, and disenthrall
My heart from your enchantments, once for all.

SCENE EIGHT: *Eliante, Alceste, Philinte*

ALCESTE (*to* ELIANTE).
            Madam, your virtuous beauty has no peer;
            Of all this world, you only are sincere;
            I've long esteemed you highly, as you know;
            Permit me ever to esteem you so,
            And if I do not now request your hand,
            Forgive me, Madam, and try to understand.
            I feel unworthy of it; I sense that fate
            Does not intend me for the married state,
            That I should do you wrong by offering you
            My shattered heart's unhappy residue,
            And that in short . . .

ELIANTE   Your argument's well taken:
            Nor need you fear that I shall feel forsaken.
            Were I to offer him this hand of mine,
            Your friend Philinte, I think, would not decline.

PHILINTE Ah, Madam, that's my heart's most cherished goal,
            For which I'd gladly give my life and soul.

ALCESTE (*to* ELIANTE *and* PHILINTE).
            May you be true to all you now profess,
            And so deserve unending happiness.
            Meanwhile, betrayed and wronged in everything,
            I'll flee this bitter world where vice is king,
            And seek some spot unpeopled and apart
            Where I'll be free to have an honest heart.

PHILINTE Come, Madam, let's do everything we can
            To change the mind of this unhappy man.

The Miser

Comedy in Five Acts

Translated into English prose by Alan Drury

CHARACTERS

HARPAGON, father of Cléante and Elise, suitor for the hand of Mariane

CLEANTE, his son, in love with Mariane

ELISE, his daughter, in love with Valère

VALERE, son of Anselme and in love with Elise

MARIANE, in love with Cléante and courted by Harpagon

ANSELME, father of Valère and Mariane

FROSINE, an adventuress

MAITRE SIMON, an intermediary

MAITRE JACQUES, cook and coachman to Harpagon

BRINDAVOINE ⎫
LA MERLUCHE ⎭ servants to Harpagon

LA FLECHE, servant to Cléante

MAGISTRATE

The scene throughout is Paris.

This translation was commissioned by and first produced at the Theatre Royal, York, in 1978.

Act One

VALERE *and* ELISE *discovered.*

VALERE. My dear Elise, what's the matter? How can you be so sad after all we've said to each other? Do you regret making me happy? I smile and you frown. Do you want to be released from the promises our love has led us into?

ELISE. No, Valère. I'm not sorry for anything we've said, or done. I feel I'm being swept along on the crest of a wave, and I don't want to get off. But, to tell you the truth, I am a bit worried about where all this is heading. I'm beginning to be afraid I love you a little bit more than I should do.

VALERE. How can you even think such a thing, Elise, after all you say you feel for me?

ELISE. For any number of reasons. My father's anger, my family's reactions, the censure of the world. But more than anything, Valère, I'm frightened that, having persuaded me to love you, you will promptly lose interest. For men the chase is everything; having caught us they take us for granted.

VALERE. But I'm not like that. Other men, yes; me, no. Accuse me of anything, Elise, murder even, but not of that. I will never fail you. I love you, and my love for you will last as long as my life.

ELISE. You're all the same. Men all say the same things. You can only tell them apart by what they do.

VALERE. If you think that, at least give me the benefit of the doubt. Don't judge me on the basis of your, if I might say so, cynical misgivings. Slay me no longer with the slings and arrows of outrageous suspicion. Let me prove to you my intentions are strictly honourable.

ELISE (*aside*). How easy it is to be persuaded by the person one loves. (*To him.*) Oh, yes, Valère, I know you're incapable of deceiving me. I know a true love beats in your breast and you will be faithful to me for ever. I know all that. I've no misgivings on that score. I am worried what other people will think.

VALERE. Why?

ELISE. I'd have nothing to fear if everyone saw you through my eyes. You are your own justifications. Putting your conspicuous virtues on one side, I know that Heaven intends us for each other. You saved my life.

VALERE. Oh, I hardly think that qualifies . . .

ELISE. How could I forget the extreme danger in which we first met? How could I forget the way you risked your life to snatch mine from the bosom of the foaming waves? How could I forget all you did for me after you had pulled me from the water? And how could I forget the love you have shown me ever since?

VALERE. Look, I really don't think . . .

ELISE. A love which neither time nor difficulty has abated. A love which has made you forsake your own country and your quest for your father. A love which has made you disguise yourself as one of my father's servants simply so you could be close to me.

VALERE. Oh, it was nothing.

ELISE. It may be nothing to you, but I must confess it has made somewhat of an impression on me. It vindicates everything. However I'm not sure that everyone else will be entirely sympathetic.

VALERE. Look, in all you've just said, it's only my love that makes me lay any claim on you. As for your scruples, surely your father is a big enough excuse for anything. His extreme meanness, and the way he treats you and your brother would justify far stranger things than our engagement. I'm sorry to have to talk about your father like this, Elise, but you know what everyone thinks of him. But if at last, as I hope and pray, I find my father again, I'm sure we'll be able to bring your father round. I'm expecting some new information any minute. In fact, if it doesn't come soon I might even go out and look for it myself.

ELISE. Don't leave me, Valère.

VALERE. What should I do then?

ELISE. Carry on with what you're doing. Putting yourself in my father's good books.

VALERE. Ah yes, you see the way I go about it. The way I had to crawl to get him to take me on. The way I have to pretend to agree with every idiotic thing he says. The sort of person I have to pretend to be all the time I'm with him. And all so I can put myself in his good books. I've come to the conclusion that to get someone on your side, you only have to do four things; dress the way he likes, believe everything he says, flatter all his faults, and applaud everything he does. It's simple. You can be as transparent as you like, and the cleverest people fall for it the most. You can make anyone swallow anything, provided you salt and pepper it with flattery first. I know what you're going to say. I agree one's integrity does suffer, but he who pays the piper calls the tune. If someone wants to be flattered, that's his fault, not mine.

ELISE. Why don't you try to get my brother on your side?

VALERE. I couldn't cope with both of them at once. It's too complicated. Their personalities are such poles apart I'd get confused and tell the wrong thing to the wrong one. Why don't you persuade him? You're his sister. You've got a bigger hold over him than I have. He's coming. I'll withdraw. Talk to him, but don't tell him any more than you absolutely have to.

Exit VALERE.

ELISE. I'm frightened. I don't know if I can go through with it or not.

Enter CLEANTE.

CLEANTE. Good, you're alone. I wanted to talk to you confidentially. I'm dying to tell you something.

ELISE. What?

CLEANTE. The best thing possible. I'm in love.

ELISE. You're in love?

CLEANTE. Don't say it like that. Yes, I'm in love. Now, before I tell you any more, I know I'm dependent on father; I know as his son I should do as he says; I know we should never fall in love without the permission of those who brought us into this world; I know that having the wisdom of age they are less likely to be deceived than us; I know we should trust the light of their experience rather than the blindness of our passions; and I know the folly of youth leads us even unto the brink. I'm saying all this now so you won't have to say it later, for love is deaf and will brook no contradiction.

ELISE. Have you exchanged promises with her?

CLEANTE. Not yet, but I'm going to, so don't you try and put me off.

ELISE. What sort of person do you think I am?

CLEANTE. You're not in love. You don't know the gentle havoc love can wreak in an unsuspecting heart. And I'm scared of your common sense.

ELISE. Don't talk to me about common sense. We all lapse once in a life-time, and if you knew what I'm feeling now, you'd wonder who was the farther gone.

CLEANTE. You mean, you mean . . . can it be . . .

ELISE. Let's finish with you first. Tell me, who is she?

CLEANTE. A young girl who's only just moved into this part of town, and seems created expressly to inspire love in all

who see her. Nature never framed a lovelier being, and
I've been in absolute raptures since first clapping eyes
on her. She's called Mariane, and lives with her mother,
who's almost always ill. You've no idea the way she looks
after her. She fetches and carries, talks and jokes; I mean
it's so, so . . . divine it makes you want to cry. Everything
she does is charming. A thousand graces shine in all her
actions. She's gentle, kind, modest . . . Elise, I wish you'd
seen her.

ELISE. I feel I have done, Cléante, from the way you describe
her. It's enough for me you love her.

CLEANTE. I've found out, without them knowing, that they
aren't very well off, and that even their modest mode of
life is stretching their resources to breaking point. Imagine, Elise, what a joy it would be to restore the fortune
of the girl one loves, you know, give help, tactfully, with
minor household expenses and all that sort of thing; and
then imagine how I feel that because of father's meanness
there's absolutely no way I can do it. I am thwarted from
trumpeting to my beloved any evidence of my love.

ELISE. Yes, I can see it must be frustrating.

CLEANTE. Frustrating? More than you could possibly
imagine. Could anything be more cruel and unnatural than
the way he keeps us starved of money? What good is it to
us that we'll get it when he's gone, if by the time we've
got it we're too old to enjoy it? I have to borrow money
simply to keep going from day to day. The only way we
can both dress at all decently is on tick. I've had enough I
tell you. I was going to ask you to help me sound father
out about Mariane. If he refuses consent, we're going to
elope and we'll just have to live on what the Heavens chose
to provide. I've been scratching around for money for this
for some time. Now, if you're in love Elise, and he opposes
both of us; we'll both leave him and free ourselves from
the yoke of his tyranny for ever.

ELISE. It's regrettably true that every day he gives us more and more cause to mourn the death of our mother, and if he goes on . . .

CLEANTE. Talk of the devil; I can hear him. Let's withdraw a little and complete our plan. Then we'll join forces and move into the attack.

Exit CLEANTE *and* ELISE.

Enter HARPAGON *and* LA FLECHE.

HARPAGON. Out, go on, clear out, and none of your lip. Out of my house this minute. You ought to be hanged.

LA FLECHE (*aside*). I have never in my life seen anyone so spiteful as this vile old man. I'm convinced he's possessed by the devil.

HARPAGON. You're muttering again.

LA FLECHE. Why do you pick on me?

HARPAGON. That's just like you, asking questions. Get out quick before I clobber you one.

LA FLECHE. What've I done to you?

HARPAGON. More than enough.

LA FLECHE. My master, your son, told me to wait for him here.

HARPAGON. Well, you can wait for him in the street. I don't want you in here, plain as a pikestaff, drinking everything in and waiting to pounce. I don't like people spying on me; people whose eyes are in and out of every nook and cranny, ferretting out things to steal.

LA FLECHE. A chance would be a fine thing! How could anyone steal from you. You've got everything under lock and key; guarded day and night.

HARPAGON. And a good thing too. I know what I'm doing, and I don't want to be surrounded by informers, grasses, stool-pigeons, blabber-mouths poking their noses into my affairs all the time. (*Aside.*) I'm frightened he knows something about my money. (*To him.*) Now my good fellow, I'm sure you aren't the kind of man who goes around spreading malicious rumours about where I hide the money in my house.

LA FLECHE. You're hiding some money in the house?

HARPAGON. I didn't say that. I didn't say anything like that. Did I say anything like that? (*Aside.*) I am beginning to get angry. (*To him.*) I was asking you not to go noising it abroad that I have.

LA FLECHE. How could I go noising it abroad that you have, if you haven't? I'd have nothing to noise abroad then.

HARPAGON. Don't you be clever with me, or I'll belt you one. (*He raises his hand as if to hit him.*) Now get out while the going's good.

LA FLECHE. All right, I'm going.

HARPAGON. Just a minute. You aren't taking anything with you by any chance, are you?

LA FLECHE. Now why should I be doing a thing like that?

HARPAGON. Over here. Let me see. Show me your hands.

LA FLECHE. There you are.

HARPAGON. And the other.

LA FLECHE. And the other?

HARPAGON. Playing the innocent are you?

LA FLECHE. There you are. Satisfied?

HARPAGON. You've got nothing stuffed down there?

LA FLECHE. Why don't you find out for yourself?

HARPAGON *feels round the lower part of* LA FLECHE's *breeches.*

HARPAGON. It's amazing what you can hide in vast baggy pants like these. Legs aren't the only things inside them that've walked. The people who make them should be hung.

LA FLECHE (*aside*). A man like this deserves everything he gets. I'm very tempted to steal from him myself.

HARPAGON. What?

LA FLECHE. What?

HARPAGON. What was that you said about stealing?

LA FLECHE. I said you were having a good rummage round to see if I'd stolen anything.

HARPAGON. Perceptive of you. (*He rummages in* LA FLECHE's *pockets*.)

LA FLECHE (*aside*). Oh, a wit as well as a skinflint.

HARPAGON. What was that? What was that you said?

LA FLECHE. What? What? What? What?

HARPAGON. Don't you monkey with me.

LA FLECHE. Devil take the lot of you.

HARPAGON. Lot of who?

LA FLECHE. Misers.

HARPAGON. Don't know what you mean.

LA FLECHE. Oh yes you do.

HARPAGON. Don't know what they are.

LA FLECHE. Oh yes you do.

HARPAGON. Will you shut up.

LA FLECHE. Temper, temper. Did you think I was talking about you?

HARPAGON. I think what I think. I wish you'd tell me who you're talking to when you mutter like that.

LA FLECHE. Mutter like what?

HARPAGON. When I can't hear you properly.

LA FLECHE. I'm talking . . . I'm talking to my hat.

HARPAGON. Oh, really. I'll make you eat it if you're not careful.

LA FLECHE. You want me to stop talking about mean old men.

HARPAGON. No, I just want to stop you chattering and being insolent. Be quiet.

LA FLECHE. No names, no packdrill.

HARPAGON. Belt up.

LA FLECHE. If the cap fits, wear . . .

HARPAGON (*shouts*). Shut your mouth.

LA FLECHE. All right then, but I don't want to.

HARPAGON (*thrusts his hand into one of* LA FLECHE's *jerkin pockets*). Aha.

LA FLECHE *shows him the other.*

LA FLECHE. There's another one as well. Now are you satisfied?

HARPAGON. Come on, give it back to me without me having to go through all this rigmarole.

LA FLECHE. Give what back to you?

HARPAGON. Whatever it is you've taken from me.

LA FLECHE. But I haven't taken anything from you.

HARPAGON. Really?

LA FLECHE. Really.

HARPAGON. Oh, well, good-bye then. You can go to the devil as far as I'm concerned.

LA FLECHE. Thank you and goodnight.

HARPAGON. I leave you to the dictates of your own conscience.

Exit LA FLECHE.

HARPAGON. There he goes, the jail-bird of a servant I've been lumbered with. I hope I never see the lame dog again. It's no laughing matter, you know, keeping large amounts of money in the house. Happy the man, I always say, happy the man who's got it well invested and keeps back just enough for ready cash. It's virtually impossible to find anywhere safe to hide it. I can't be doing with safes; they're a magnet for robbers and always the first place they go for. To tell you the truth, I'm not sure I've done the right thing burying the fifteen thousand francs I was paid yesterday in the garden. Fifteen thousand francs, in gold, on my property is quite a responsibility, and I don't . . .

Enter CLEANTE *and* ELISE, *talking quietly to each other.*

HARPAGON. I'll be my own ruin if I'm not careful. Here am I, churning things over in my head and I've got so carried away I've been talking aloud. (*To them.*) What is it?

CLEANTE. Nothing much, father.

HARPAGON. Have you been here long?

CLEANTE. We've only just come in.

HARPAGON. Have you, by any chance, um overheard . . . er . . .

CLEANTE. Overheard what, father?

HARPAGON. Er . . .

ELISE. What?

HARPAGON. What I've just been saying?

CLEANTE. No.

HARPAGON. Is that so? Is that so?

ELISE. Yes, it is.

HARPAGON (*aside*). They must have heard some of it. (*To them.*) The thing is, you see, I was just talking to myself, aloud, you know musing, about how difficult it is to lay your hands on ready money these days. Happy the man, I was saying, happy the man who has fifteen thousand francs in his house.

CLEANTE. We didn't know whether to interrupt you or not.

HARPAGON. I'm telling you this so you don't get hold of the wrong end of the stick. I wouldn't want you imagining I had fifteen thousand francs. Far from it. Nothing could be further from the truth.

CLEANTE. We don't want to pry into your affairs.

HARPAGON. Would to God I had it, fifteen thousand francs.

CLEANTE. I don't believe that . . .

HARPAGON. I would be a happier man then.

ELISE. There are one or two things . . .

HARPAGON. Heaven only knows I need them.

CLEANTE. I think that . . .

HARPAGON. I could rest easy at nights.

ELISE. You are . . .

HARPAGON. And I wouldn't have to bore you any more going on about how hard times are.

CLEANTE. Good God, father, you've got nothing to complain about. Everyone knows you've got more than enough.

HARPAGON. What, me? More than enough? Who says so? They're lying. Lies, all lies. People who say that sort of thing should have their tongues pulled out: slowly.

CLEANTE. There's no need to get into a state.

HARPAGON. Things have come to a pretty pass when your own children betray you and become your enemies.

CLEANTE. Is a person who says you're well off your enemy?

HARPAGON. Of course they are. Talk like that, coupled with the amount you splash around, will make people think I'm made of money. Then one fine day they'll break in and cut my throat. You mark my words, young man.

CLEANTE. What large amounts have I splashed around?

HARPAGON. You ask me? You stand there, bold as brass, and ask me that. What about all these, these outfits you swan around town in? I had to have words with your sister about this yesterday, but you're ten times as worse. It cries down vengeance from Heaven. If all the money you've got on your back were invested, you could live off the interest. If I've said it once, I've said it twenty times: I don't like it and I won't have it. Anyone would think you were a lord. If you can afford to dress like that you must be robbing me somehow.

CLEANTE. How am I robbing you?

HARPAGON. How should I know? But where else do you get the money from, you tell me that.

CLEANTE. It so happens I'm lucky at cards, father, and I spend all my winnings on me.

HARPAGON. That's not very clever. You should put your winnings out on the money market. Then you'd have something to fall back on for a rainy day. Anyway, to get back to the point; I should like to know what purpose all these ribbons serve, and if you really need all those lacy bits and bobs to fasten your breeches? And why do you waste money on wigs when you could wear your own hair for nothing? I'm prepared to bet that your wigs and ribbons alone are worth twenty francs; and twenty francs at eight per cent would earn one and three fifths a year.

CLEANTE. Yes, father, you're right as usual.

HARPAGON. Let's leave all that, and talk about something else. (*Aside.*) What's this? I do believe they're signalling to each other to snatch my purse. (*To them.*) And what do all those gestures mean?

ELISE. We were deciding which of us would speak first, father. We've both got something to say to you.

HARPAGON. And I've got something to say to both of you.

CLEANTE. We want to talk to you about marriage, father.

HARPAGON. And I want to talk to you about marriage as well.

ELISE. Oh no.

HARPAGON. What's the matter my dear? Does the idea upset you?

CLEANTE. No, it's not the idea that frightens us: it's your interpretation of it. We're afraid we may not be able to reconcile our feelings with your intentions.

HARPAGON. Patience, my dear fellow, patience. There's no cause for alarm. I know what's best for both of you, and neither of you will have the slightest grounds for complaint with my plans. However, to get to the main point: tell me, have either of you seen a young lady called Mariane, who lives not far from here?

CLEANTE. Yes, father.

HARPAGON. And you?

ELISE. I've heard people mention her.

HARPAGON. And what do you think of her, son?

CLEANTE. She's a very charming person.

HARPAGON. What about her looks?

CLEANTE. Totally open, and full of spirit.

HARPAGON. And her general manner?

CLEANTE. Admirable.

HARPAGON. Don't you think a girl like that demands attention?

CLEANTE. Yes.

HARPAGON. And she's a good catch?

CLEANTE. A very good catch indeed.

HARPAGON. And she'd be a good little housekeeper?

CLEANTE. No doubt about it.

HARPAGON. And she'd give her husband every satisfaction?

CLEANTE. I assume so; I mean, I wouldn't know.

HARPAGON. There is one snag however. She hasn't got a big enough dowry.

CLEANTE. Father, when it's a question of marrying a good woman, money should not be an issue.

HARPAGON. Sorry I'm sure. Anyway, if you can't get it one way, you can always get it another. That's what I always say.

CLEANTE. So I've noticed.

HARPAGON. Good. I'm glad you agree with me. The girl's won me over and I've decided to marry her, provided she brings some money in from somewhere.

CLEANTE. What?

HARPAGON. What do you mean, what?

CLEANTE. You've decided, you say . . .

HARPAGON. To marry Mariane.

CLEANTE. What, you? You? You!

HARPAGON. Yes, me. Me. Me. Any objections?

CLEANTE. I suddenly feel sick. I don't know what can have brought it on. You must excuse me. I will withdraw.

Exit CLEANTE.

HARPAGON. Go and get yourself a glass of cold water in the kitchen. It's the best remedy and it doesn't cost anything. (*Aside.*) There's the younger generation for you. No staying power. There's more stuffing in chicken. (*To* ELISE.) Well, my dear, that's what I've got in mind for me. As for your brother, I'll marry him off to a certain widow I was being told about this morning; and you, you I am going to give to Seigneur Anselme.

ELISE. To Seigneur Anselme?

HARPAGON. That's right. He's a mature, gentle, sensible man who can't be a day over fifty and is also very rich.

ELISE *curtsies.*

ELISE. I'm sorry, father, but I don't really want to get married.

HARPAGON *imitates her curtsey.*

HARPAGON. I'm sorry, daughter, but I really want you to.

ELISE. I'm sorry to inconvenience you, father, but . . .

HARPAGON. And I'm sorry to inconvenience you, daughter, but.

ELISE. I'm Seigneur Anselme's very humble servant but, with your permission, I don't think I'll marry him.

HARPAGON. And I'm your very humble servant miss, but, with your permission, I think you will. And what's more, you'll do it first thing this evening.

ELISE. First thing this evening?

HARPAGON. First thing this evening.

ELISE. That cannot be, father.

HARPAGON. It will be, daughter.

ELISE. No.

HARPAGON. Yes.

ELISE. Shan't.

HARPAGON. Shall.

ELISE. You wouldn't force me.

HARPAGON. I will force you.

ELISE. I'll kill myself rather than marry such a husband.

HARPAGON. Don't be stupid. You won't kill yourself and you will marry him. (*Aside*.) Have you ever seen such insolence? Was ever a father treated thus?

ELISE (*aside*). Was ever a daughter married thus?

HARPAGON. There can be no objection to him. Everyone will applaud my choice.

ELISE. No reasonable person could approve it.

Enter VALERE.

HARPAGON. Here's Valère. Do you agree that he should judge between us in this?

ELISE. Yes, I agree.

HARPAGON. And you'll stand by his judgment?

ELISE. I'll abide by what he says.

HARPAGON. Right then. You're on. Come over here, Valère. My daughter and I are having an argument and we want you to tell us who's right.

VALERE. You, Monsieur, no doubt about it.

HARPAGON. How can you tell when you don't even know what we're talking about?

VALERE. Monsieur is unable to be wrong. Monsieur is reason itself.

HARPAGON. I want to marry her off this evening to a man who's as rich as he is wise; and the brazen hussy tells me to my face that she won't have him. Now then, what do you think of that?

VALERE. What do I think of that?

HARPAGON. Yes.

VALERE. Ah, let me see.

HARPAGON. What do you say?

VALERE. In the end, when it comes down to it, I am of course in agreement with you; you cannot, after all, be otherwise than right. However, the young lady is not altogether wrong, and if I were pushed . . .

HARPAGON. What is all this? Seigneur Anselme is quite a match. He is, as I was telling her, noble, gentle, steady and wise and he is also extremely well off, and, on top of all that, he's got no children by his first marriage. Now where would she find better than that?

VALERE. That's true. But she might possibly, I mean just conceivably be able to say you're rushing things a bit, and that she should have a little time, not much, but a little time to see if she likes him or not.

HARPAGON. We must strike while the iron's hot. There's one advantage to him which I can find nowhere else: he'll take her without a dowry.

VALERE. Without a dowry?

HARPAGON. Yes.

VALERE. Who could say more. This is a totally convincing reason and we must all bow before it.

HARPAGON. Think how much I'll save.

VALERE. You can't say fairer than that. Of course it is true your daughter could say to you marriage is the most important decision in her life, and that it could make her happy or unhappy for ever, and that such a large step should never be taken without far-reaching precautions.

HARPAGON. But without a dowry.

VALERE. There's no answer to that; I mean who on earth could go against a consideration like that? It is of course completely inconceivable there are fathers who concern themselves with their daughters' happiness rather than money, who wouldn't dream of sacrificing them to financial interest, and who would search out a partner for them who they could spend the rest of their lives with in tranquil contentment; fathers who . . .

HARPAGON. But without a dowry.

VALERE. True. That settles the matter. Who could resist a reason like that.

HARPAGON *looks towards the garden.*

HARPAGON. What was that? I thought I heard a dog bark. Somebody's after my money. Stay here. I won't be a minute.

Exit HARPAGON.

ELISE. Valère.

VALERE. Yes, my dear?

ELISE. Was all that your idea of a joke?

VALERE. I don't want to cross him, otherwise we won't get what we want. There are some people you can only approach by stealth; stubborn, pig-headed people who won't see the truth even when it stares them in the face, people who won't behave reasonably, and whom you have to coax to get them to do what you want them to. These people you have to pretend to agree with, so you can lead them up the . . .

ELISE. But what about this marriage, Valère?

VALERE. We'll find some way to stop it.

ELISE. But we haven't got time. It's happening this evening.

VALERE. You'll have to get a delay somehow. Pretend you're ill.

ELISE. They'll call the doctors in and find out.

VALERE. You must be joking. What do doctors know about

it? You can have any symptoms you please and they'll invent an illness to fit it, just so long as they get paid.

Enter HARPAGON.

HARPAGON (*aside*). It was nothing, thank God.

VALERE. And if the worst comes to the worst, we can always elope. Dearest Elise, tell me now before we go any further, is your love for me strong enough to ensure the hardships we are bound to . . . (*He sees* HARPAGON.) A girl should obey her father. It's ludicrous to think she should have any say in choosing a husband, and when one crops up who will take her without a dowry, she should thank heaven on her bended knees, and not look a gift horse in the mouth.

HARPAGON. Very good. That was very well said.

VALERE. Monsieur, you must pardon my frankness. I'm afraid I got rather carried away.

HARPAGON. Not at all. I'm delighted, in fact so delighted I think you ought to look after her for me. Yes, I give you full rein. Elise, I'm putting this man in charge of you, and I want you to obey him as you would obey me.

VALERE. Ah yes, cross me at your peril.

ELISE *moves away*.

VALERE. Monsieur, I'll follow her and continue the lesson I was giving her.

HARPAGON. I'm much obliged. Certainly I . . .

VALERE. I think we ought to keep an eye on her. You never know . . .

HARPAGON. Quite, quite. Maybe we should . . .

VALERE. Don't you bother yourself with it. I'm sure we'll pull through in the end.

HARPAGON. Well, what can I say but get on with it? I've got

some business to do in town. I won't be long.

VALERE. Yes, money is the most precious thing in the world, and you should thank God for the father he's seen fit to give you. He knows what it's all about. When someone offers to take a daughter without a dowry, there is nothing more to be said. It supersedes considerations of beauty, youth, birth, honour, wisdom, probity . . .

Exeunt VALERE *and* ELISE.

HARPAGON. Ah, the brave boy. He talks like an oracle. Happy the man, I always say, happy the man with a servant like that.

Exit HARPAGON.

Act Two

Enter CLEANTE *and* LA FLECHE.

CLEANTE. Ah, there you are. Where have you been hiding
yourself, eh? Didn't I tell you to . . .

LA FLECHE. Yes Monsieur. I was standing here, on this very
spot, as you said, waiting for you, when who should come
in but Monsieur your father, bless him. He chased me
outside. I didn't want to go but I almost ended up getting
hit.

CLEANTE. How are our plans going? Things are getting more
urgent than ever. Since I last saw you, I've found out my
father is my rival.

LA FLECHE. Your father is in love?

CLEANTE. Yes, and I've had the devil's own job to stop him
from seeing the turmoil it's thrown me into.

LA FLECHE. Him, mixed up with love? Where did he get that
idea from? Is he having us on? I mean what's love got to
do with men like him?

CLEANTE. It's gone to his head. It's just my luck.

LA FLECHE. But why haven't you told him you're in love as
well?

CLEANTE. I don't want to show my hand too early, otherwise
it's going to be difficult to stop him. I'm going to save the
trump until I really need to play it. What do you think of
it all?

LA FLECHE. I don't know what to think. It just shows, if you
ask me, the depths people are reduced to if they're forced
to rely on money lenders.

CLEANTE. Talking of which, how are things going on that
front?

LA FLECHE. Oh I'm sorry, I should have told you earlier. Maître Simon, you know, the broker that was recommended to us, er, he's a busy little fellow if you ask me, bit too busy, er where was I? Oh yes, Maître Simon says he's working day and night on our behalf and your looks alone won him to our cause.

CLEANTE. Will I get the fifteen thousand francs I asked for?

LA FLECHE. Yes, but there are one or two small conditions you will have to accept if you want things to work out properly.

CLEANTE. Have you spoken to the person who's actually going to lend the money?

LA FLECHE. Ah, things don't quite work like that. It's all much more complicated than you think. The lender goes to extraordinary lengths to conceal his identity. No one will tell me his name. However, he does want to see you today, and he's rented a room in a house for the meeting. I think he wants to hear, from the horse's mouth as it were, what your resources are and what your background is. I've no doubt at all that as soon as you tell him who your father is, it'll all be plain sailing.

CLEANTE. Yes. He'll be much more interested to hear that mother is dead and no one else can touch my part of the legacy.

LA FLECHE. You know I mentioned one or two small conditions. Well, he's dictated them to our broker, and I'm to get you to agree to them before we go any further.

CLEANTE. Let's hear them then.

LA FLECHE. 'Assuming that the lender has access to all his securities, and the borrower is of age and comes of a family whose means are ample, solid and assured, clear and clean of any embarrassment; a valid and exact contract shall be drawn up before a notary. The notary should be the most experienced available and is to be chosen by the lender because of his greater risk in this transaction.'

CLEANTE. I've nothing to say against that.

LA FLECHE. 'The lender, so as to have a clear conscience, will not lend his money out for a rate greater than five and a half per cent.'

CLEANTE. Five and a half per cent? Good heavens, an honest man at last. There's no room for complaint here.

LA FLECHE. That's true. But. 'If the said lender has not the sum in question and to oblige the said borrower the said lender is constrained himself to borrow from a third party, at a rate of say twenty per cent, then it is agreed that the first said borrower shall pay the said interest, without prejudice to any other part of the transaction, arising from the fact that it is only to oblige the first said borrower that the said lender engages himself in the debt in the first place.'

CLEANTE. I see. Right little Shylock isn't he. That's more than twenty-five per cent.

LA FLECHE. That's true. It's like I said. You have to look into everything.

CLEANTE. What choice have I got? I need the money so I'm forced to agree.

LA FLECHE. That's what I told the broker.

CLEANTE. Is there anything else?

LA FLECHE. Just one little thing. 'Of the fifteen thousand francs asked for, the lender cannot supply more than twelve thousand in ready money. As for the remaining three thousand the borrower must accept goods and chattels in kind as outlined in the appended memorandum. The lender assures the borrower that he has put as fair a price as possible on them.'

CLEANTE. What's all that about?

LA FLECHE. Listen to the appended memorandum. 'Item: a four poster bed with Hungarian lace hangings, proper olive cloth covers, complete with six chairs and a counterpane to match, the whole in good condition and lined in red and blue shot silk. Item: a tester bed . . .'

CLEANTE. Whatever that might be.

LA FLECHE. Whatever that might be. 'A tester bed covered in good pale rose colour Aumale serge with tassels and silk fringes.'

CLEANTE. What am I supposed to do with that lot?

LA FLECHE. There's more where that came from. 'Item: a tapestry showing the loves of Gombaut and Macea . . .'

CLEANTE. Whoever they might be.

LA FLECHE. Whoever they might be. 'Item: a large walnut table with twelve turned legs which pulls out at both ends and comes complete with six wooden stools.'

CLEANTE. I don't believe it. I mean . . .

LA FLECHE. Now, now patience. 'Item: three large muskets inlaid with mother of pearl and three matching musket-forks. Item: a brick furnace with two retorts and three bell jars, very useful to people interested in distilling.'

CLEANTE. I am beginning to get angry.

LA FLECHE. Gently does it. 'Item: a Bologna lute with all its strings, or as many as possible. Item: a compendium of games, including draughts and the Merry Game of Goose as reconstructed from the ancient Greek, very good for passing the time when one has got nothing to do. Item: a crocodile three and a half feet long stuffed with hay; a conversation piece breaks the ice at parties. The complete lot as above mentioned fairly valued at four thousand five hundred francs but reduced to three thousand francs as a gesture of goodwill from the lender.'

CLEANTE. I'm not interested in his goodwill. Have you ever seen anything like it? Not contented with the exorbitant interest he's charging he palms me off with a job lot of old junk he's picked up from somewhere and rooks me three thousand francs for the privilege. Needless to say I've got to agree. He's got me by the throat and he knows it.

LA FLECHE. I'm sorry to have to say this Monsieur but I see

you taking the first steps on the primrose path to the
everlasting bonfire; taking money in advance, buying dear,
selling cheap, and generally eating your corn in the blade.

CLEANTE. What else can I do? Such are the straits young
men are reduced to by the meanness of their fathers. And
then people are surprised they can't wait for them to die.

LA FLECHE. I must confess your circumstances would try
the patience of a saint. I'm not, as you know, all that
criminally inclined, but I do know how to look after myself
when necessary; and to tell you the truth, the way your
father carries on makes me think robbing him would be
doing him a favour.

CLEANTE. Oh give me the appended memorandum. I'd
better have another look at it.

Enter HARPAGON *and* MAITRE SIMON.

SIMON. Yes Monsieur, it's a young man wants the money.
He's got problems you understand with his business, and
he'll agree to all the conditions you've laid down.

HARPAGON. Now you're sure are you, Maître Simon, that
there's absolutely no risk whatsoever? I mean do you know
the name and circumstances of his family?

SIMON. No, I have to admit I don't, as it was the only chance
I came across him myself. But there's no need to worry.
He'll clarify everything himself and his man assures me
you'll be more than satisfied once you've met him. All I
can tell you is that his family's very rich, his mother has
departed this vale of tears, and he's prepared to guarantee
his father will follow her in the next eight months.

HARPAGON. That is something I suppose. Christian charity,
Maître Simon, obliges us to help people if it is in our power.

SIMON. How very true.

LA FLECHE. What's going on? Isn't that our Maître Simon
talking to your father?

CLEANTE. Has anyone told him who I am? You haven't let the cat out of the bag have you?

SIMON. Ah, there you are. What a pleasant surprise! Who told you the meeting was going to be here? Oh Monsieur I do hope you realize it wasn't me told them who you are and where you're living. I mean it's not the way I go about it. But least said soonest mended eh? There's no harm done: they're discreet people. Well I'll be off and let you all get down to it.

HARPAGON. I beg your pardon?

SIMON. Monsieur here is the person who wants to borrow the fifteen thousand francs I was talking about.

HARPAGON. What, my son?

SIMON. Ah. Yes. I think I will withdraw.

Exit SIMON.

HARPAGON. Can it be you who has abandoned himself to the pit of luxury?

CLEANTE. What, my father? Can it be you who trades in such shameful actions?

HARPAGON. Can it be you who ruins himself by this damnable borrowing?

CLEANTE. Can it be you who enriches himself by this criminal usury?

HARPAGON. How dare you, after this, appear before me?

CLEANTE. How dare you, after this, show your face in the world?

HARPAGON. Tell me, have you no shame indulging in these debaucheries? Precipitating yourself into frightful expense? Dissipating the money your parents have amassed by the sweat of their brows?

CLEANTE. Tell me, do you not blush, dishonouring your position by all these deals? Sacrificing glory and reputation to pile up money? Gaining riches by stratagems more infamous than the most celebrated usurer's?

HARPAGON. Out of my sight, degenerate youth, out of my sight.

CLEANTE. Who is the more criminal, tell me this; the man who buys money he needs or the man who steals money he cannot use?

HARPAGON. Withdraw, I tell you, trouble me no longer.

Exit CLEANTE.

HARPAGON (*aside*). Actually I'm not all that upset by this turn of events. It just confirms that I've got to keep an eye on him.

Enter FROSINE.

FROSINE. Monsieur . . .

HARPAGON. Would you mind waiting for a minute? I'll be back soon and talk to you then. I must go and check on my money. I haven't looked at it for at least forty minutes.

LA FLECHE (*aside*). How very entertaining. He must have a huge warehouse somewhere full of old junk. We didn't recognize anything in that list.

FROSINE. Is it you La Flèche? What are you doing here?

LA FLECHE. Is it you Frosine? I might ask you the same question.

FROSINE. The usual. Sounding things out. Making myself useful to people. Exploiting as best as possible what small talents I am able to command. You know very well people like me, whom Heaven has seen fit to give no income whatsoever, have only their wits to live on.

LA FLECHE. Have you any business with the master of the house?

FROSINE. Yes. I have a little project in hand, from which I hope to get some recompense.

LA FLECHE. From him? I tell you you'll have to be very expert to get anything out of him. Money comes dear in these parts.

FROSINE. There are certain services one can do people that have a miraculous effect.

LA FLECHE. I'm your humble servant, but you don't know Seigneur Harpagon. Of all human beings, Sen. Harpagon is the least human. Of all mortals he is the most hard-hearted and the most tight-fisted. There's nothing you can do that'll make him put his hand in his pocket. You can get as much praise, esteem, good wishes out of him as you like, but as for your actual money, nothing doing. His good books are not so much dry as arid. He is not, as they say, in the giving mood. He'll never say he gives you his word on something, he says he'll lend it.

FROSINE. No trouble. I can draw people out. I can make people open their hearts to me like a flower to the morning dew. I've got an instinct, you see, for their soft spots.

LA FLECHE. I tell you, there's nothing doing there. I defy you to get round the party in question on the topic of money. He's more jewish than the jews. You could starve to death and he wouldn't bat an eyelid. He loves money more than reputation, more than honour, more than virtue itself. The sight of a suitor gives him a heart attack. To ask for money is to get him where it hurts. It's to stab him through the heart. It's to tear out his innards; and if . . . But he returns. I will withdraw.

Exit LA FLECHE.

Enter HARPAGON.

HARPAGON (*aside*). Everything's all right. (*To her.*) Well now, Frosine, what can I do for you?

FROSINE. You're looking very well today; quite the picture of health.

HARPAGON. Who me?

FROSINE. Never have I seen you looking so hale and hearty.

HARPAGON. You're having me on.

FROSINE. Honestly. I've never seen you looking so young. I've seen men of twenty-five look older than you.

HARPAGON. But Frosine, I'm well over sixty.

FROSINE. What's that, sixty? It's nothing. It's the best age to be. You're entering your prime.

HARPAGON. That's true, but still I wouldn't mind losing twenty years.

FROSINE. Are you joking? You don't need to lose years. You'll make a hundred with no problems.

HARPAGON. Do you really believe that?

FROSINE. I wouldn't say it if I didn't. You have all the signs. Hold yourself upright. Oh yes, it's definitely there, between your eyes, the sign of long life.

HARPAGON. You know all about that sort of thing?

FROSINE. It's one of my specialities. Show me your hand. Oh my God, look at that life line.

HARPAGON. Where?

FROSINE. Can't you see how far round it goes?

HARPAGON. What does it mean?

FROSINE. I know I said a hundred years, but this looks more like a hundred and twenty.

HARPAGON. Really?

FROSINE. They're going to have to do you in to get rid of you, I can tell you. You'll bury your children and your grandchildren.

HARPAGON. Couldn't be better. Now, how is our little project going?

FROSINE. Do you need to ask? Has anybody ever seen me

undertake anything without seeing it through to a successful conclusion? I think my greatest talent is as a match-maker. I don't think there are any two people in the world who given a little time I wouldn't in the end be able to get hitched. Given the time, I believe I could've married off Joan of Arc to the Pope. I can't see any major snags in our little business. Whenever I visit their house I keep on and on about you, and I've told the mother your intentions towards Mariane, having seen the child one day, sunning herself at her window while you were walking along the street.

HARPAGON. How did she take it?

FROSINE. She received the proposition with joy, and when I told her you would like her daughter to be one of the witnesses of the contract of marriage to be signed this evening at your house, she gave her wholehearted consent and entrusted her to me.

HARPAGON. You see Frosine, I have to give Seigneur Anselme supper, and I'd be very pleased if Mariane could be one of the guests.

FROSINE. Yes, it's a splendid idea. She'll pay a visit to your daughter in the early evening, then she'll want to go to the fair, and then she can round everything off by coming back here for supper.

HARPAGON. Good. They can both go to the fair. I'll lend them my coach.

FROSINE. Splendid.

HARPAGON. But tell me Frosine, have you talked to the mother about what sort of dowry she can give? I hope you've told her she must help her daughter, make some sort of effort. I mean really she should bleed herself dry at a time like this. You can't marry a girl off unless she brings something with her.

FROSINE. What are you talking about? A girl like that will bring you twelve thousand a year.

HARPAGON. Twelve thousand a year?

FROSINE. Yes of course. First of all, she's used to simple food, you know salad, cheese, milk, apples, all that sort of thing; so you won't have to keep an expensive table; no fancy soups, no bizarre puddings; she's not finicky like other women. Now that's no small thing for a start. That should add up to at least three thousand francs a year. Then, it's enough for her she keeps herself tidy and neat. She's not interested in superb clothes, or sumptuous jewels, or expensive furniture; all of which seem to arouse such passions in other women her age. Now that there is worth four thousand francs a year. But even better than this though; she can't stand gambling, which you must admit isn't all that common in women today. Do you know, I know one woman, lives quite close to me, she lost twenty thousand francs last year. Cards, dreadful. But let's take no more than a quarter of that. Five thousand from gambling, four thousand from clothes and jewels, that makes nine thousand, throw in the three thousand we mentioned for food and there you are, twelve thousand francs over the odds.

HARPAGON. Yes, it's not bad, but it isn't really real.

FROSINE. Excuse me. Aren't simple tastes real? Isn't a love of simple clothes real? Isn't a simple hatred of gambling real?

HARPAGON. You're having fun with me. You can't make up a dowry out of expenses that won't be incurred. I can't give a receipt for something I haven't had. It's not real unless I've got it in my hand.

FROSINE. You'll have something in your hands all right. They were talking to me about some estates they held in a certain foreign country. Those, of course, would be yours.

HARPAGON. We'll have to look into that. But Frosine, there's another thing worries me. The girl is young, as you know, and young people generally prefer the company of, indeed love, people of their own age. I'm afraid a man of my years may not be to her taste, and that could cause all sorts of unpleasant schemes which would only upset me.

FROSINE. Ah, I can see you don't know her. There's a little foible of hers I must tell you about. She can't stand young men; she only likes old ones.

HARPAGON. Really?

FROSINE. Yes, really. I wish you could've heard her talking about it. She says she can't even bear to look at a young man, but she's never happier, she says, that when she's gazing at a beautiful old man with a majestic beard. The older the better as far as she's concerned, so I warn you not to try to make yourself look younger than you really are. They must be at least sixty. Why, only four months ago, she was just about to get married and she called the whole thing off. And do you know why? The bridegroom looked as if he was only fifty-six and showed no sign of putting glasses on to sign the contract.

HARPAGON. Were those the only reasons?

FROSINE. They were. She said she couldn't be happy with only fifty-six, and she could only adore noses with glasses on them.

HARPAGON. You know, this is totally new to me. I had no idea.

FROSINE. And it goes much farther than that. She's got some pictures and engravings in her room, but what do you think they're of? Adonis, Hercules, Paris, Apollo? Well, you'd be wrong. They're of Saturn, Priam, Nestor, and in pride of place, Methusalah.

HARPAGON. This is really very good. It's something I would never have thought and I'm very relieved she feels like this. You know, if I'd been a woman, I don't think I'd've liked young men either.

FROSINE. I can well believe it. Look what the young are like. Spoiled brats, stupid country bumpkins.

HARPAGON. I know, I don't understand it at all. I don't know what women see in them.

FROSINE. They must be mad. Can you have common sense and love a youth? They're all brawn and no brains. How can people become attached to animals?

HARPAGON. That's what I always say. I mean, their high pitched voices, like hens on heat, and their three little strands of beard standing out like cats' whiskers, their grotesque wigs, their breeches almost falling down, and they're always wandering around with their buttons undone.

FROSINE. You only have to put them next to a person like you to see the difference. There's something about you that's strangely satisfying to look at. You seem framed and dressed for love.

HARPAGON. Do you really think so?

FROSINE. What? You are made of enchantment and you ought to be painted. Would you turn round a little please. Have you seen anything like it? It couldn't be better. Give us a little walk. Such ease, such deportment. You move completely freely, as people should do, and there isn't the slightest awkwardness.

HARPAGON. There's nothing major wrong with me, thank God. Just a touch of inflammation in my tubes which takes me from time to time.

FROSINE. That's nothing. In fact it rather suits you. I've always thought you coughed rather gracefully.

HARPAGON. Tell me a little about Mariane. She's never seen me? She never noticed me as I pass?

FROSINE. No, she's never seen you, but we're always talking about you. I've given her a description of your personality, speaking very highly of your merits, and I haven't failed to bring home the advantages of a husband like you.

HARPAGON. You've done very well. I'm most indebted to you.

FROSINE. I have Monsieur, a little favour I'd like to ask you.

HARPAGON *looks severe.*

FROSINE. I'm up to my neck in a court case, and I think I might lose it all because I haven't got quite enough money. I was wondering if you could see your way to helping me win it. You will not believe how happy Mariane will be when she finally sees you.

HARPAGON *goes back to normal.*

FROSINE. You're just her sort of man. Your old-fashioned ruff will make her feel happy for days. But I tell you what will really enchant her the way your breeches are attached to your doublet with little pieces of tagged lace. It's so out of date she'll be mad for you. A tagged lover is just her cup of tea.

HARPAGON. And you enchant me by saying so.

FROSINE. To tell you the truth, Monsieur, this court case is make or break as far as I'm concerned.

HARPAGON *looks severe again.*

FROSINE. All I need is a little bit of help and I'll be back on my feet again. I wish you had seen the happiness with which she heard me talk about you.

HARPAGON *looks normal again.*

FROSINE. As I listed your virtues, joy sparkled in her eyes. She can't wait for the marriage to be signed, sealed and concluded.

HARPAGON. You've made me very happy, Frosine, and I'm much obliged to you.

FROSINE. I beg you Monsieur, please give me the help I'm asking for. I'd be on even keel again and then I'd be much obliged to you.

HARPAGON. Good-bye. I must finish writing some letters. I'll give orders for my carriage to be ready to take you to the fair.

FROSINE. I assure you Monsieur you would never save me from a greater need.

HARPAGON. And I'll make sure we eat at a reasonable time so you won't have bad dreams during the night.

FROSINE. Please don't refuse me the favour I'm asking. You can't believe Monsieur, the pleasure it would give . . .

HARPAGON. I must be off. There, someone is calling me. I will see you later this evening.

Exit HARPAGON.

FROSINE. I hope you catch a particularly nasty and lingering disease. Preferably one with no cure. The skinflint was deaf to all my appeals, but not to worry. I shan't ditch the negotiations. There's still the other side of the match. They're bound to give me something.

Exit FROSINE.

Act Three

Enter HARPAGON, CLEANTE, ELISE, VALERE, MAITRE JACQUES, BRINDAVOINE *and* LA MERLUCHE. LA MERLUCHE *carries a broom.*

HARPAGON. All right, gather round everybody. I'm going to tell you all what I want you to do. Come here, La Merluche, let's start with you. Good, I see you're prepared, got your things with you. Now I want you to give everything a good going over; floors, tables, chairs, the lot; but be careful you don't polish them too hard, otherwise you'll wear them out. In addition to that, I want you to be cellarman this evening, and if any bottles wander or get broken, I warn you, I'll dock it off your wages.

MAITRE JACQUES (*aside*). Very encouraging.

HARPAGON. Off you go. Now you Brindavoine, I want you to rinse glasses and actually give people things to drink; but be careful you don't get carried away. Only give them something when they're thirsty and don't encourage them by asking them if they want some when the thought couldn't be further from their heads. Wait until they've asked you at least twice and also remember to carry plenty of water.

MAITRE JACQUES (*aside*). Yes, do. Pure wine goes to the head.

LA MERLUCHE. Can we change out of our smocks Monsieur?

HARPAGON. Yes, when you see people coming, and remember, do try not to spoil your clothes.

BRINDAVOINE. But Monsieur, what about that huge oil stain on my doublet I was showing you yesterday?

LA MERLUCHE. And me, Monsieur, I've gone through the seat of my trousers so that when I bend over, people will see my . . .

HARPAGON. That's enough. Stand with your back to the wall. Let them see your front all the time. (HARPAGON *holds his hat in front of his doublet to show* BRINDAVOINE *how to hide the stain.*) And you, hold your cap like that when you're waiting at table. Now daughter, I want you to keep an eye on what people are leaving and make sure it gets back to the kitchen in a fit state. Then we can use it again. But before that, you must get yourself ready to receive my new mistress who is coming to visit you and take you with her to the fair. Do you understand?

ELISE. Yes, father.

HARPAGON. And as for you, my son the dandy here, for whom, out of the goodness of my heart I will let bygones by bygones; I strongly advise you not to disgrace yourself in front of Mariane.

CLEANTE. How, disgrace myself? Why should I want to do a thing like that?

HARPAGON. Look, everyone knows how children feel when their parents remarry, and what they normally think of their step-mothers. If you want me to forget the latest batch of unfortunate incidents, I think you'd better make her as welcome as you can.

CLEANTE. To tell you the truth father, I can't say I'm exactly delighted at the prospect of her becoming my step-mother, I'd by lying if I said so. But as for putting a good face on it and making her welcome, I'll obey you to the letter.

HARPAGON. You'd better watch out, that's all I can say.

CLEANTE. You'll have nothing to complain about, I assure you.

HARPAGON. Good, I'm pleased to hear it. Valère, you'll keep an eye on him. Now, Maître Jacques, come over here. I've saved you until last.

Exeunt ELISE, CLEANTE, BRINDAVOINE, LA MERLUCHE.

MAITRE JACQUES. Do you want to talk to your coachman, Monsieur, or your cook? I am after all both of them.

HARPAGON. And it's both of them I want to talk to.

MAITRE JACQUES. But which first?

HARPAGON. To the cook.

MAITRE JACQUES. Just one moment, if you please.

He takes off his coachman's jacket and appears dressed as a cook.

HARPAGON. What was all that about?

MAITRE JACQUES. You've got to be properly dressed for the job.

HARPAGON. Well, I have got, I'm sorry to say, to give a supper this evening.

MAITRE JACQUES (*aside*). Wonders will never cease.

HARPAGON. Tell me, can you do a good meal?

MAITRE JACQUES. Yes, if you give me a lot of money.

HARPAGON. It's always the same, money. 'Money, money, money,' that's all anyone says these days. Never anything different. They're obsessed with it.

VALERE. I've never heard such a defeatist reply. Anyone can lay on a good meal if they have a lot of money. Unhappy the man, I always say, unhappy the man who cannot. No, the real challenge, the thing to really stretch a man, is to lay on a good meal with little or no money at all.

MAITRE JACQUES. Little or no money at all? Good heavens, Master Steward, sir, we'd all be much obliged I'm sure, if you let us into the secret. And you can take over my job as cook into the bargain. You poke your nose into everything as it is anyway. Fancy yourself as a right lord high bottle-washer.

HARPAGON. Oh shut up. What are we going to need?

MAITRE JACQUES. Why don't you ask Master Steward sir?
He can lay on a good meal for little or nothing at all.

HARPAGON. I asked you the question. I want you to answer
it.

MAITRE JACQUES. How many people will be there?

HARPAGON. Eight or ten; but we need only plan for eight. If
there's enough for eight it'll stretch to ten with no
trouble.

VALERE. That goes without saying.

MAITRE JACQUES. Let me see then; That means four large
soups and five other dishes. Soups, entrées . . .

HARPAGON. What? You could feed a whole town on that.

MAITRE JACQUES. Fish, a roast . . .

HARPAGON *puts his hand over* MAITRE JACQUES' *mouth.*

HARPAGON. Do you want to gobble up all my money?

MAITRE JACQUES. Side dishes . . .

HARPAGON. Yet more?

VALERE. Do you want to make everybody burst? Monsieur
didn't invite people here to kill them by forced feeding.
Go away and read the golden rules of health. Ask a doctor
if there's anything more prejudicial to a man than eating
to excess.

HARPAGON. He's right.

VALERE. You must understand, Maître Jacques, you and
people in your position, that loading a table with too much
food is like cutting peoples' throats. One shows oneself a
true friend to one's guests, I always say, if frugality reigns
in the festive feast. We should follow the saying of the
ancients: man eats to live, not lives to eat.

HARPAGON. Well said, well said. Come, let me embrace you for
it. It's the finest proverb I've ever heard. Man lives to eat, not
eats to li . . . No, that's not it. What was that you said?

VALERE. Man eats to live, not lives to eat.

HARPAGON. Exactly. Did you hear that? Which great man said that?

VALERE. I can't quite remember.

HARPAGON. You must write it down for me. I'll blazon it on the dining room chimney piece.

VALERE. I won't forget. As for your supper, leave it to me. I'll make sure things are as they should be.

HARPAGON. Do it now.

MAÎTRE JACQUES. So much the better. It just means I've got less to do.

HARPAGON. I think we should have things that people don't really like; good, heavy, filling things. Things like thick bean soup and chestnut pâté.

VALERE. Leave it all to me.

HARPAGON. Good. Now, Maître Jacques, my coach has got to be cleaned.

MAÎTRE JACQUES. Just one moment. For that you'll have to speak to the coachman. (*He puts his jacket on.*) You were saying?

HARPAGON. My coach needs cleaning, and the horses must be got ready to go to the fair.

MAÎTRE JACQUES. The horses, Monsieur? They aren't in a fit state for anything. I won't say they're lying clapped out on their straw, because they haven't got any straw to lie on, and I wouldn't want to mislead you, but you've put them on such short commons they're no more than ghosts in the guise of horses.

HARPAGON. Of course they're ill. They don't do anything.

MAÎTRE JACQUES. Just because they don't do anything, Monsieur, does that mean they shouldn't eat anything? They'd be far better off, poor beasts, if they worked a lot and ate a lot. It gets me right here when I see them so worn down. When it comes down to it, I love my horses, and when they suffer it's as if I'm suffering too. Every day I give them some of my own food. You must be very hard indeed, Monsieur, to have no sympathy for your fellow creatures.

HARPAGON. It's not particularly hard work, just going to the fair and back.

MAITRE JACQUES. No, I'm sorry, Monsieur, I can't do it. I'd feel guilty whipping them in the state they are. How can you want them to drag a coach when they can't even drag themselves?

VALERE. Monsieur, I'll ask neighbour Picard to drive them for us. We'll also need him to help us prepare the supper.

HARPAGON. Oh well, it's all for the best. Che sera sera, as the Italians say. If they're going to die it's better it happens when someone else is driving them.

VALERE. Maître Jacques is becoming a bit of a barrack room lawyer.

MAITRE JACQUES. And Master Steward sir, is becoming a bit of a busybody.

HARPAGON. Now, now.

MAITRE JACQUES. Monsieur, I'm sorry, but I can't stand flatterers, and when I see what he's up to, I get very angry. Can't you see that the way he doles out the bread, the wine, the wood, the salt and the candles are just his way of crawling to you? I get upset virtually every day hearing the way he talks to you; for when it comes down to it, I have a bit of a soft spot for you despite the way you treat me; and, after my horses, you're the person I'm most fond of.

HARPAGON. Maître Jacques, will you tell me what people say about me?

MAITRE JACQUES. Yes, Monsieur, provided I knew it wouldn't upset you.

HARPAGON. Not in the least.

MAITRE JACQUES. I beg to differ. I know very well it'll make you angry.

HARPAGON. Not at all. On the contrary, I'd be pleased. I want to know what people say.

MAITRE JACQUES. Well, Monsieur, if you insist. Frankly, generally speaking, people mock you. We get hundreds of jokes thrown at us from all sides about you. It's a general game to hold you up, as it were, by the seat of your pants, and tell stories about your stinginess. One person says you've had special calendars printed with lent twice as long, so you can save money on what we give up. Another says you always quarrel with your servants round about Christmas or when they're leaving you, so you don't have to give them anything. This person here says how you once tried to take your neighbour's cat to court for eating the remains of a leg of mutton. That there says how you were caught one night stealing your own horses' oats for your porridge next morning. He says your coachman, the one before me, caught you at it and hit you I don't know how many times with a stick, during all of which you didn't make a sound. I mean, in the end, what do you want me to tell you? You can't go anywhere without hearing you being torn to pieces. You're a . . . a . . . universal laughing stock, and no one ever mentions you without calling you a miser, skinflint, villain, and an out-and-out shylock.

HARPAGON *hits him.*

HARPAGON. And you are a dolt, a petty thief, a scoundrel, and a . . . a . . . an impudent man.

MAITRE JACQUES. What did I tell you? You wouldn't believe me. I told you you'd get upset if you heard the truth.

HARPAGON. You'd be advised to get a civil tongue in your head.

Exit HARPAGON.

VALERE. From what I've been able to see, Maître Jacques, virtue is not its own reward.

MAITRE JACQUES. Look here, Johnny-come-lately, clever clogs, aren't you getting a bit too big for your boots? It's none of your business. You laugh when you get hit and not when I do.

VALERE. Ah, Monsieur Maître Jacques, I'm sorry; I didn't mean to upset you.

MAITRE JACQUES (*aside*). He's back-pedalling. I'll come the heavy a bit, and if he's stupid enough to take it, I'll hit him. (*To* VALERE.) Well, can't you see, Smiler, I'm not laughing, me? It's no laughing matter. If I have any more laughing out of you, I'll make you laugh on the other side of your face.

MAITRE JACQUES *pushed* VALERE *to the back of the stage, menacing him.*

VALERE. Now, now, no need to get rough.

MAITRE JACQUES. No? What if I want to?

VALERE. Softly, softly.

MAITRE JACQUES. Catchee monkee? You're a cheeky little chappie to be sure.

VALERE. Monsieur Maître Jacques . . .

MAITRE JACQUES. What Monsieur Maître Jacques? There's no Monsieur Maître Jacques here for the likes of you. If I had a stick, I'd thrash all your self-importance out of you.

VALERE. What, a stick?

VALERE *makes him recoil as he did him.*

MAITRE JACQUES. A stick? I didn't mention a stick.

VALERE. You know, I think you're the one who's going to get hit, not me.

MAITRE JACQUES. Really?

VALERE. What are you?

MAITRE JACQUES. I don't know.

VALERE. A cook, nothing but a cook. A cook smelling of cabbage and soup.

MAITRE JACQUES. Yes, you're quite right.

VALERE. And who am I?

MAITRE JACQUES. You ...

VALERE. You don't really know who I am at all. And you were going to hit me.

MAITRE JACQUES. I was only joking.

VALERE. I don't like your jokes. (VALERE *hits him with a stick.*) I think you ought to learn you've got no sense of humour.

    Exit VALERE.

MAITRE JACQUES. A plague on sincerity. It's not worth it. From now on I'll have nothing to do with it. I'm not going to speak the truth any more. I'll take it from my master, he's got some right to hit me; but as for Master Steward, I shall be revenged.

    Enter FROSINE *and* MARIANE.

FROSINE. Do you know, Maître Jacques, if your master is at home?

MAITRE JACQUES. Only too well.

FROSINE. Will you tell him we are here.

    Exit MAITRE JACQUES.

MARIANE. Frosine, I feel distinctly peculiar. I have to say I am not looking forward to this meeting.

FROSINE. But why? What have you got to be worried about?

MARIANE. How can you ask me that? Think what a prisoner

feels like, seeing for the first time the rack on which she is to be stretched.

FROSINE. I can well appreciate Harpagon is not the instrument you would choose to embrace; and I know from the way you've talked about it the young man you have mentioned reciprocates your feelings a little.

MARIANE. Yes, Frosine, there's no denying it, I simply couldn't. His visits to our house have had some small effect on my heart.

FROSINE. But do you know who he is?

MARIANE. No, not at all. But I do know his very manner arouses love, and if I had my way, I would want him more than all others. All this contributes not a little to the frightful turmoil I feel concerning the husband it is wished I should take.

FROSINE. My dear, these charming young men are all the same, and I've no doubt are absolutely splendid fellows, but the majority of them are as poor as church mice. It's much better for you to take an older husband, who'll give you plenty of money. I do admit that most older men are not very attractive, and that you would have to endure some little . . . distastefulnesses with such a husband; but it will soon be over. He will soon die, and then the same young men will find you even more lovely than before and it will all have been worthwhile.

MARIANE. Frosine, it's a strange business. We can't be happy until someone else is dead, and then there's no guarantee it's going to happen in time.

FROSINE. Are you joking? You're only marrying him on the condition he makes you a widow soon. It must be part of the contract. He will be very tactless if he doesn't die in three months. Ah, here he is now.

MARIANE. Frosine, look at his face.

Enter HARPAGON.

HARPAGON. I hope you will not be offended, my beauty, if
I come to you with glasses on. I know your charms are
clear enough in their own right, and it is not necessary to
wear glasses to see them, but it is through glasses we view
the heavenly bodies, and you are a star, Mariane, a verit-
able star, a star amongst stars.

FROSINE. If Mariane seems at all taken aback, Monsieur, it
is because young girls always hesitate to show what they
are feeling in their hearts.

HARPAGON. You are right. See, my beautiful dainty morsel,
where my daughter comes to greet you.

Enter ELISE.

MARIANE. I must apologize, Madame, for leaving it so long
before paying you a visit.

ELISE. You have done, Madame what I should have done. It
was up to me to call on you first.

HARPAGON. I'm afraid my daughter is rather large for her
size; but rank grass grows rife.

MARIANE (*to* FROSINE). He is foul.

HARPAGON. What did my beauty say?

FROSINE. She was saying how much she admired you.

HARPAGON. You do me too much honour, adorable dainty
dish.

MARIANE (*aside*). He's an animal.

HARPAGON. You're too kind. Too kind.

MARIANE (*aside*). I can't stand it.

HARPAGON. Ah, here is my son as well. He has come to pay
his respects to you.

Enter CLEANTE.

MARIANE (*aside to* FROSINE). Frosine, that's the young man
I was talking about.

FROSINE (*to* MARIANE). Who would have thought it.

HARPAGON. I see you are amazed I have two such grown up children. But do not concern yourself, I'll soon have them both off my hands.

CLEANTE. Madame, to tell you the truth, this is a turn of events I in no way expected. My father surprised me not a little when he told me, a short while ago, what he intended.

MARIANE. I have to say the same thing. This unexpected meeting has surprised me as much as it has surprised you, and I was in no way prepared for it.

CLEANTE. It is undoubtedly true, Madame, that in my opinion my father could not have made a better choice, and that it is with real joy I have the pleasure of seeing you; but, even bearing all this in mind, I cannot assure you I am delighted at the prospect of you being my step-mother. The compliment, I must admit to you, is too difficult for me to make. It is an honour that I would not wish on you at all. This manner of speaking may seem brutal to the ears of some; but I am certain you will take it in the spirit in which it is intended. This is a marriage, Madame, that you can well imagine, Madame, for which I can have nothing but repugnance. You cannot but realize, knowing now who I am, how far it goes against my own interests. I am sure you will understand if I tell you, with my father's permission of course, that if things depended on me, these nuptials would not take place at all.

HARPAGON. What are you talking about? What are you saying to her?

MARIANE. And I have to say, in response to you, that your feelings towards me are exactly matched by mine towards you. I have no less a repugnance in seeing you my step-son than you have in seeing me your step-mother. Do not believe, I pray you, that it was I who sought to give you this displeasure. I would be very upset to do so; and if I did not see myself forced by circumstances beyond my control, I give you my word I would not consent to this marriage.

HARPAGON. She's right; a stupid compliment deserves a stupid reply. I must excuse my son's impertinence, my dear. He's a young fool who doesn't yet know the meaning of what he says.

MARIANE. I promise you he has in no way offended me. On the contrary he has given me pleasure by so revealing to me his true sentiments. I respect him for such a statement, and if he had spoken to me in another fashion, I would have held him in far lower esteem.

HARPAGON. You're too kind to him, wanting to excuse him. Time'll make him wiser and then he'll change his tune.

CLEANTE. No, mother, I will in no way change my views. I earnestly beg you to believe me, mother.

HARPAGON. More foolishness. He's getting worse.

CLEANTE. Do you wish me to betray my heart?

HARPAGON. Wouldn't you rather change the subject?

CLEANTE. Very well, if that's what you want. Madame, let me put myself in my father's place and talk to you on his behalf. I swear to you I have never seen anyone as charming as you are. I swear to you I can conceive of nothing to equal the pleasure of pleasing you. I swear to you I could think of no greater glory than to be called your husband. It is a title I would prefer to those of the greatest princes on earth. Possessing you would be the best of all possible fortunes. It is my greatest ambition. There is nothing I would not do to achieve such a conquest. I would surmount the most powerful obstacles; I would . . .

HARPAGON. Not so much, son, if you please.

CLEANTE. It's a compliment I'm paying Madame on your behalf.

HARPAGON. I've got a tongue of my own; I don't need you to do my talking for me. Go and get some chairs.

FROSINE. No, I think it'd be much better if we went to the fair now. Then we'd get back at a reasonable time and be able to do all the talking we wanted to later.

HARPAGON. Someone get the horses harnessed. You must forgive me, my dear, but I've completely forgotten to give you a little bite of something before you move on. What a pity there's not enough time for me to . . .

CLEANTE. Don't worry father, I'd thought of it. I've had brought over some fruit, you know, satsumas and things that are out of season, and some fruit cordials and some rather complicated and expensive sweets. And I've had them all charged to your account.

HARPAGON (*low, to* VALERE). Valère.

VALERE (*to* HARPAGON). He's taken leave of his senses.

CLEANTE. Don't you think that'll be enough, father? I'm sure Madame will have the goodness to forgive us.

MARIANE. You shouldn't have.

CLEANTE. Have you ever seen, Madame, a more brilliant diamond than the one on my father's finger?

MARIANE. It's very nice.

CLEANTE *takes it off his father's finger and gives it to* MARIANE.

CLEANTE. Take a closer look at it.

MARIANE. It's very beautiful indeed. I haven't seen one sparkle so much.

CLEANTE *prevents* MARIANE *from returning it.*

CLEANTE. And it will be made even more beautiful by staying in your beautiful hands. It's a present from my father.

HARPAGON. From me?

CLEANTE. Isn't it true, father, you want Madame to keep it as a token of your love?

HARPAGON (*to* CLEANTE). What are you doing?

CLEANTE. How nice. He's asked me to make you accept it.

MARIANE. I couldn't.

CLEANTE. You must. He will not take it back.

HARPAGON (*aside*). I am losing my temper again.

MARIANE. It's far too . . .

CLEANTE *always prevents* MARIANE *from returning the ring.*

CLEANTE. You will offend him.

MARIANE. Please, let me . . .

CLEANTE. Please take it.

HARPAGON (*aside*). The plague take . . .

CLEANTE. You see how he is upset by your refusal.

HARPAGON (*to his son*). You're no better than a thief.

CLEANTE. You see how badly he is taking it.

HARPAGON (*to his son*). I'll get you for this.

CLEANTE. Father, it's not my fault she won't take it. I'm doing all I can, but she's being very obstinate.

HARPAGON (*to his son, very angry*). You ought to be hung.

CLEANTE. You see, Madame, how you make my father quarrel with me?

HARPAGON (*to his son, very angry*). I'll disinherit you.

CLEANTE. You'll make him ill; Madame, I implore you, do not refuse it any longer.

FROSINE. For goodness sake girl, take the ring if that's what Monsieur wants.

MARIANE. I will take it for now, because I don't want to make you angry. However, I will give it back to you the next time I see you.

Enter BRINDAVOINE.

BRINDAVOINE. Monsieur, there's a man wants to talk to you.

HARPAGON. Tell him I'm busy and he should come back later.

BRINDAVOINE. He says he's got some money for you.

HARPAGON. I must beg your pardons. I'll be back very soon.

Enter LA MERLUCHE. *He collides with* HARPAGON, *knocking him over.*

LA MERLUCHE. Monsieur . . .

HARPAGON. You've half killed me.

CLEANTE. Are you all right, father? Have you hurt yourself?

HARPAGON. That traitor there has been paid by my debtors to break my neck.

VALERE. It's nothing.

LA MERLUCHE. I'm sorry, Monsieur. I thought I was right, running straight in like that.

HARPAGON. What is it, dolt?

LA MERLUCHE. Two of the horses have lost their shoes.

HARPAGON. Then take them to the blacksmith's at once.

CLEANTE. While we are waiting for them to be shod, I will, on behalf of my father, do the honours of the house. I'm sure Madame would like to see the garden. I've had a little something to eat laid out there.

Exeunt CLEANTE, ELISE, MARIANE *and* FROSINE.

HARPAGON. Valère, keep an eye on all this. please retrieve as much food as possible. Then we can send it back and get a refund.

VALERE. Of course, Monsieur.

Exeunt VALERE, BRINDAVOINE, LA MERLUCHE.

HARPAGON. Oh my son, my son, my son. Do you want to ruin me?

Act Four

Enter CLEANTE, MARIANE, ELISE *and* FROSINE.

CLEANTE. Let's go in here. We'll be much safer. There won't be any servants around, so we can talk freely.

ELISE. Yes, Madame, my brother has told me all he feels for you. I know how you must feel after such a set-back, and it is with the deepest sympathy, I assure you, I interest myself in your affairs.

MARIANE. It's some consolation to have someone like you on my side. I hope, Madame, you will always feel like this and help me deal with fate's cross currents.

FROSINE. It's really all your own fault, both of you. You should have told me before what was going on. Then I could have done something about it and we wouldn't find ourselves in our present circumstances.

CLEANTE. What could you have done? It is my evil destiny that has made things so. But, Mariane, what do you intend to do?

MARIANE. What can I do? How, in the state you see me, can I do anything? All I can do is wish.

CLEANTE. Is that really all? Have you nothing else to give me, save your wishes? What of your pity? What of your support? What of your affection?

MARIANE. What can I say to you? Put yourself in my place and then see what options are open to you. I will do whatever you want. I know you would not ask me to do anything that goes against my honour.

CLEANTE. What good is that? What can we do if we are bound by the limits of honour and propriety?

MARIANE. What else can I say? Even if I was able to ignore

the rules that govern us women, I have my mother to think of. She has been very good to me and I will not upset her. Go and talk to her. Try to win her over. You can do and say anything you like; I give you free rein. And if you need me to back you up, I would be only too happy to tell her all I feel for you.

CLEANTE. Frosine, Frosine, can you do anything for us?

FROSINE. I very much hope so. I very much want to. You know that underneath everything I'm very soft hearted. Heaven hasn't made me of stone. Whenever I see two people really in love, I'm only too pleased to do anything I can to help them. Now, what avenues are open to us?

CLEANTE. Please think of something.

MARIANE. Shed some light on our darkness.

ELISE. Devise some means to undo what you have done.

FROSINE. It's so difficult. Now your mother is not altogether unreasonable and it should be possible to win her over and persuade her to give to the son what she intended giving to the father. But the stumbling block in all this is the fact that your father is your father.

CLEANTE. That goes without saying.

FROSINE. There's no point in you turning him down, as then he'll only nurse resentment and refuse consent to his son. The impetus must come from him. We'll have to find some way of making him go off you.

CLEANTE. You're right.

FROSINE. Of course I'm right. I wouldn't have said it otherwise. Now, we know what we've got to do, but how on earth do we go about it? Wait, I have it. What if I found a woman who was slightly older than me and had my acting talents? We could ask her to pretend to be a lady of quality; we could rustle up a train for her and give her some bizarre title or other, a marchioness or viscountess or something from Lower Brittany. Now I think I could make your father believe she was very rich, with several houses and an income of at least a hundred and fifty thousand francs, and furthermore she's so madly in love with him that she'll make everything his if only she could lay her hands on him. I've no doubt at all he'll prick up his ears at that; for although he loves you dearly he loves money even more. And, when, dazzled by this bait, he consents to everything you ask, it won't matter very much if in the end he finds he's been tricked.

CLEANTE. All that is very well thought out.

FROSINE. Leave it all to me. Come to think of it, I have a friend who will just fit the bill.

CLEANTE. Frosine, if this works I shall be eternally grateful. But, my dearest Mariane, we must begin to persuade your mother. There is so much to do if we're going to stop this marriage taking place. Use every means you can; exploit her natural feelings for you, deploy without reserve all the myriad charms heaven has given you. Above all do not forget any of those tender words and caresses I have always found so irresistible.

MARIANE. I will do all I can. I will forget nothing.

Enter HARPAGON.

HARPAGON (*aside*). What, my son kissing the hand of his stepmother to be? And she doesn't exactly seem to be objecting. Can there be more to this than meets the eyes?

ELISE. Here is my father.

HARPAGON. The carriage awaits. You can go whenever you like.

CLEANTE. As you aren't going, father, I'll drive them myself.

HARPAGON. No, stay. They'll be all right and I want to talk to you about something.

Exeunt MARIANE, ELISE *and* FROSINE.

HARPAGON. Tell me, leaving aside the fact that she's going to be your step-mother, what do you think of her?

CLEANTE. What do I think of her?

HARPAGON. Yes; her looks, her general air, her personality?

CLEANTE. Oh, so so.

HARPAGON. Only so so?

CLEANTE. To tell you the truth, I'm rather disappointed in her. She's not at all what I'd been led to expect. She seems a bit of a flirt, her face is nothing to write home about, she's generally a bit awkward, and her mind is really rather ordinary. Please don't think, father, I'm trying to put you off. If I've got to have a step-mother I'm sure she'll be just as good as anyone else.

HARPAGON. But what about all you've just said to her?

CLEANTE. Anything pleasant I said to her was in your name and done to please you.

HARPAGON. So you've got no leanings in the direction whatsoever?

CLEANTE. Me? None at all.

HARPAGON. That's a pity, as it rather puts paid to an idea that was coming into my head. Seeing her just now, I suddenly realized how old I am, and what people would say if I married such a young girl. So, I thought to myself, I'd better give the whole thing up. But since I had asked for her hand and given my word to her mother, I was thinking I should pass her on to you. But in the light of what you've just said . . .

CLEANTE. Pass her on to me?

HARPAGON. To you.

CLEANTE. Marry her off to me?

HARPAGON. Marry her off to you.

CLEANTE. Listen father, it's true she's not exactly my sort of woman, but if it makes you happy, I think I might force myself to marry her, if that's what you want.

HARPAGON. What I want? I'm much more reasonable than

you think. I wouldn't want to force you to do something you don't want to.

CLEANTE. No, no; I insist. I will do it to show my love to you.

HARPAGON. No, no. A marriage can't be happy, I always say, a marriage can't be happy unless it is based on love.

CLEANTE. That will maybe come in the end, father. People say love is a fruit of marriage.

HARPAGON. I'm sorry, it's too big a risk for a man to take. I must say this puts me in a bit of a difficult position. Now if you'd felt something for her, that would have been all well and good, I'd've married her off to you. But you don't. I suppose I will have to follow my original plan and marry her myself.

CLEANTE. I see. Father, I'm going to have to make a clean breast of things and tell you our secret. The fact of the matter is that I love her, and have done ever since I saw her out walking one day. I was going to ask you for your permission to marry her, but then you made your intentions clear and I didn't want to upset you.

HARPAGON. Have you been visiting her?

CLEANTE. I have.

HARPAGON. Many times?

CLEANTE. For as long as I've known her, yes.

HARPAGON. And have you been well received?

CLEANTE. Very well, but they didn't know who I was. Mariane has just had a very unpleasant surprise.

HARPAGON. Have you told Mariane of your feelings and that you want to marry her?

CLEANTE. I have indeed, and I've also started to canvas her mother.

HARPAGON. And how did the mother receive your suggestions?

CLEANTE. Very civilly.

HARPAGON. And the girl, does she reciprocate your love?

CLEANTE. As far as I can tell, I think I can persuade myself she has some small feeling for me.

HARPAGON. I'm very glad you've told me your secret. It's exactly as I expected. I think, son, that you're going to have to look facts squarely in the face. You're going to forget your love, stop your pursuit of the person I intend for myself, and prepare yourself to marry, very soon, the woman I have chosen for you.

CLEANTE. So you've been playing with me, have you father? Well, if we're putting our cards on the table, I tell you this. I will in no way renounce my love for Mariane, and I will fight you for her to the hilt. If you have the mother's consent, maybe I have other forces on my side.

HARPAGON. What, you have the nerve to tread in my footsteps?

CLEANTE. It's you who are treading in mine. I got there first. First come first served.

HARPAGON. Am I not your father? Ought you not to respect me?

CLEANTE. In matters such as these, the child is not obliged to defer to the father. All's fair in love and war.

HARPAGON. I'll beat the living daylights out of you.

CLEANTE. Threats will get you nowhere.

HARPAGON. You will renounce Mariane.

CLEANTE. I will do no such thing.

HARPAGON. Somebody bring me a stick.

Enter MAITRE JACQUES.

MAITRE JACQUES. Gentlemen, gentlemen, what is it?

CLEANTE. You're just a bad joke.

MAITRE JACQUES. Now, now.

HARPAGON. How dare you talk to me like that.

MAITRE JACQUES. If you please.

CLEANTE. I stand by everything I've said.

MAITRE JACQUES. Talking like this to your father?

HARPAGON. Let me deal with him.

MAITRE JACQUES. Talking like this to your son? It won't do. It won't do at all.

HARPAGON. Maître Jacques, will you judge between us? See whether I'm right.

MAITRE JACQUES. Of course I will. Now both of you move off a little. I'll talk to you one at a time.

HARPAGON. I love a girl and I want to marry her; and this, this idiot has the insolence to love her as well, and to carry on despite me ordering him not to.

MAITRE JACQUES. He's very much in the wrong.

HARPAGON. Isn't it frightful, a son in competition with his father? Shouldn't he, out of respect, clear the field for me?

MAITRE JACQUES. Of course he should, you're perfectly right. You stay here, I'll have a word with him. (MAITRE JACQUES *crosses to* CLEANTE.)

CLEANTE. Well, I suppose if he wants you to decide between us, I've no objections. Your judgment's as good as the next man's, and I'm happy enough to go through with it.

MAITRE JACQUES. You're too kind.

CLEANTE. I've fallen in love with someone and she's fallen in love with me, and now my father's making trouble by sticking his oar in.

MAITRE JACQUES. It's very wrong of him.

CLEANTE. Has he no shame, thinking of marrying at his age? Does it suit him, falling in love again? Shouldn't he leave all that sort of thing to younger men?

MAITRE JACQUES. Of course he should. He must be having a little joke. Let me have one or two words with him. (*He crosses to* HARPAGON.) Well, things aren't as bad as they seem. Your son will listen to reason. He says that he knows he ought to respect you and that he was carried away by the heat of his passion. He says he will submit himself to your wishes, provided you will treat him better than you have done of late, and not marry him off without his consent.

HARPAGON. Tell him, Maître Jacques, that if that's the case we've got nothing to quarrel about, and he can marry who ever he likes, provided it's not Mariane.

MAITRE JACQUES *crosses to* CLEANTE.

MAITRE JACQUES. Leave it to me. Well, your father isn't as unreasonable as you make out. He says he only got angry because you got angry. The only point he wants to make is your manner upsets him, and he'll give you all you want, provided you accept it gracefully and show your father all the deference and respect due to him.

CLEANTE. Maître Jacques, you can assure him that if he gives me Mariane he will find me the most submissive of men, and I won't do the slightest thing against his will.

MAITRE JACQUES. It's done. He agrees to everything you say.

HARPAGON. Thank goodness for that.

MAITRE JACQUES. No problems. He accepts your promises.

CLEANTE. Heaven be praised.

MAITRE JACQUES. Gentlemen, you talk to each other again; you are reconciled. To think you were going to quarrel over such a paltry misunderstanding.

CLEANTE. Maître Jacques, I shall be eternally grateful.

MAITRE JACQUES. It's nothing, Monsieur.

HARPAGON. You've done well, Maître Jacques, and that merits a reward.

HARPAGON *puts his hand in his pocket.* MAITRE JACQUES *thinks he's going to get some money.* HARPAGON *pulls out his handkerchief.*

HARPAGON. Go, I shall remember it, I assure you.

MAITRE JACQUES. I bid you both farewell.

Exit MAITRE JACQUES.

CLEANTE. I'm sorry I made you so angry, father.

HARPAGON. It's nothing.

CLEANTE. No, I'm really upset.

HARPAGON. I'm very glad to find you so reasonable again.

CLEANTE. It was very good of you to forgive me so quickly.

HARPAGON. One easily forgets the faults of children, once they have returned to the fold.

CLEANTE. No more hard feelings about my extravagancies?

HARPAGON. All wiped out by the respect you are showing.

CLEANTE. I promise you father, I will be grateful for this until the day I die.

HARPAGON. And I on my part promise you I'll give you every single thing you ask for.

CLEANTE. Ah, father, I'll ask you for nothing. You gave me enough when you gave me Mariane.

HARPAGON. What?

CLEANTE. I said father, I'll never ask you for anything else now you've given me Mariane.

HARPAGON. Who said I'd given you Mariane?

CLEANTE. You did.

HARPAGON. Me?

CLEANTE. Of course.

HARPAGON. But it's you who's promised to give her up.

CLEANTE. Me, give her up?

HARPAGON. Yes.

CLEANTE. Nothing of the sort.

HARPAGON. You've not changed your intentions on that score?

CLEANTE. On the contrary. I feel more determined than ever.

HARPAGON. What, monkey, again?

CLEANTE. Nothing will change me.

HARPAGON. I think you'll find I will, traitor.

CLEANTE. Do your worst.

HARPAGON. Never let me see you again.

CLEANTE. That's all right by me.

HARPAGON. I abandon you to your fate.

CLEANTE. Abandon away.

HARPAGON. I renounce you as my son.

CLEANTE. So be it.

HARPAGON. I disinherit you.

CLEANTE. Do anything you want.

HARPAGON. All you're getting from me is my curse.

CLEANTE. Curse away.

Exit HARPAGON.

Enter LA FLECHE *from the garden with a cash box.*

LA FLECHE. Ah Monsieur, I'm glad I've found you. Follow me quickly.

CLEANTE. What is it?

LA FLECHE. Come with me. We've done it.

CLEANTE. Done what?

LA FLECHE. This is what we wanted.

CLEANTE. What?

LA FLECHE. I've had my eye on this all day.

CLEANTE. What is it?

LA FLECHE. It's your father's money. I've nicked it.

CLEANTE. How?

LA FLECHE. I'll tell you later. Let's get out of here. I can hear him coming.

HARPAGON (*off*). Thief. Thief.

Exeunt CLEANTE *and* LA FLECHE.

Enter HARPAGON *from the garden without a hat.*

HARPAGON. Thief. Thief. Murder. Rape. Justice, give me justice, heaven. I am lost. I am slain. They have cut my throat. They have stripped me of my money. Who done it? What's happened to him? Where is he? Where is he hiding himself? What must I do to find him? Where should I look? Where not? There he is. No, over there. Stop. Give me back my money . . . (*He grabs hold of his own hand.*) Ah, it's me. My brain is reeling. I don't know where I am, who I am and what I'm doing. My money, my poor money, my dearest friend, they have sundered us for ever. When they take away my money, they take away my prop, my consolation and my joy. It's all over for me. I have nothing else in this world. Without you, I can't live. It is finished. I die; I am dead; I am buried. Will no one resurrect me by giving me back my money? Or at least by telling me who's taken it? What? What did you say? Nothing. The person who took it must have been keeping a watch on the house. He chose exactly the time I was talking to the traitor, my son. I will call the magistrates and have everyone in the house put to torture; the servants, my daughter, my son, even me. And you, out there, what about you? I can't look at anyone without being suspicious. Everyone looks like a robber to me. I can't trust anybody. I used to think that only I talked to you, but they've all been doing it, haven't they. What are you saying down there? It's about the thief, isn't it. What's that noise up there? It's him, making his get-away. If any of you know anything, on bended knees I beg you to tell me. You all look at me and snigger behind your hands. You're all involved in it. Accomplices. Come to me here, I invoke you; magistrates, officers, beadles, judges, torturers, hangmen, executioners. I will have the whole world hung, and if I still haven't found my money, I'll hang myself.

Exit HARPAGON.

Act Five

Enter HARPAGON *and* MAGISTRATE.

MAGISTRATE. Let me deal with it. I do know my own job,
you know. This isn't the first time I've investigated a robbery. I've hung more thieves than you've had hot dinners.

HARPAGON. I want every magistrate in town put on this
case, and if you don't recover my money, I'll have the
whole lot of you looked into.

MAGISTRATE. We'll go through all the necessary procedures.
Now, how much did you say was in this cash box?

HARPAGON. Fifteen thousand francs.

MAGISTRATE. Fifteen thousand francs?

HARPAGON. Fifteen thousand francs.

MAGISTRATE. That's quite a big haul.

HARPAGON. There is no punishment strong enough to fit
this crime. If he isn't caught, it will be the end of civiliza-
tion as we know it.

MAGISTRATE. This sum was in what denominations?

HARPAGON. Pistoles and louis d'or; all in mint condition.

MAGISTRATE. Do you suspect anyone of this theft?

HARPAGON. The whole world. I want you to arrest the entire
town, and all the out-lying suburbs.

MAGISTRATE. We're going to have to go carefully on this
one; we don't want to scare anyone off. Once we've got
some leads we'll follow them up with the full rigour of the
law, and then you'll get your money back.

Enter MAITRE JACQUES.

MAITRE JACQUES (*to people off*). I'll be straight back. You
should cut the throat immediately; and then I want one of

you to grill the feet, while someone else puts the body in boiling water and then hangs it from the ceiling.

HARPAGON. Whose body? The thief's?

MAITRE JACQUES. I'm talking about a sucking pig your steward has had sent in. I'm having it prepared according to my own special recipe.

HARPAGON. Never mind about all that. I want you to answer any questions this gentleman here asks you.

MAGISTRATE. There's no need to get alarmed. I don't want to upset you. I just want everything to go smoothly.

MAITRE JACQUES. Monsieur is one of your supper guests?

MAGISTRATE. Now you mustn't, my friend, hide anything from your master.

MAITRE JACQUES. Monsieur, I assure you I am preparing everything to the best of my ability and you will be entertained as royally as possible.

HARPAGON. We're not talking about food.

MAITRE JACQUES. If things aren't perhaps entirely up to scratch, that isn't my fault. Blame your steward whose false economies have clipped my wings.

HARPAGON. There are more important things afoot than supper. Now tell me all about the money someone's stolen from me.

MAITRE JACQUES. Someone's stolen some money from you?

HARPAGON. You know very well they have. I'll have you hung if you don't give it me back.

MAGISTRATE. I think you're doing him an injustice. He's an honest enough looking fellow, and I'm sure we won't have to put him into prison to find out what we want to know. Now, friend, you just tell us everything and I give you my word nobody will do anything to you, and your master will make it worth your while; someone has stolen his money and you're bound to know something about it.

MAITRE JACQUES (*aside*). This is just the chance I've been looking for to revenge myself on the steward. Ever since he came here, he's been the favourite, and only his ideas have been taken any notice of. There's also the little matter of that beating he recently gave me.

HARPAGON. What are you muttering to yourself for?

MAGISTRATE. Let him be. He's working out what he can say to please you. I told you he was an honest man.

MAITRE JACQUES. All right Monsieur, since you put it that way, I'll tell you everything. It was your steward that did it.

HARPAGON. Valère?

MAITRE JACQUES. Yes.

HARPAGON. But he seemed so honest.

MAITRE JACQUES. It was him all right.

HARPAGON. What grounds have you got for saying this?

MAITRE JACQUES. What grounds?

HARPAGON. Yes.

MAITRE JACQUES. I mean it's obvious isn't it.

MAGISTRATE. You've got to have better proof than that.

HARPAGON. Have you seen him prowling around the place I put my money?

MAITRE JACQUES. Indeed I have. Where did you put your money?

HARPAGON. In the garden.

MAITRE JACQUES. Exactly so. I've seen him prowling around the garden. And what did you keep the money in?

HARPAGON. A cash box.

MAITRE JACQUES. I knew it. I've seen him prowling around the garden with a cash box.

HARPAGON. This cash box, tell me, what was it like? Then I'll know if it's mine or not.

MAITRE JACQUES. What was it like?

HARPAGON. Yes.

MAITRE JACQUES. Well it was like, it was like . . . you know . . . a cash box.

MAGISTRATE. Yes, we know that. Just give us some sort of description.

MAITRE JACQUES. It was a large one.

HARPAGON. Oh. Mine was small.

MAITRE JACQUES. Yes, well of course it was small if you want to talk about things like size. I was calling it large, not because of its size, but because of the amount of money inside it.

MAGISTRATE. What colour was it?

MAITRE JACQUES. What colour?

MAGISTRATE. Yes.

MAITRE JACQUES. Well it was sort of you know, it's difficult to put; what colour would you say it was?

HARPAGON. Me?

MAITRE JACQUES. Wasn't it red?

HARPAGON. No, it was grey.

MAITRE JACQUES. That's it. That was exactly the word I was looking for. It was a sort of reddish-grey.

HARPAGON. It's mine, there's no doubt about it, that settles it. Take a statement from him. My God you can't trust anybody these days. Nothing's sacred any more. After this, it'll turn out I'm robbing myself.

MAITRE JACQUES. Monsieur, it's him, coming towards us. Please don't give him the slightest hint it was me told you all this.

Enter VALERE.

HARPAGON. Come here. Down on your knees and confess. Confess the blackest deed, the most horrible crime ever committed.

VALERE. What's the matter, Monsieur?

HARPAGON. What, do you not blush at your misdeed?

VALERE. What are you talking about now?

HARPAGON. What am I talking about, infamous creature? As if you didn't know. It's no use feigning ignorance, all has been revealed. I know everything; everything. Oh, how could you? How could you infiltrate yourself into my house expressedly to betray me? How could you deceive me so?

VALERE. Monsieur, since someone has seen fit to tell you everything, I will make no excuses. I stand by all I have done.

MAITRE JACQUES (*aside*). Aha, have I hit the nail on the head without knowing it?

VALERE. I have been intending to talk to you about it all, and I was waiting for more favourable circumstances, but things being as they are, I ask you not to be angry and to hear my reasons.

HARPAGON. Reasons? What reasons can you possibly have, infamous thief?

VALERE. Monsieur, I do not deserve such names. I know I have sinned against you, but, in the end, my fault is pardonable.

HARPAGON. How, pardonable? A blow like this?

VALERE. Please, do not upset yourself. When you have heard what I have to say, you will see that things are not as bad as you think.

HARPAGON. Not as bad as I think? How dare you say such a thing, traitor, viper, villain?

VALERE. Your reputation, Monsieur, is in good hands. My standing in life is such that you cannot be done any harm by what has happened. There is nothing for which I cannot make reparation.

HARPAGON. That's exactly my intention. You will restore everything you have untimely ripped from me.

VALERE. Your honour, Monsieur, will be fully satisfied.

HARPAGON. This isn't a question of honour. But tell me, why did you do it?

VALERE. Alas, you ask me that?

HARPAGON. Yes, I ask you that.

VALERE. For the sake of a God that excuses all he makes us do: Love.

HARPAGON. Love?

VALERE. Yes, love; bitter – honey-sweet love.

HARPAGON. Honey sweet love my foot. You were just after my money.

VALERE. No, Monsieur, it was not your riches that tempted me. Their lustre does not dazzle me. I lay no claims on them, provided you let me have what it is in your power to give.

HARPAGON. I will not, devil take you, I will not. He has the effrontery to ask me to give him the ill gotten gains of his robbery.

VALERE. Do you call it a robbery?

HARPAGON. Of course I call it a robbery. Treasure like that?

VALERE. Treasure indeed, the most precious thing you have, but you would not be losing it in letting me have it. I ask you on bended knees for this charming, beautiful treasure; and if you have any sense of what is right, you will give it to me.

HARPAGON. I will do nothing of the sort. What is all this you're saying?

VALERE. We have promised ourselves to each other, and sworn we will never part.

HARPAGON. Very nice I'm sure.

VALERE. Yes, we have decided we will be together always.

HARPAGON. I'll stop that, I can tell you.

VALERE. Nothing but death can separate us.

HARPAGON. He seems to be obsessed with my money.

VALERE. I've already told you, Monsieur, all that's got nothing to do with it. My feelings do not spring from the well you assume. A more noble motive has inspired this resolution.

HARPAGON. He'll be suggesting he wants my money through Christian charity next, but I'll put an end to that. I will have satisfaction, my man, in the courts.

VALERE. Do as you wish, I will endure anything you care to

impose on me; but I beg you to believe that if there is any fault here it is entirely I who am to be blamed. Your daughter has had nothing to do with it.

HARPAGON. I can well believe that. It would be very strange indeed if my daughter were mixed up in such a crime. But I want to see my property again. Where have you taken my treasure?

VALERE. Me? Nowhere. Your treasure is still in the house.

HARPAGON. Heavens be praised. Not even out of the house?

VALERE. No, Monsieur.

HARPAGON. Er, tell me frankly, you haven't done anything you shouldn't with it have you? Like prising it open?

VALERE. Monsieur, you are mistaken. I am not the sort of person to do that sort of thing. My passion, though burning, is totally pure.

HARPAGON (*aside*). Burning? Burning for my cash box?

VALERE. I would rather die than harbour any offensive thought. My loved one is too honest for that.

HARPAGON (*aside*). My cash box too honest?

VALERE. My desires are restricted to the joy of seeing. Nothing criminal has profaned the emotions that those beautiful eyes have inspired in me.

HARPAGON (*aside*). The beautiful eyes of my cash box? He talks like a lover does of his mistress.

VALERE. Dame Claude, her maid, knows all that has happened, and she can tell you that . . .

HARPAGON. What, one of my servants is an accomplice in this affair?

VALERE. Yes, Monsieur, we had her witness our engagement. When I'd convinced her my intentions were honourable, she helped me persuade your daughter to give me her love and to accept mine.

HARPAGON. What? Has the fear of punishment made him mad? Why are you dragging my daughter into all this?

VALERE. I am telling you, Monsieur, that such was her

innate modesty that I had great difficulty in making her accept my love.

HARPAGON. Whose innate modesty?

VALERE. Your daughter's. It was only yesterday that she finally saw her way to promising she would marry me.

HARPAGON. My daughter has promised to marry you?

VALERE. Yes, Monsieur. And I on my part have promised to marry her.

MAITRE JACQUES (*to* MAGISTRATE). I hope you're getting all this down.

HARPAGON. Truly, troubles do not come alone, but in big battalions. Monsieur, do your duty. I ask you to charge him on my count as a thief and a kidnapper.

VALERE. I should not be called such names. When you know who I am . . .

Enter ELISE, MARIANE *and* FROSINE.

HARPAGON. Ah, wicked, wicked girl. Ah, daughter unworthy of a father like me. Is this how you repay all I have given you? You let yourself fall in love with a wicked thieving man, and promise to marry him without my consent. But I will spike both your plans. You will be confined to the house, and you will hang.

VALERE. You're letting your feelings run away with you. You should at least listen to me before condemning me.

HARPAGON. Hanging's too good for you. You should be broken on a wheel.

ELISE (*on her knees before her father*). Father, dear father, abate your fury a little, I implore you. Do not insist on taking things to the extremes your power as a father allows you. Ameliorate. Be humane. Give yourself some time to think of what you want to do. The man who has offended you is better than you think. If you saw him through my eyes, you would judge him completely differently. You will find it less incomprehensible that I love him when I reveal to you that 'without him you would have lost me some time ago. Yes father, it was he, it was he who saved me from a watery grave; and it is he to whom you owe the life of the oh so unhappy daughter who now implores you . . .

HARPAGON. I don't care. None of this matters. It would have been better he left you to drown than do what he has done.

ELISE. Father, I beseech you, by your love to me as your daughter, do not . . .

HARPAGON. No, no, I will hear no more. Justice will take its course.

MAITRE JACQUES (*aside*). And so, I am revenged for my beating.

FROSINE. Here's a fine state of affairs.

Enter ANSELME.

ANSELME. What is it, Seigneur Harpagon, you seem very upset?

HARPAGON. Ah, Seigneur Anselme, you find me the most unfortunate of men. There are all sorts of complications in the contract you have come to sign. I am attacked on all sides; both my money and my honour. And this is the culprit; a traitor, a scoundrel who has violated the most sacred rights known to man. He has wormed his way into my house disguised as a servant to steal both my cash and my daughter.

VALERE. What's all this fuss you keep on making about your money?

HARPAGON. Yes, these two have promised they will marry each other. You have been insulted, Seigneur Anselme, and you must join with me to bring all possible lawsuits against him to revenge yourself for his insolence.

ANSELME. I wouldn't want to marry by force, or lay claims to a heart that has been given elsewhere; but as for your interests in this affair, I will embrace them as if they were my own.

HARPAGON. This gentleman here is a magistrate, who, from what I can judge, is a master of his profession. Charge him as you see fit, Monsieur, and make things look as black as possible.

VALERE. I cannot see that the passion I hold for your daughter is a crime; and as for the tortures you think I should suffer because of our engagement, when you know who I am . . .

HARPAGON. I've had enough of this; people going around claiming to be God knows who. Impostors, who, taking advantage of their own obscurity, dress themselves in the first noble name they can lay their hands on.

VALERE. I know I have too much integrity to pretend to be something I am not. All Naples can give witness of my birth.

ANSELME. I see. Young man, I advise you to take care in what you are going to say. You've more at risk than you think, for I know Naples very well indeed, and will be able to judge of your claims very easily.

VALERE (*proudly putting on his hat*). I am afraid of nothing. If you know Naples, you will know of Dom Thomas d'Alburcy.

ANSELME. I know him very well. Few people know him better than I do.

HARPAGON. I can't be bothered with Dom Thomases or Dom Martins or whatever.

ANSELME. Please, let him speak. We will hear what he has to say.

VALERE. It was Dom Thomas d'Alburcy brought me into the light of day.

ANSELME. He?

VALERE. Yes.

ANSELME. Come, come, you are mocking us. If you want to save yourself I'd advise you to find some other story. This one will not serve.

VALERE. Be careful of what you say. This is no story. I say nothing I cannot prove.

ANSELME. What? You dare to call yourself the son of Dom Thomas d'Alburcy?

VALERE. Yes, I dare. I will maintain the claim against all comers.

ANSELME. Such bare-faced audacity is truly marvellous. Learn, to your confusion, that at least sixteen years ago the man of whom you speak perished on the sea with his wife and children. They were fleeing the persecutions and disorders that so afflicted Naples at that time and forced so many noble families into exile.

VALERE. Yes, but learn to your confusion, that his son, then aged seven, with a servant, was saved from the shipwreck by a Spanish ship, and it is this son who speaks to you now. The captain of the ship, moved by my misfortune, took pity on me and had me raised as his own son. I showed a natural talent for arms and so was made a soldier. Quite recently I learnt my father was not dead as I had always believed, and I set out to look for him. Passing through this region, a strange turn of events arranged by heaven itself, made me catch sight of Elise. Just one glimpse was enough to make me slave to her captivating beauties. The strength of my passion and the severity of her father made me decide to seek employment in this house, and to entrust to another the quest for my father.

ANSELME. But have you any other proofs, apart from what you've just said, to show this is not a story built up from one fact?

VALERE. The Spanish captain; a ruby signet ring that was my father's; an agate bracelet my mother put on my arm;

and old Pedro, the servant saved with me from the wreck.

MARIANE. He is right. He is no impostor. For, from all you have said, I know you must be my brother.

VALERE. Are you my sister?

MARIANE. I am. My heart was moved the very moment you began to speak. Our mother, whose heart you must soon fill with delight, has told me a thousand times of the misfortunes of our family. Heaven did not let us perish in that shipwreck either, but saved our lives at the expense of our liberty. We were scooped, my mother and I, from that wreckage by some pirates and endured ten years of slavery. Then a happy chance gave us our liberty, and we returned to Naples to find all our property sold, and no news of our father. We moved on to Genoa, where my mother was able to piece together the remains of the money owing to her, but we were forced from there by the unkindness of her relatives. Finally we settled here, where mother is almost overwhelmed by the difficulties of keeping body and soul together.

ANSELME. Oh Heaven, such are the signs of your power. Truly the days of miracles are not passed. Come, embrace me, my children and let us share our joys together.

VALERE. You are our father?

MARIANE. It is you my mother has wept for?

ANSELME. Yes my daughter, yes my son, I am Dom Thomas d'Alburcy who Heaven also protected against the waves, along with all the money I was carrying at the time. I had thought you all dead for sixteen years, and after trying to forget my sorrows by travelling, had decided to marry some gentle, wise girl and finally gain the consolation of a new family. I could see no future for myself in Naples, so renounced that city, and having sold all I had, settled here, under the name of Anselme; a name I had chosen to remove the sad associations the other had for me.

HARPAGON. Is, that, there, your son?

ANSELME. Yes.

HARPAGON. I hold you responsible for the fifteen thousand crowns he has stolen from me.

ANSELME. He has robbed you?

HARPAGON. He has.

VALERE. Who says so?

HARPAGON. Maître Jacques.

MAITRE JACQUES. I'm saying nothing.

HARPAGON. Here is the Magistrate I have brought in to settle the matter.

VALERE. Could you believe me capable of so dastardly an action?

HARPAGON. Capable or not, I want my money back.

Enter CLEANTE *and* LA FLECHE.

CLEANTE. Don't get worked up father. There's no need to accuse anyone of anything. I've got wind of your little misfortune and I've come to say that if you let me marry Mariane, your money will be returned to you.

HARPAGON. Where is it?

CLEANTE. There's no need to worry about that. I know where it is; and it's perfectly safe. Now, you must tell me which you prefer. You can give up Mariane or you can give up your cash box.

HARPAGON. Nothing's been removed?

CLEANTE. Nothing at all. Mariane's mother has let her decide between us, and so all that remains is for you to give your consent.

MARIANE. There is more to it now. Heaven has given me a father and a brother for you to ask consent from as well.

ANSELME. I've not been given back to you, children, so I can cross your wishes. Seigneur Harpagon, you know very well a young girl will prefer the son to the father. Don't make an issue of things; consent with me to these two marriages.

HARPAGON. If I give my consent, I'll get my cash box back?

CLEANTE. You'll get it back safe and sound.

HARPAGON. You realize I can't give my children any money in a marriage settlement?

ANSELME. I have enough for all four. Don't let that stand in your way.

HARPAGON. You'll pay for both ceremonies?

ANSELME. Yes.

HARPAGON. Everything?

ANSELME. Everything. Are you satisfied?

HARPAGON. And you'll buy me a new set of clothes for the occasion?

ANSELME. Agreed. Come and join in the rejoicing of this happy day.

MAGISTRATE. Just one moment gentlemen, just one moment. Who's going to pay my fee?

HARPAGON. But you haven't done anything.

MAGISTRATE. I haven't been standing around here all day for nothing.

HARPAGON. There's a man you can hang for your pains.

MAITRE JACQUES. What can I do? If I tell the truth they beat me and they hang me for lying.

ANSELME. Seigneur Harpagon, you must forgive him.

HARPAGON. You'll pay the Magistrate.

ANSELME. I will. Now let us go and share our joy with your mother.

HARPAGON. And I, I will share my joy with my beloved cash box.

The Hypochondriac

Comedy-Ballet in Three Acts

Translated into English prose by Alan Drury

CHARACTERS

ARGAN
BELINE, his wife
ANGELIQUE, his daughter
LOUISON, his younger daughter
BERALDE, his brother
CLEANTE
DIAFOIRUS SENIOR
THOMAS DIAFOIRUS
M. PURGON
M. FLEURANT
NOTARY
TOINETTE

PLAYERS (*at least four men and two women*)
AUNT
THE WATCH
BYSTANDERS *etc.*

There are two locations: ARGAN's *study and the street.*

Translator's note: The Prologue, Interludes and Epilogue have been devised in parallel to Molière's rather than being a direct translation.

This translation was commissioned by and first produced in the Olivier auditorium of the National Theatre, London, on 22 October 1981.

PROLOGUE

A Street.
At the five minute call, and as the audience are still taking their seats, build up the feeling of a seventeenth-century French provincial carnival, using whatever company resources and skills are at hand. SPECTATORS *gather and watch.*
House lights down. Enter a troupe of PLAYERS, *preferably on a cart. They include a* SHEPERDESS *and* PUNCHINELLO. *The troupe's leader (later to be revealed as* MOLIERE) *makes the three raps on the floor of the cart using his stick.*

SHEPHERDESS (*sings*).
  Doctors, your learning is purely illusion,
  Your remedies rubbish, your order confusion;
  Your big latin words are unable to cure
  This sickening sadness I have to endure.
  So from my sorrow one thing is sure;
  Doctors, your learning is simply absurd.

  What do you know of day to day lives?
  Of husbands, of lovers, of daughters, of wives?
  Of meeting, of parting, a passionate look;
  A vow made for ever and later forsook?
  You never lift your eyes from your book.
  Doctors, your learning is simply absurd.

  Your magic mixtures charm the crowd.
  To you all secrets are allowed,
  But you all true knowledge lack.
  You are just a squawking quack.
  Curing the Hypochondriac.
  Doctors, your learning is simply absurd.

The PLAYERS *come down from the cart and dance with the* SPECTATORS. PUNCHINELLO *tries to persuade a young lady (whom we later know to be* ANGELIQUE*) to dance with him. She is frightened and tries to hide behind her* AUNT *and a serving maid (*TOINETTE*).* PUNCHINELLO *pursues her. A young man (*CLEANTE*) comes to her aid and drives* PUNCHINELLO *off.* CLEANTE *and* ANGELIQUE *gaze transfixed into each other's eyes for the rest of the Prologue.* PUNCHINELLO *mocks them.*

The dance ends and the PLAYERS *return to the cart,* MOLIERE *having to drag* PUNCHINELLO *back.*

SHEPHERDESS (*sings*).
   Doctors, your learning is purely illusion,
   Your remedies rubbish, your orders confusion;
   Your big latin words are unable to cure
   This sickening sadness I have to endure.
   So from my sorrow one thing is sure;
   Doctors, your learning is simply absurd.

Throughout this verse, ANGELIQUE *and* CLEANTE *have continued gazing at each other. The* PLAYERS *leave, followed by the* SPECTATORS.

ANGELIQUE *and* CLEANTE *remain. The* AUNT *and* TOINETTE *lead* ANGELIQUE *away.*

ANGELIQUE *and* CLEANTE *go off at opposite sides of the stage, still looking at each other.*

Act One

ARGAN'S *study.* ARGAN, *alone, sitting at a table with his bills, shifting counters from pile to pile. He is doing his accounts.*

ARGAN. Three and two makes five, and five makes ten, and ten makes twenty. Three and two makes five. That's twenty-five francs. Now, what have we here? (*He refers to a paper.*)
'The twenty-fourth. A minor insinuative and emollient enema to soften, moisten and refresh Monsieur's bowels.' What I like about Monsieur Fleurant, my apothecary, is that his bills are always so tactfully phrased. 'To soften, moisten and refresh Monsieur's bowels. One and a half francs.' But, Monsieur Fleurant, tact isn't everything. You mustn't fleece us invalids. One and a half francs for an enema? I'm your obedient servant, but we've had words about this before. You charged one franc last time, and when an apothecary says one franc, he really means a half. There we are then, half a franc.
'On the aforementioned day, a good evacuative enema prepared from mel rosatum, diacatholican', honey, it's all honey, 'rhubarb and etc. as per prescription to flush, wash and brush up Monsieur's lower abdomen. One and a half francs.' By your leave, three quarters.
'On the evening of the aforementioned day, an hepatic, soporific and somniferous,' somniferous? 'sedative to make Monsieur sleep.' Oh, somniferous. 'One and a half francs.' And very good it was too; I slept like a log. Three quarters.
'The twenty-fifth. A purgative and fortifying philtre prepared from cinnamon, oriental sennapods and etc, under Monsieur Purgon's instructions to expel and

evacuate Monsieur's bile. Four francs.'. So, Monsieur Fleurant, is this your idea of a joke? You've got to play fair with us invalids. Monsieur Purgon didn't instruct you to charge four francs. We'll call it three. After all, he is a specialist.

'On the afternoon of the aforementioned day, an astringent anodyne to assist Monsieur to relax. One and a half francs.' Good, three quarters.

'The twenty-sixth. An exhalatory enema to expel Monsieur's flatulence. One and a half francs.' Three quarters.

'An additional draft of the anodyne Monsieur asked for the anterior afternoon. One and a half francs.' We'll call it a half; it was a repeat order.

'The twenty-seventh. A mollifying mixture to ameliorate Monsieur's *mauvaises humeurs*.' To ameliorate Monsieur's mauvaises humeurs. There's tact for you. 'Three francs.' We'll call that one and a half; I'm glad to see you're being so reasonable.

'The twenty-eighth. A measure of clarified and sweetened whey to assuage, blend, temper and refresh Monsieur's blood. One franc.' Half.

'A pleasant and preservative potion, prepared from twelve grains of bezoar,' that's a fatty growth on the inside of cows' stomachs that ... no, I don't think I want to think about that, 'syrup of lemon, pomegranate and etc. as per prescription. Five francs.' Now, now, Monsieur Fleurant, hold on a minute, if you please. If one is to be treated in this manner, one will no longer wish to be ill. Content yourself with two and a half. Now let's see, that's twenty-five francs and ... (*He adds up the piles of counters.*) That makes thirty-six and a half francs in all. Now, where are we? This month I've taken one, two, three, four, five, six, seven, eight different types of medicine and had, one, two, three, four, five, six, seven, eight, nine, ten, eleven, twelve enemas; whereas last month I took twelve medicines and had twenty enemas. No wonder I've not been feeling so good this month as I did last. I'll have to have a word with Monsieur Purgon, so he can take the matter in hand. Will someone take all this away?

Slight pause.

Is there anybody there?

Slight pause.

It's incredible. Why is there never a servant when you want one? As soon as you turn your back they vanish into thin air.

He rings a small handbell.

Nothing. This thing's not loud enough.

He rings it again.

Absolutely nothing doing.

He rings it again.

They've all gone deaf. Toinette.

He rings it again.

I don't know why I bother. Where's the stupid bitch got to?

He rings it again.

I am beginning to get angry.

He throws the bell to one side and calls out instead of ringing it.

Ting a ling a ling. Devil take the lot of them. Ting a ling a ling. How can they leave a poor sick man like me all by myself all alone? Ting a ling a ling. It's enough to make you weep. Ting a ling a ling. My God, they're going to leave me here to die. Ting a ling a ling.

Enter TOINETTE.

TOINETTE. I'm coming.

ARGAN. Well, baggage, and what have you got to say for yourself?

TOINETTE *pretends to have knocked her head.*

TOINETTE. Can't wait a minute, can you. You chivvy people about so much I've caught my head on the shutter.

ARGAN. You can't trust anyone . . .

TOINETTE. Ah, ah . . .

ARGAN. I've been . . .

TOINETTE. My head, my head . . .

ARGAN. I have been left here . . .

TOINETTE. Ah, the pain, the pain . . .

ARGAN. For a whole hour, and nobody . . .

TOINETTE. I'm in agony.

ARGAN. For God's sake, slut, shut up. How can I tell you off if you won't be quiet?

TOINETTE. How very nice, after what I've done to myself.

ARGAN. You're giving me a sore throat, making me shout like this.

TOINETTE. And you've made me bang my head. Fair exchange is no robbery.

ARGAN. How dare you talk to me in that . . .

TOINETTE. If you're going to make a scene, I'll cry.

ARGAN. Leaving me all alone, an invalid like . . .

TOINETTE. I said I'm going to cry.

ARGAN. I will not be treated like this.

TOINETTE (*cries*). Waaaaaaa . . .

ARGAN. Will. You. Be. Quiet.

Slight pause.

So, yet again, you will not allow me to reprimand you.

TOINETTE. You can reprimand 'til the cows come home. See if I care.

ARGAN. I can't, can I. You keep on interrupting me.

TOINETTE. You want to have fun telling me off and I want to have fun crying. Each to his own. It isn't much to ask. Waaaaa . . .

ARGAN. All right, all right. I see I've no choice but to let the matter go. Now, would you kindly take all this away, baggage, if it isn't too much trouble. (*Gets up out of his chair.*) Today's enema; has it done the trick?

TOINETTE. Done the trick?

ARGAN. Yes. Have I voided much bile?

TOINETTE. Don't ask me. It's up to Monsieur Fleurant to poke his nose into all that business. After all, he gets paid for it.

ARGAN. Make sure the boiling water is ready for the next one. I shall have to take it soon.

TOINETTE. That nice Monsieur Fleurant and that nice Monsieur Purgon are having a high old time with your body. They're milking you dry. I'd like to ask them exactly what's wrong with you, you have to take so much stuff.

ARGAN. Silence, you ignorant trollope. It is not for the likes of you to tamper with the Dictates of Medicine. Go and get Angélique, my daughter. I've something I want to tell her.

TOINETTE. She's coming anyway; she must be psychic.

Enter ANGELIQUE.

ARGAN. Angélique, my girl, you couldn't have met your old father at a better moment. There's something I want to have a little chat about.

ANGELIQUE. What is it, Father?

ARGAN. Wait there. Where's my stick? I'll be back in a minute.

Exit ARGAN, *hastily.*

TOINETTE. Faster, M'sieur, faster. My word, Monsieur Fleurant is keeping him busy.

ANGELIQUE. Toinette.

TOINETTE. Yes?

ANGELIQUE. Look into my eyes.

TOINETTE. All right then.

ANGELIQUE. Ah me.

TOINETTE. What do you mean, 'Ah me'?

ANGELIQUE. Can't you guess what I want to talk about?

TOINETTE. Oh that; it's obvious. It's your young man. The conversation's been about nothing else for the last six days. You look distinctly peaky if you can't talk about him all the time.

ANGELIQUE. If you knew, why didn't you engage me in conversation first and spare me the anguish of broaching the subject?

TOINETTE. You didn't give me the time. You go on about him so much I can't get a word in edgeways.

ANGELIQUE. I admit I cannot stop talking about him. My heart thrills each time I unburden its inmost secrets to you. Tell me, do you condemn the sentiments I harbour towards him?

TOINETTE. Me? Far from it.

ANGELIQUE. Am I wrong to abandon myself to such sweet rapture?

TOINETTE. No, I wouldn't say that.

ANGELIQUE. Should I remain forever insensible to his tender

protestations of the ardent passion he holds towards me?

TOINETTE. Heaven forfend.

ANGELIQUE. Tell me honestly, Toinette, do you not find, as I do, some mark of Providence, the stamp of Destiny in our unexpected meeting?

TOINETTE. Yes.

ANGELIQUE. Do you not find that his rushing to my defence, without even knowing me, was the action of a true man of honour?

TOINETTE. Yes.

ANGELIQUE. That no-one could have behaved more generously?

TOINETTE. Agreed.

ANGELIQUE. And that he has done everything in the most charming manner?

TOINETTE. Oh yes.

ANGELIQUE. Do you not find, Toinette, that he is extremely well . . . formed?

TOINETTE. Very much so.

ANGELIQUE. That his general demeanour has a certain . . . *je ne sais quoi*?

TOINETTE. No doubt about it.

ANGELIQUE. That his conversation, his very actions have a touch of the nobility about them?

TOINETTE. Absolutely.

ANGELIQUE. That no-one has ever heard anything more passionate than the things he says to me?

TOINETTE. True enough.

ANGELIQUE. And that there is nothing more infuriating than the constraint under which I am held; a constraint that prevents the exchange of those tender transports of mutual ardour the heavens inspire in us?

TOINETTE. You're right there.

ANGELIQUE. But, my dear Toinette, do you think he loves me as much as he says?

TOINETTE. Ah well, you've got to be a little bit careful with all this sort of thing. It's easy enough to act being in love, and I've seen some performers in my time, I can tell you.

ANGELIQUE. Toinette, what are you saying? Can it be possible, after all he has said, that he is not telling me the truth?

TOINETTE. You'll soon find out. This scheme of his to ask for your hand in marriage will prove it one way or the other. Either he will, or he won't. Whatever happens, we'll see if he's telling the truth or not.

ANGELIQUE. Toinette, if he's been deceiving me, I shall never believe another man as long as I live.

TOINETTE. Oh look, here's your father.

Enter ARGAN. *He sits in his chair.*

ARGAN. Now my girl, I've got some news for you that may come as a bit of a surprise. A certain someone's asked for your hand in marriage. What is it? You're laughing. Yes, it's a lovely word marriage. Young girls like nothing better. Ah youth, youth. At least I shan't have to force you into it.

ANGELIQUE. I am happy, Father, to do whatever you instruct me.

ARGAN. And I am happy to have such a dutiful daughter. Anyway, it's all arranged; I've accepted on your behalf.

ANGELIQUE. I have no greater pleasure in life, Father, than blindly to obey your commands.

ARGAN. My wife, your step-mother, thinks I should put you in a convent. She thinks the same about your little sister, Louison, as well. She seems quite set on the idea.

TOINETTE (*aside*). The old bag has her reasons?

ARGAN. She won't like this marriage one little bit, but as I said, I've given my word.

ANGELIQUE. Father, how shall I ever thank you for your kindness?

TOINETTE. Really, M'sieur, even I must give you credit for this. It's the best thing you've ever done.

ARGAN. I've not yet seen the party concerned, but they tell me I shall be perfectly satisfied, and so shall you.

ANGELIQUE. I am certain of it, Father.

ARGAN. What do you mean, you're certain of it? Have you seen him?

ANGELIQUE. Your decision enables me to reveal my inmost heart to you. But six days ago, Fate crossed our paths and made us acquainted. The request that has been made to you is but a natural result of those feelings which, from that very first sight, we have harboured towards each other.

ARGAN. Nobody told me. Anyway, I'm very pleased, and it just goes to show how things turn out for the best in the end. They tell me he's a strapping young lad.

ANGELIQUE. Yes.

ARGAN. Well-built.

ANGELIQUE. Oh yes.

ARGAN. Charming way with him.

ANGELIQUE. Absolutely.

ARGAN. Handsome face.

ANGELIQUE. Very handsome.

ARGAN. Straight out of the top drawer.

ANGELIQUE. The very best.

ARGAN. In fact quite the perfect gentleman.

ANGELIQUE. The most perfect gentleman in the world.

ARGAN. Speaks good Latin and Greek.

ANGELIQUE. I didn't know that.

ARGAN. And he'll be a fully fledged doctor in three days' time.

ANGELIQUE. What?

ARGAN. And he'll be a fully fledged doctor in three days' time.

ANGELIQUE. He will?

ARGAN. Yes. Didn't he tell you?

ANGELIQUE. No, he's never mentioned it. Who told you?

ARGAN. Monsieur Purgon.

ANGELIQUE. Does Monsieur Purgon know him?

ARGAN. Does Monsieur Purgon know him? Ask a silly question ... Of course he knows him; he's his nephew.

ANGELIQUE. Cléante is Monsieur Purgon's nephew?

ARGAN. Cléante, Cléante, who's this Cléante? We're talking about the man who's asked for your hand in marriage.

ANGELIQUE. Yes, of course.

ARGAN. Good. It's Monsieur Purgon's nephew. Neph-ew. He's the son of Monsieur Purgon's brother-in-law; Monsieur Diafoirus the doctor. He's called Thomas, not Cléante. The three of us, Monsieur Purgon, Monsieur Fleurant and me, arranged the marriage this morning, and tomorrow morning my son-in-law to be is being brought round to see me by his father. What's the matter with you? You're looking totally thunderstruck.

ANGELIQUE. Father, I have just realized we have been talking about two completely different people.

TOINETTE. What are you up to? Is this some kind of practical joke? The money you've got, and you want to marry your daughter off to a doctor?

ARGAN. Yes, I do. What've you stuck your oar in for, impudent baggage!

TOINETTE. All right, calm down. There's no need to fly off the handle. Why can't we have a nice quiet rational conversation once in a while? Let's discuss it calmly. What is your reason, if you don't mind me asking, for such a match?

ARGAN. It's quite simple. My state of health being what it is, I want to have doctors in the family so they're always on tap. For consultations, prescriptions, the making up of medicines.

TOINETTE. Well I suppose that's a reason. Isn't it nice to be talking civilly to each other, for a change? But M'sieur, answer me with your hand on your heart, are you really ill?

ARGAN. Really ill, me? You ask me if I'm really ill? How dare you have the impudence to suggest . . .

TOINETTE. Yes, yes, all right, all right, you're ill. Let's not quarrel about it. You are very ill indeed. I totally agree with you. In fact you're sicker than you think. But your daughter should marry for her own sake. She's not ill, so there's no need for her to marry a doctor.

ARGAN. The doctor's for my benefit, not hers. Any daughter with a drop of natural feeling in her would be overjoyed to marry someone who'll look after her father's health.

TOINETTE. M'sieur, will you take a bit of advice from an old friend?

ARGAN. What sort of advice?

TOINETTE. Put this marriage completely out of your head.

ARGAN. And your reason?

TOINETTE. My reason is your daughter won't be doing with it.

ARGAN. She won't be doing with it?

TOINETTE. She will not.

ARGAN. My daughter?

TOINETTE. Your daughter. She'll tell you she'll have nothing to do with this Monsieur Diafoirus, nor with his son, Thomas Diafoirus, nor with all the Diafoiri in the world.

ARGAN. But you don't know what I know. There's more to this match than meets the eye. Monsieur Diafoirus has only got one son, so he'll inherit the lot, and better still, Monsieur Purgon, who has neither wife nor child, will settle all his income on his nephew in honour of the marriage, and Monsieur Purgon is worth eight thousand francs a year.

TOINETTE. Eight thousand?

ARGAN. Eight thousand.

TOINETTE. He must have killed that many to get it.

ARGAN. And eight thousand is quite something, even without taking into account what the father's worth.

TOINETTE. M'sieur, that's all well and good, but I must keep coming back to the point at issue. Between you and me, I advise you to choose her another husband. She's just not cut out to be Madame Diafoirus.

ARGAN. I insist on it.

TOINETTE. Oh come now, don't say that.

ARGAN. What? You're saying I shouldn't say that?

TOINETTE. No . . . I mean yes.

ARGAN. And why shouldn't I say it?

TOINETTE. People will say you don't know what you're saying if you say that.

ARGAN. They can say what they want. I have given my word and my word is my bond.

TOINETTE. She won't do it.

ARGAN. I'll force her to.

TOINETTE. She won't do it I tell you.

ARGAN. She will do it, or I'll put her in a convent.

TOINETTE. You?

ARGAN. Me.

TOINETTE. You?

ARGAN. What do you mean, me?

TOINETTE. You'll never put her in a convent.

ARGAN. I'll never put her in a convent?

TOINETTE. No.

ARGAN. Oh yes I will.

TOINETTE. Oh no you won't.

ARGAN. Oh yes I will.

TOINETTE. Oh no you won't.

ARGAN. Oh no? That's nice. I won't put my own daughter in a convent if I want to?

TOINETTE. I'm telling you, you won't.

ARGAN. And who'll stop me?

TOINETTE. You will.

ARGAN. I will?

TOINETTE. Yes. You won't have the heart.

ARGAN. I'll have the heart all right.

TOINETTE. Pull the other one.

ARGAN. What do you mean?

TOINETTE. Fatherly feelings will hold you back.

ARGAN. No they won't.

TOINETTE. A tiny tear or two; two tiny arms thrown around your neck; a tiny voice whispering 'my dearest little papa' oh so tenderly; that's all it will take to change your mind.

ARGAN. All that will have no effect whatsoever.

TOINETTE. Yes it will.

ARGAN. It won't touch me in the least.

TOINETTE. Fiddlesticks.

ARGAN. Don't you say fiddlesticks to me.

TOINETTE. I can read you like a book. You are naturally good.

ARGAN (*angrily*). I am not naturally good. I can be absolutely horrid when I want to.

TOINETTE. Calm down, M'sieur, you're forgetting you're ill.

ARGAN. I absolutely command her to take the husband I decide.

TOINETTE. And I absolutely forbid her to do it.

ARGAN. So that's the way things are. How dare a slut of a servant talk like this in front of her master?

TOINETTE. When her master doesn't know what he's doing, it's her duty to put him right.

ARGAN *pursues* TOINETTE *round and round the chair, brandishing his stick.*

ARGAN. Oh, hoity-toity. I'll soon beat that out of you.

TOINETTE. I won't let you make a fool of yourself.

ARGAN. Come here; I'll teach you to answer back.

TOINETTE. You'll be an absolute laughing stock.

ARGAN. Hussy.

TOINETTE. I'll never consent to this marriage.

ARGAN. Harpy.

TOINETTE. I don't want her to marry Thomas Diafoirus.

ARGAN. Harlot.

TOINETTE. And she'll do what I say, not you.

ARGAN. Angélique, stop that slut.

ANGELIQUE. Father, you'll only make yourself ill.

ARGAN. Do as I say, or never darken my door again.

TOINETTE. And I'll cut her off without a penny if she does.

ARGAN (*flings himself into his chair*). I've had enough. All this will kill me.

Enter BELINE.

ARGAN. Wife, come over here.

BELINE. What's the matter, husband of mine?

ARGAN. I need your help.

BELINE. What's the matter with Mummy's little boy?

ARGAN. Light of my life.

BELINE. My angel.

ARGAN. Someone has been getting me into a state.

BELINE. My poor little hubby. Why don't you tell wifey?

ARGAN. Your Toinette is being even more insolent than ever.

BELINE. Now you mustn't upset yourself.

ARGAN. But sweetheart, she's made me go and get all angry.

BELINE. Then we shall have to calm you down again.

ARGAN. She's been thwarting me for a whole hour.

BELINE. There, there; there, there.

ARGAN. And she's the effrontery to say I'm not really ill.

BELINE. Now that is pushing it a bit far.

ARGAN. You know, dear heart, how it is.

BELINE. Yes, dear heart. She's definitely in the wrong.

ARGAN. Sweetheart, she'll be the death of me.

BELINE. Mummy kiss it better?

ARGAN. She's churning me up; no wonder I'm having all this bile trouble.

BELINE. You mustn't get yourself worked up so.

ARGAN. And I've told you to get rid of her I don't know how many times.

BELINE. Mummy's little boy knows no servants are perfect. Mummy's little boy will just have to put up with their bad points on account of their good. Toinette knows her job; she's hard-working and above all faithful; and Mummy's little boy knows he's got to be very careful about who he takes on these days. Toinette, come here.

TOINETTE. Madame?

BELINE. Have you been upsetting my husband?

TOINETTE (*sweetness and light*). Me, Madame? I don't know what you mean. I wouldn't dream of crossing M'sieur in anything.

ARGAN. She's lying.

TOINETTE. He told me he was marrying his daughter to young Thomas Diafoirus. I told him that although it would be a good match, she'd be better off in a convent.

BELINE. There's no great harm in that, and I happen to think she's right.

ARGAN. Darling, you believe her? She's an impudent trollop. I can't tell you how often she's been rude to me.

BELINE. Don't worry, Mummy believes you. There, there, compose yourself. Now listen here Toinette, if you ever upset my husband again, you're out, sharpish, understand? Now give me his fur cloak and his pillows so I can settle him in his chair. You're all skew-wiff. Pull your night-cap down; you'll catch your death if you get a draft in your ears.

ARGAN. You're my only friend. You're so good to me.

BELINE *arranges the pillows round* ARGAN.

BELINE. This little pillow goes down on your left
And this little pillow goes down on your right,
And this little pillow goes under your head,
And this little pillow. . . .
TOINETTE. . . . shuts out the light.

> *She rams the pillow over his face.* ARGAN *leaps up and throws all the pillows at* TOINETTE.

ARGAN. What, slut, do you want to smother me?

> *Exeunt* TOINETTE *and* ANGELIQUE.

BELINE. What's all this then?

> ARGAN, *out of breath, flings himself back in his chair.*

ARGAN. Ah, ah, ah, I can't take any more.
BELINE. What are you getting so worked up about? She was only doing her best.
ARGAN. Darling, you cannot imagine how malicious that wretch can be. She's quite put me out. It's going to take at least eight different medicines and twelve enemas before I feel all right again.
BELINE. There, there, my baby; calm down, calm down.
ARGAN. My sweetheart, you're the only thing I've got in the whole wide world.
BELINE. Mummy's little boy.
ARGAN. My dearest darling, in recognition of how much you love me, I wish, dear heart, as I've said before, to alter my will.
BELINE. No, no, don't let's talk about it, I beg you; I

can't abide even to think of it. Even the very word, will, makes me quiver with grief.

ARGAN. Have you talked it over with your notary, as I asked?

BELINE. As it happens, he's waiting outside.

ARGAN. Let me see him, my love.

BELINE. Alas, when one is as much in love as I with you, my husband, all this scarcely bears thinking of.

Enter NOTARY.

ARGAN. Come here, Monsieur de Bonnefoi, come here. Take a pew. My wife tells me, Monsieur, that you're an honest fellow and quite one of her friends, so I've asked her to have a few words with you about some changes I want to make to my will.

BELINE. Alas, I cannot bear to hear such things mentioned.

NOTARY. She has, Monsieur, explained your wishes and the intentions you have towards her, but I am obliged to advise you that you will be unable to leave anything to your wife in your will.

ARGAN. Why's that?

NOTARY. As you know, the law is an accumulation of precedent, and precedent is against it, and where precedent stands we mere mortals must bow. Even if you tried it, the dispensation would be rendered null and void. The advantages a man and a woman conjoined in marriage bestow upon each other are a mutual gift for their lifetimes only; and for the relict to inherit there must be no children, that is of either of the conjoined parties, at the time of the decease of the first party.

ARGAN. You mean it all has to go to my children and my wife gets nothing?

NOTARY. Exactly.

ARGAN. If a husband cannot leave anything to the wife he loves so tenderly, to the wife who has taken such great care of him, then precedent's an ass. I'll have to consult my lawyer to see what I can do.

NOTARY. I wouldn't advise that. Lawyers are usually very pernickety about the above mentioned matters, imagining it a great crime to dispose of anything contrary to the Dictates of the Law. They make mountains out of mole-hills, and know nothing of those byways down which our all too natural feelings must at times lead us. No, there are certain other people you can consult who will be much more accommodating; people expert in using expediency to trip lightly past the law, making the illegal legal; people who know how to smooth out all difficulties and to find the means to elude precedent via some indirect ways or other. Without these people, where would we be? There must be ways round everything, otherwise nothing would get done and my humble profession would go to the dogs.

ARGAN. My wife was quite right, Monsieur, when she told me you were an ... ingenious man. What must I do to give her my estate and frustrate my children's expectations?

NOTARY. What must you do? First, you must secretly choose one of your wife's closest friends and bequeath him without arousing any suspicion, as much as you can ...

ARGAN. But ...

NOTARY. And he, at the end of the day, will give it all back to her. Then, without arousing any suspicion, make out a large number of bills of credit to various persons ...

ARGAN. But ...

NOTARY. And they, at the end of the day, will sign them over to your wife. You must also, while you're still with us, give her ready money and bills which, without arousing any suspicion, you have made payable to the bearer.

BELINE. Do not torment yourself with this. If my little

boy were taken from me, I would no longer linger in this cruel, cruel world.

ARGAN. My darling.

BELINE. Yes, my pet, if I were so unfortunate as to lose you . . .

ARGAN. My better half.

BELINE. Life, to me, would be as naught . . .

ARGAN. My love.

BELINE. And I would follow in your footsteps so you would know how much I love you.

ARGAN. My dear, you break my heart. Console yourself, I pray you.

NOTARY. These tears are untimely. Things have not come to that.

ARGAN. If I should die, my only regret would be you not having a child. Monsieur Purgon tells me he can fix it for me somehow.

NOTARY. Everything can be fixed, eventually.

ARGAN. I shall have to make my will, my love, the way Monsieur tells me to; but to be on the safe side, I'm going to give you twenty thousand francs in gold I have behind a secret panel next to my bed, and two bills payable to the bearer, one from Monsieur Damon and one from Monsieur Gérante.

BELINE. No, no, I'll have none of it. How much did you say was behind the secret panel?

ARGAN. Twenty thousand francs, my love.

BELINE. Do not talk to me of riches, I pray you. How much are those two bills worth?

ARGAN. One is worth, my love, four thousand francs and the other six thousand.

BELINE. All the riches in the world, my love, are dross compared to thee.

NOTARY. Shall we proceed with this will?

ARGAN. Yes Monsieur, but we would be better off in my

closet. My love, conduct me, I pray you.

BELINE. Come, my poor little boy.

Exeunt ARGON, BELINE *and* NOTARY. *Enter* ANGELIQUE *and* TOINETTE.)

TOINETTE. They've got a notary and they were talking about a will. Your stepmother doesn't waste time. No doubt she's hatching some plot against you to try on your father.

ANGELIQUE. He can squander his wealth according to his whim provided he leaves my heart to me. Ah my trembling heart; Toinette, do you see how they torture it? Do not abandon me, I beg you, in this extremity.

TOINETTE. I, abandon you? I'd sooner perish. But, to serve you to the best advantage, I shall conceal my affection towards you, and pretend to be party to your father's and step-mother's schemes.

ANGELIQUE. Try, I beseech you, to inform Cléante of the marriage they have arranged for me.

TOINETTE. I shall, I will.

BELINE (*off*). Toinette.

TOINETTE. But soft, someone calls. Goodnight. You can rely on me.

Exeunt severally.

First Interlude

A street. Mid-carnival. A string of dancers, led by the SHEP-HERDESS, *cross the stage. Enter* CLEANTE *and* MUSICIANS.

CLEANTE. Oh love, love, love, love. Cléante, what passion possesses you? You do not sleep, you do not eat, and you do not drink, well hardly. You abandon your friends, and let everything go to ruin. And for what? You, who were the first to ridicule those in love; smile at their sighs and mock at their moans; are now in knee-deep, and are come, in the carnival, in the middle of the night, to serenade your mistress. What a falling off is here. But, if one wishes to love, one needs must be mad like the rest of them. There is nothing more touching than a lover pouring out his sorrows to his mistress' front door, sobbing to the hinges and bewailing his fate to the bolts. These fellows shall accompany me. Oh night, sweet night, waft my amorous plaints even to the bed of my mistress.

> *(Sings).* Notte e di v'amo e v'adoro
> Cerco un si per mio ristoro;
> Ma se voi dite di no,
> Bell' ingrata, io moriro.

DRUNKEN REVELLERS *pass singing raucously, and interrupt them.*

PUNCHINELLO *has come on. He follows* CLEANTE *around, mocking him silently.*

CLEANTE (*sings*). Fra la speranza
     S'afflige il cuore,
     In lontananza
     Consuma l'hore;
     Si dolce inganno
     Che mi figura
     Breve l'affanno,
     Ahi! troppo dura.
    Cosi per tropp'amar languisco e muoro.

    Notte e di v'amo e v'adoro etc.

BELINE, *with mask in front of her face, has come out onto the balcony.* CLEANTE *gestures, in mid line, for the* MUSICIANS *to stop.* PUNCHINELLO *reacts throughout ad lib, but silently.*

CLEANTE. Leave us a while.

The MUSICIANS *wander off a bit.*

CLEANTE. Fair one, let me see your face.

BELINE. My husband is asleep. Come up and talk a little, then I will remove my mask.

CLEANTE (*aside*). Oh heavens, it is not Angélique. It is . . . someone else.

BELINE. Monsieur, you have rekindled romance in the heart of one who thought it gone for ever.

CLEANTE. Madame, I am mistaken.

BELINE. I think not.

CLEANTE. I fear I have the wrong house. My apologies. Farewell.

  CLEANTE *retreats in confusion and collides with* PUNCHINELLO. *He tries to move off, but* PUNCHINELLO *dodges round, blocking his way.*

BELINE (*meanwhile*). The wrong house. So much for the licence of carnival. I shall to bed and dream for another year.

The string of dancers, lead by the SHEPHERDESS, *thread their way back again.*

CLEANTE (*to* PUNCHINELLO). Let me through, you oaf.

PUNCHINELLO *bites his thumb at him.*

CLEANTE. You bite your thumb at me.
CLEANTE *pushes* PUNCHINELLO *aside. He collides with the* SHEPHERDESS. *The string of dancers collapse domino fashion. The male dancers attack* PUNCHINELLO *and each other.* PUNCHINELLO *tries to put the blame on* CLEANTE *and draws him into it. A full-scale brawl develops.*
TOILETTE *and the* AUNT *dash out. The* AUNT *lays about people with a frying pan.* TOINETTE *grabs* CLEANTE *and tells him in mime in midst fight about* ANGELIQUE's *wedding. They go off severally. With much blowing of whistles the* WATCH *arrives. If the* MUSICIANS *have not been playing, they start now to accompany: the* WATCH *chasing* PUNCHINELLO *and the assembled company. The traditional number, including the mad dash through the auditorium. Finally* PUNCHINELLO *is caught and carried off to an ensemble reprise of the song.*

Act Two

ARGAN's *study. Enter* TOINETTE *and* CLEANTE *severally.*

TOINETTE. What do you want, Monsieur?

CLEANTE. What do I want?

TOINETTE. Good heavens, it's you. What a surprise. What are you doing here?

CLEANTE. I have come to learn my Destiny; to converse with the admirable Angélique, to learn the inmost secrets of her heart, and to ask her intentions concerning this fateful marriage of which you have warned me.

TOINETTE. Yes, but you can't talk to her just like that. You're going to have to use some kind of subterfuge. You know how she's kept on a tight rein the entire time; how she is allowed neither to go out nor talk to anyone. It was only because an old aunt took a fancy to see those players your love had an opportunity to bloom in the first place; and we're taking good care not to mention that to anybody.

CLEANTE. Exactly. I am not here as Cléante, her suitor, but as a friend of her music master, for whom I am deputising.

TOINETTE. Here's her father. Go over there a bit, and let me tell him you're here.

Enter ARGAN.

ARGAN. Monsieur Purgon has told me to walk from wall to wall of my room twelve times every morning, but I've forgotten to ask him if he meant lengthways or breadthways.

TOINETTE. M'sieur, there's a . . .

ARGAN. Quieter, woman; you'll scramble my brains, like eggs. Has nobody ever told you you must never shout at the sick?

TOINETTE. All I wanted to tell you, M'sieur, was that . . .

ARGAN. Quieter, quieter.

TOINETTE. M'sieur . . . (*She pretends to speak.*)

ARGAN. Eh?

TOINETTE. I said . . . (*She pretends to speak.*)

ARGAN. What's that you said?

TOINETTE (*shouts*). There's a man outside wants to see you.

ARGAN (*shouts*). All right. (*Normal.*) Show him in then.

TOINETTE *makes a sign for* CLEANTE *to advance.*

CLEANTE. Monsieur . . .

TOINETTE. Lower your voice. You'll scramble M'sieur's brains, like eggs.

CLEANTE. Monsieur, I am happy to find you up and about, and to see that you are better.

TOINETTE. Better? What do you mean, better? Nothing could be further from the truth. M'sieur is always ill.

CLEANTE. I was told Monsieur was better; indeed, he's looking well.

TOINETTE. Well? What do you mean well? M'sieur looks terrible. Whoever said he was better didn't know what he was talking about. He's never had it so bad.

ARGAN. She's right, you know.

TOINETTE. He may walk, sleep, eat and drink like everyone else, but that doesn't mean to say he isn't very ill.

ARGAN. How very true.

CLEANTE. Monsieur, you have my condolences. I come on behalf of Mademoiselle, your daughter's, singing teacher. He's had to go to the country for a few days, and, as I'm a close friend, he's sent me instead. He doesn't want to interrupt the lessons for fear Mademoiselle might forget what she knows.

ARGAN. Very good. Call Angélique.

TOINETTE. Wouldn't it be better, M'sieur, for me to take the gentleman to her room?

ARGAN. No, she can come here.

TOINETTE. He won't be able to teach her all he wants to if they aren't in private.

ARGAN. That's all right.

TOINETTE. M'sieur, the noise will only give you a headache, and the state you're in nothing should upset you. Or scramble your brains, like eggs.

ARGAN. No, no, I love music, and will be only too happy to ... Ah, here she is. You, go and see if my wife is dressed yet.

Enter ANGELIQUE. *Exit* TOINETTE.

ARGAN. Come here my girl. Your music master is out of town, so here's someone else come instead to teach you.

ANGELIQUE. Oh, heavens.

ARGAN. What is it? You look startled.

ANGELIQUE. I, um, er ...

ARGAN. What's the matter?

ANGELIQUE. Father, something extraordinary has just happened.

ARGAN. What?

ANGELIQUE. I dreamt last night I was in the most dreadful predicament, and a man exactly like Monsieur introduced himself to me, and I asked him to help, and he extricated me from all my troubles. Judge of my surprise, then, on entering this room, unexpectedly to see the very person I had had in my thoughts all night.

CLEANTE. I can think of no greater happiness than to be in your thoughts, sleeping or waking; and it would be my greatest good fortune were you to be in any trouble that you should judge me worthy to deliver you from it; and furthermore there is nothing I would not do ...

Enter TOINETTE.

TOINETTE. I declare I've been converted. M'sieur, I'm on your side now. I take back all I said yesterday. Monsieur Diafoirus Senior and Monsieur Diafoirus Junior have come to pay you a visit. What a son-in-law you're going to have. You're about to set eyes on the handsomest boy in the world, and the wittiest. He's only said two words so far, and they've both bowled me over. Your daughter will be charmed with him.

CLEANTE *goes to exit.*

ARGAN. There's no need to go, Monsieur. I'm marrying my daughter off, and they've brought her husband to see her. She's never set eyes on him before in her life.

CLEANTE. I'm honoured, Monsieur, that you wish me to be present at so touching a meeting.

ARGAN. He's the son of a brilliant doctor, and they're getting married in four days.

CLEANTE. How very nice.

ARGAN. You must tell her music master, so he can come to the wedding.

CLEANTE. I won't fail.

ARGAN. And you must come too.

CLEANTE. You're too kind.

TOINETTE. Come on, everyone, best behaviour. They're here.

Enter the DIAFOIRI. ARGAN *puts his hand to his cap without removing it.*

ARGAN. Monsieur Purgon, sir, has forbidden me to uncover my head. You are in the profession yourself, you know the consequences.

DIAFOIRUS SENIOR. It is our mission in life to bring comfort to the ill, not to inconvenience them.

ARGAN *and* DIAFOIRUS SENIOR *speak at the same time during the following.*

ARGAN. I acknowledge, Monsieur . . .

DIAFOIRUS SENIOR. We have come here, Monsieur . . .

ARGAN. With extreme joy . . .

DIAFOIRUS SENIOR. My son Thomas and I . . .

ARGAN. The honour you do me . . .

DIAFOIRUS SENIOR. To tell you personally . . .

ARGAN. And I would have wished . . .

DIAFOIRUS SENIOR. The great delight we derive . . .

ARGAN. To be able to call on you . . .

DIAFOIRUS SENIOR. From the favour you do us . . .

ARGAN. To thank you for it . . .

DIAFOIRUS SENIOR. In wishing to receive us . . .

ARGAN. But you know, Monsieur . . .

DIAFOIRUS SENIOR. Into the bosom, Monsieur . . .

ARGAN. How it is for us invalids . . .

DIAFOIRUS SENIOR. Of your family . . .

ARGAN. But I can do no better . . .

DIAFOIRUS SENIOR. And to assure you . . .

ARGAN. Than to assure you . . .

DIAFOIRUS SENIOR. In our professional expertise . . .

ARGAN. That I will waste no opportunity . . .

DIAFOIRUS SENIOR. As in anything else . . .

ARGAN. To prove to you Monsieur . . .

DIAFOIRUS SENIOR. That we are completely at your service.

ARGAN. That I am completely at your service.

DIAFOIRUS SENIOR. Yes.

ARGAN. Yes.

DIAFOIRUS SENIOR. Absolutely.

ARGAN. Absolutely

DIAFOIRUS SENIOR *turns to his son.*

DIAFOIRUS SENIOR. Step forward, Thomas. Present your compliments.

THOMAS. Do I do the father first?

DIAFOIRUS SENIOR. Yes.

THOMAS. Monsieur, I come to salute, love, honour and obey in you a second father, but a second father whom I dare say I will find myself more indebted to than the first. The first has engendered me, but you have chosen me. He received me through necessity, but you through the goodness of your heart. I am indebted to him for the good graces of his body, but I am indebted to you for the good graces of your will. As the more intellectual facilities are held superior to the corporeal, so the more indebted I am to you than to him, and so the more precious I hold this future affiliation, in honour of which I have come today to pay in advance this humble and respectful tribute.

TOINETTE. What a clever man. He's a credit to his college.

THOMAS. Was I all right, Father?

DIAFOIRUS SENIOR. *Optime.* Thomas.

ARGAN (*to* ANGELIQUE). Go on, make Monsieur welcome.

THOMAS. Do I have to kiss her?

DIAFOIRUS SENIOR. Yes, yes.

THOMAS (*to* ANGELIQUE). Madame, it is with justice that heavens have bestowed on you the name of mother-in-law, as . . .

ARGAN. That isn't my wife, it's my daughter you're talking to.

THOMAS. Where is your wife?

ARGAN. She'll be here soon.

THOMAS. Father, shall I wait until she gets here?

DIAFOIRUS SENIOR. No. Present your compliments to Mademoiselle.

THOMAS. Must I?

DIAFOIRUS SENIOR. Yes.

THOMAS. Mademoiselle, as the statue of Memnon made an

harmonious sound when struck by the rays of the rising sun, so I feel myself suffused with a great delight at the appearance of yourself, the sun among beauties. And, as the naturalists tell us, the flower named heliotrope turns unceasingly towards that fire decked star of the day, so will my heart, henceforth, turn unceasingly towards the resplendent stars of your adorable eyes, as a magnet turns towards its pole. Allow me, Mademoiselle, to offer today at the altar of your charms the oblation of my heart, the heart of one who yearns after no other glory than to be, all his life, Mademoiselle, your very humble, very obedient and very faithful servant and husband.

TOINETTE. So that's why people are students; they learn to say such pretty things.

ARGAN. What do you say to that, eh?

CLEANTE. Monsieur is a marvel. If he is as good a doctor as he is an orator, it will be a pleasure to be one of his patients.

TOINETTE. Place your bets now.

ARGAN. Get my chair, and seats for the others. Quickly. Sit yourself here, daughter. You see, M'sieur, how much everyone admires your son? You must be proud to have such a boy.

DIAFOIRUS SENIOR. Monsieur, it's not just a father's fondness, but I can truthfully say I have every reason to be pleased with him. Everyone who knows him says that, as a boy, he wasn't at all spiteful. He had never had a fertile imagination, nor indeed the high spirits one sees in so many. It's because of this I have always had such high hopes of his solidity, a requisite quality for the exercise of our art. When he was little, he was never what one calls lively, or even alert. One would always describe him as docile, peaceable, even taciturn. He never said a word, and never once played any of all those childish little games one finds so irritating. It was an uphill struggle to teach him to read, and he was nine years old before he even knew his letters. 'Good' I said to myself 'tardy trees bear best fruits. It is harder to write on marble than in sand, but marble lasts for ever. This slowness of comprehension, this heaviness of imagination is the mark of a good judgment to come.' When I sent him to college, he did find it difficult but he persisted against all odds, and his tutors always gave him A for effort. At last, by hammering it into him, he gloriously attained his first degree, and I can say without boasting that in the next two years he made quite a reputation for himself in formal disputations. He was never shouted down and he did not let a single proposition go until he had argued to the bitter end for the opposite. He is firm in dispute, strong as a Turk in his principles, and pursues an argument even to the last gasp of logic. But, the thing that pleases me most, and in which he follows my example, is that he subscribes blindly to the opinions of the ancients and he has no wish to understand, or even read, these new-fangled ideas and so-called discoveries concerning the circulation of the blood, and other such theories.

THOMAS *takes a large rolled thesis out of his pocket, which he presents to* ANGELIQUE.

THOMAS. I have written a thesis against the circulators, and, with Monsieur's permission, I will presume to present to Mademoiselle these first fruits of my genius as a tribute I owe to her.

ANGELIQUE. It's no use to me, Monsieur. I know nothing of these things.

TOINETTE. Give it to me then. The picture will brighten up my garret.

THOMAS. With Monsieur's permission, I will, one of these days, as a diversion, invite you to come to see me dissect a woman, while giving a running commentary.

TOINETTE. Diversion indeed. Some young men take their fiancée to a play but a dissection will be something else altogether.

DIAFOIRUS SENIOR. As for the other matters, the qualities required for marriage and for propagation and so forth, I can assure you, that according to medical opinion, he has everything to be desired. He possesses to a praiseworthy degree the prolific virtue, and he has the necessary temperament to engender and indeed procreate children in top condition.

ARGAN. Is it not your intention, Monsieur, to present him at court and arrange a position for him there?

DIAFOIRUS SENIOR. To be frank, I've never found practising amongst the great all that agreeable. I've always found it much more worthwhile to stay with the general public. The general public is so much more accommodating. You do not have to answer to anyone for your actions, and provided you are seen to follow the broad outlines of the art, no-one takes much notice of the results. What's irritating about the great is that when they are ill they absolutely insist their doctors cure them.

TOINETTE. How very presumptuous. You aren't there for that. You're there to issue prescriptions and to collect your fees. It's up to them to get better if they can.

DIAFOIRUS SENIOR. That's true. Our only obligation is to treat people according to the rules.

ARGAN (*to* CLEANTE). Monsieur, have you a little something for my daughter to sing for the company?

CLEANTE. I was anticipating your request, Monsieur, so I thought, to divert the assembled throng, we, that is Mademoiselle and myself, would perform a scene from a recently composed opera. (*He gives* ANGELIQUE *a paper.*)

CLEANTE. There's your part.

ANGELIQUE. Who, me?

CLEANTE (*low to* ANGELIQUE). Please, not a word. I'll let you know what you've got to do. (*Normal.*) I don't have a good singing voice myself, but it will suffice to make myself heard. You understand I'm only doing this to help Mademoiselle, so I'm sure you will have the goodness to bear with me.

ARGAN. What are the words like?

CLEANTE. It is, properly speaking, an extempore opera, *un opéra impromptu*. What you're about to hear is rhythmic prose, a sort of free verse, such as passion and necessity would wring out of two people who are revealing their deepest feelings to each other, and making it up as they go along.

ARGAN. Very good. Let's hear it.

CLEANTE. The story so far. A shepherd is absorbed in a play, which has only just begun when his attention is drawn to a sound he hears to one side. He turns and sees an oaf, who with insolent words is maltreating a shepherdess. At once the shepherd takes to heart the interest of that sex to whom all men must pay tribute, and after having chastised the oaf for his impudence, he goes to the shepherdess. He finds a young lady, who, from the two most beautiful eyes he has ever seen, is shedding tears, also the most beautiful he has ever seen. 'Alas,' he says to himself, 'is anyone capable of insulting such an amiable young person? Would not any man, nay barbarian even, be moved by such tears?' The shepherd dries the tears, the tears he finds so beautiful, and the amiable shepherdess thanks him for his trifling service, but so tenderly, so charmingly and so sincerely, that the shepherd is unable to resist, as each word, each look is a shaft of flame with which his heart is pierced. 'Can anything,' he marvels to himself, 'be worthy of so enchanting an acknowledgement? What service would one not render, what dangers would one not be overjoyed to run, to deserve for a single moment the touching thanks of so grateful a soul?' The play passes without him giving it the slightest attention, but he complains it is too short, for on finishing he is separated from the shepherdess he loves. And from that first sight, from that first moment, it is as if he has been deeply in love for many years. He immediately suffers all the miseries of absence, and he is tormented to see no more of her of whom he's seen so little. He cherishes the vision night and day, and does all he can to regain it; but the heavy constraint under which the shepherdess is held totally confounds him. The extremity of his passion resolves him to demand in marriage the adorable beauty without whom he can live no longer, and, by a ruse, giving her a note, obtains her consent. But, at the very same time, he is told his fair one's father has arranged her marriage to another. Judge what cruel blow to the heart of this sad swain. Behold him overwhelmed by mortal sorrow. He cannot abide the appalling thought of seeing the one he loves in the arms of another, and in his despair finds means to infiltrate himself into the house of his shepherdess. There he finds preparations in train for all he dreads most. There he sees the ridiculous rival a foolish father's caprice sets against his tenderest love. He sees him triumphant, this booby, this buffoon, this imbecile, thinking the amiable shepherdess a conquest of which he is assured. The sight fills the shepherd with a swelling rage, which he has considerable difficulty in mastering. He sorrowfully gazes on her whom he adores. His respect for her and the presence of her addled, ailing, ageing father prevent him from saying anything, except with his eyes. But at length he breaks through all restraint, and the transports of his love oblige him to speak to her, as follows:

CLEANTE (*sings*). Fair Phyllis, 'tis too much to suffer

Break your silence to your lover.
Teach to me my Destiny
Must I live or must I die?

ANGELIQUE (*sings*). Fair Tircis, how can I reply?

(*Nasty pause.*)

You see me sad and melancholic
For these nuptials are no . . . frolic,
And my only hope is you;
Teach me all that I should do.

ARGAN. What's this? I'd no idea my daughter was clever
enough to sing on sight.

CLEANTE (*sings*). What, fair Phyllis, can it be
Fortune's face smiles full on me?
Come the joyful news impart,
Have I a place within your heart?

ANGELIQUE (*sings*). Danger all restraint removes
Tircis, yes, 'tis you I . . . louve.

CLEANTE (*sings*). Louve, oh word with joy's light beaming!
But have I understood your meaning?
Shout it to the heavens above.

ANGELIQUE (*sings*). Tircis, yes, 'tis you I love.

CLEANTE (*sings*). Shout it to the heavens above.

ANGELIQUE (*sings*). Tircis, yes, 'tis you I love.

CLEANTE (*sings*). Once more, I beg you.

ANGELIQUE (*sings*). Tircis, I love you.

CLEANTE (*recitative*). Repeat it a hundred times; please never
cease.

ANGELIQUE (*sings*). I love you, I love you,
Yes, Tircis, I love you . . . . (*etc.
ad nauseam.*)

All except CLEANTE *become restless.* CLEANTE, *with an
imperious gesture, stops her.*

CLEANTE (*sings*). Ye kings, and you with powers divine,
Can you compare your happiness to mine?
But Phyllis, an unsettling thought
Comes to disrupt our sweet trans-ports.
I fear I have a rival.

ANGELIQUE (*sings*). Ah, I hate him more than death
Like daggers are his every breath.
Have we offended, that is sent
To you and I this punishment?

CLEANTE (*recitative*). But a father to his wishes, wishes to subjugate you.

ANGELIQUE (*sings*). Sooner die, sooner die
Than ever give consent will I . . . . . .
(*etc. ad nauseam.*)

CLEANTE (*joining as duet*). Dead she'll be, dead she'll be
Than ever give consent will
she . . .

ARGAN (*interrupting*). And what says that father to all this?

CLEANTE. Nothing.

ARGAN. He must be a very stupid father to put up with all this without saying anything.

CLEANTE (*sings*). Ah, my love . . .

ARGAN. No, no, that's enough. This piece is setting a very bad example. The shepherd Tircis is an impertinent fellow, and the shepherdess Phyllis is an impudent hussy to talk like that in front of her father. Show me the score. What's this? Where are the words you've just sung? There's nothing here but the music.

CLEANTE. Have you not heard, Monsieur, of the latest invention? It's now possible to write the words and the music all in one.

ARGAN. Very well. I am your servant, Monsieur, until we meet again. We could have done without your impertinent opera.

CLEANTE. I thought you might find it diverting.

ARGAN. Stupidity never diverts. Ah, here's my wife.

Enter BELINE. *Exit* CLEANTE.

ARGAN. Darling, this is Monsieur Diafoirus' son.

THOMAS. Madame, it is with justice the heavens have bestowed on you the name of mother-in-law, as Minerva herself could have no greater wisdom than . . .

BELINE. Monsieur, my arrival is indeed happy particularly as it gives me the honour of meeting you.

THOMAS. As Minerva herself could have no greater wisdom . . . herself could have no . . . Madame, you have stopped me in full flood. I've forgotten what I was saying.

DIAFOIRUS SENIOR. Thomas, save it for another time.

ARGAN. I wish, darling, you'd been here a little while ago.

TOINETTE. You don't know what you've missed, Madame. We've had the second father, the statue of Memnon, and the flower called heliotrope.

ARGAN. Come, daughter, take Monsieur's hand. Plight him your troth as your future husband.

ANGELIQUE. Oh Father.

ARGAN. What do you mean, oh Father? Out with it.

ANGELIQUE. For pity's sake, do not rush things. Give us at least some time to become acquainted, and for there to be born in us that mutual attraction so necessary for a perfect union.

THOMAS. As far as I'm concerned, Mademoiselle, it's already there. I don't see why I have to wait any longer.

ANGELIQUE. You may be prompt in your affections, Monsieur, but I am not. I must own that your merits have not as yet altogether overwhelmed me.

ARGAN. Be that as it may, there'll be all the time in the world for that after you're married.

ANGELIQUE. Father, give me time, I beg you. Marriage is a

chain with which one should never bind a heart through force. If Monsieur is an honourable man, he would not wish to gain a wife through compulsion.

THOMAS. I deny your consequence, or as we logicians put it, *nego consequentiam*. I can be an honourable man and very much wish to gain you from the hands of Monsieur, your father.

ANGELIQUE. It is shameful to force someone to love you.

THOMAS. We read, Mademoiselle, that the ancients would carry off their brides-to-be from their father's house by force. This was so it would not look as if they were willingly giving in to a man.

ANGELIQUE. The ancients, Monsieur, were the ancients, and we live now. Such play-acting is not necessary. If we want a marriage, we know very well how to go about it, without anyone having to drag us about by our hair. Be patient. If you loved me, Monsieur, you would want what I want.

THOMAS. So I would, Mademoiselle, in all things save my passion.

ANGELIQUE. But surely the supreme mark of love is to be submissive to the wishes of she whom one adores?

THOMAS. I shall distinguish, or *distinguo*, to put it technically, the different points in your argument. In matters that do not appertain to the possession of the loved one, *concedo*, I concede your point; but in matters which do appertain to it, *nego*, I deny it.

TOINETTE. You have reasoned in vain. Monsieur is fresh from college and will always end up on top. Why not give in? Won't it be an honour to be attached to the body of the Faculty?

BELINE. She has, perhaps, ideas of her own.

ANGELIQUE. And if I have, Madame, they will be such that reason and honour would applaud them.

ARGAN. This is making me look a total fool.

BELINE. If I were you, my dear, I would not force her to

marry. Indeed, I know exactly what I would do.

ANGELIQUE. I am aware, Madame, of what you wish to say, and the good intentions you have towards me. Perhaps your advice might not be fortunate enough to be taken.

BELINE. I see these days dutiful daughters, like yourself, scorn to be submissive to the wishes of their fathers. It was not so previously.

ANGELIQUE. A daughter's duty has limits, Madame. Reason and the law cannot stretch them to include all things.

BELINE. You mean you deign to get married, but only to a spouse of your own fancy.

ANGELIQUE. If my Father does not wish to give me a husband of my choosing, I would at least entreat him not to compel me to marry one I could not love.

ARGAN. Gentlemen, I really must apologise for all this.

ANGELIQUE. Each woman marries for her own reasons. I would not want a husband except to love him truly and to be with him all my life. I, therefore, intend to go about marriage with due caution. However, there are some who take a husband solely to rid themselves of their parents' constraint, so they can do as they please. And there are others, Madame, for whom marriage is a matter of pure commercial interest. These people marry only for what they can get out of it. These people enrich themselves by the death of their partners, running without scruple from husband to husband, appropriating the spoils of war. These people do not stand on ceremony, and have little regard for anyone else.

BELINE. You're in fine form today. What, exactly, are you implying?

ANGELIQUE. Me, Madame, imply? I say what I mean.

BELINE. You are so stupid, my pet, that one really cannot put up with you any longer.

ANGELIQUE. You are trying, Madame, to make me lose my

temper with you, but I must warn you I shall not give you that advantage.

BELINE. Your insolence knows no bounds.

ANGELIQUE. Madame, you are wasting your breath.

BELINE. And you, Mademoiselle, have a ridiculous pride, an overweaning presumption that makes you a laughing stock to the entire world.

ANGELIQUE. All this will get you nowhere. I will not rise to the bait. I shall remove your hopes of success by removing myself from your sight.

ARGAN. Listen, my girl, there's no compromise. You have four days to make a choice. Either you marry Monsieur, or get thee to a nunnery.

Exeunt ANGELIQUE *and* TOINETTE.

ARGAN. Don't you upset yourself. I'll bring her to heel.

BELINE. I'm sorry, but I'm going to have to leave you, my dear. I have some business in town which I am obliged to attend to. I'll be back soon.

ARGAN. Off you go, my love. And don't forget to call in at the notary's to see how he's getting on with the you know what.

BELINE. Goodbye. Who's Mummy's little friend then?

Exit BELINE.

ARGAN. Goodbye darling. You would not believe how much that woman loves me.

DIAFOIRUS SENIOR. We are going, Monsieur, to have to take our leaves of you.

ARGAN. Would you do me a favour, Monsieur? Have a little look to see how I am.

DIAFOIRUS SENIOR. Come, Thomas, take Monsieur's other wrist. Let's see what you make of his pulse. *Quid dicis?*

THOMAS. *Dico* ... Monsieur's pulse is the pulse of a man who is not at all well.

DIAFOIRUS SENIOR. Good.

THOMAS. It is heavyish, not to say sluggish.

DIAFOIRUS SENIOR. Very good.

THOMAS. Almost turgid.

DIAFOIRUS SENIOR. Bene.

THOMAS. And even a little wilful.

DIAFOIRUS SENIOR. Optime.

THOMAS. All of which suggests an inclemency in the splenic parenchyma, that is to say the spleen.

ARGAN. No, no, Monsieur Purgon says it's my liver.

DIAFOIRUS SENIOR. Oh yes, if one says parenchyma one also means the liver because of the strong sympathy between the two owing to the connections through the short vessel of the pylorus and quite often the meatus cholidici as well. Monsieur Purgon has no doubt ordered you to eat lots of roast meat?

ARGAN. No, nothing but boiled.

DIAFOIRUS SENIOR. Oh yes, roast, boiled; it's all the same thing. He's taking good care of you. You couldn't be in better hands.

ARGAN. Monsieur, how many grains of salt should one put on an egg?

DIAFOIRUS SENIOR. Six, eight, ten, any of the even numbers; just as with pills it's the odd numbers.

ARGAN. I am your humble servant, Monsieur.

Exeunt the DIAFOIRI. *Enter* BELINE.

BELINE. I've just popped in before going out, my lamb, to tell you something I think you ought to know. On passing Angélique's room, I saw a young man with her, and furthermore he left as soon as he saw me.

ARGAN. A young man with my daughter?

BELINE. Yes. Your younger daughter, Louison, was with them. She should be able to tell you all about it.

ARGAN. Send her here, my love, send her here.

Exit BELINE.

ARGAN. Ah, the effrontery. I cease to be astonished at her obduracy.

Enter LOUISON.

LOUISON. What do you want, Daddy? My step-mother said you'd asked for me.

ARGAN. Yes. Come here. Turn round. Don't look at the floor, look at me. Well?

LOUISON. What?

ARGAN. Well?

LOUISON. Well what, Daddy?

ARGAN. Have you nothing you want to tell me.

LOUISON. I'll tell you the story of the Princess and the ass's skin, if you want something to amuse you, or even better the fable of the Crow and the Fox, which I've only just learnt. A Crow once found a large cheese, and . . .

ARGAN. I don't mean tell me that sort of thing.

LOUISON. What then?

ARGAN. Ah, slyboots, you know very well.

LOUISON. I'm sorry, Daddy, I don't.

ARGAN. Is this how you obey me?

LOUISON. What?

ARGAN. Have I not ordered you to tell me, at once, everything you see?

LOUISON. Yes Daddy.

ARGAN. And have you done so?

LOUISON. Yes, Daddy, I have.

ARGAN. And you haven't seen anything today?

LOUISON. No, Daddy, I haven't.

ARGAN. No?

LOUISON. No, Daddy.

ARGAN. You're sure?

LOUISON. I'm sure.

ARGAN. Then I'm going to have to make you see something, aren't I? (*He takes a cane.*)

LOUISON. No, Daddy.

ARGAN. So, minx, you won't tell me what you've seen in your sister's room?

LOUISON. Daddy?

ARGAN. I'll teach you to lie.

LOUISON *throws herself on her knees.*

LOUISON. Ah, Daddy, I'm sorry. My sister told me not to tell you about it, but I will tell you after all.

ARGAN. First of all I shall beat you for lying. Then, after that, we shall see about it.

LOUISON. Forgive me, Daddy.

ARGAN. No, no.

LOUISON. Dearest Daddy, do not beat me.

ARGAN. I shall; I must.

LOUISON. Please Daddy, please don't.

ARGAN *grabs her.*

ARGAN. Come here.

LOUISON. Ah, Daddy, you've hurt me. Stop; I'm dying. (*She pretends to be dead.*)

ARGAN. Alas. What have I done? Louison, Louison, oh my God, Louison. My daughter, my daughter; I have lost my daughter. Oh unhappy man, your poor daughter is dead. What have I done, wretch that I am? A plague on all punishment. Ah my poor little daughter, my poor little daughter.

LOUISON. There, there, Daddy; don't cry so much. I'm not completely dead.

ARGAN. You little slyboots you. Who's a little slyboots?

LOUISON. I am.

ARGAN. You are. Oh well, I forgive you this time, provided you tell me everything.

LOUISON. Oh yes, Daddy.

ARGAN. Now make sure you get everything right, for here's my little finger, and my little finger knows everything and will tell me if you lie.

LOUISON. Daddy, don't tell my sister I told you.

ARGAN. No, I won't.

LOUISON. You see, Daddy, a man came into my sister's room while I was there.

ARGAN. Really.

LOUISON. Yes, so I asked him what he wanted, and he said he was her singing teacher.

ARGAN. Aha, so that's what's going on. And?

LOUISON. And my sister came in.

ARGAN. And?

LOUISON. And she said to him 'Go, go, for God's sake go. You drive me to despair.'

ARGAN. And?

LOUISON. And he didn't want to go.

ARGAN. And what did he say to her?

LOUISON. He said all sorts of things.

ARGAN. Such as?

LOUISON. Such as he loved her dearly, and she was the most beautiful woman in the world, and all that sort of thing.

ARGAN. And then?

LOUISON. And then he went down on his knees in front of her.

ARGAN. And then?

LOUISON. And then he kissed her left hand.

ARGAN. And then?

LOUISON. And then he kissed her right hand.

ARGAN. And then?

LOUISON. And then my step-mother came in and he ran away.

ARGAN. And there's nothing else?

LOUISON. No Daddy.

ARGAN. My little finger is trying to tell me something. (*He puts his finger to his ear.*) Wait, Eh. Ah. Ah. What? Oh. Oh. Really. Thank you very much. My little finger says you've seen something else and you haven't told me.

LOUISON. No, Daddy, your little finger is a fibber.

ARGAN. Be careful.

LOUISON. Daddy, don't believe it, it's lying, honestly.

ARGAN. All right then, we shall see. Off you go, take care of yourself, off you go.

Exit LOUISON.

ARGAN. Thank goodness I've no more children. What a business. I haven't even the time to worry about my own illness. To tell you the truth, I'm completely worn out.

Enter BERALDE.

BERALDE. Well, well brother, and how are you?

ARGAN. Ah, brother, very ill.

BERALDE. What do you mean, ill?

ARGAN. You wouldn't believe how run down I am.

BERALDE. That must be very annoying for you.

ARGAN. I haven't even the strength to speak.

BERALDE. I've come brother, to suggest a match to you for my niece, Angélique.

ARGAN *gets out of his chair.*

ARGAN. Brother, do not mention that, that Jezebel in front of me. She is a self-willed impertinent jade. I'll put her in a nunnery before two days are out.

BERALDE. Ah splendid. I see you're coming round a little. Obviously my visit must be doing you some good. Well then, we'll talk about business later. Meanwhile, there are some people outside who are going to do a play. They're very good; I saw them in the carnival . . .

ARGAN. Carnival. Bah, humbug.

BERALDE. They'll cheer you up, and put you in a better mood for the things we've got to talk about. It's a modern piece, one of Molière's, I know you're going to enjoy it. It'll do you a lot more good than one of Monsieur Purgon's prescriptions. You come with me.

ARGAN. Must I?

BERALDE. Yes.

Second Interlude

A street. The PLAYERS *enter with their cart. They drum up an audience on stage. This includes* ARGAN, BERALDE *and, seperately,* TOINETTE.

MOLIERE. Ladies and gentlemen, you are privileged to witness tonight a unique occasion; an attempt on the world speed record for performing Molière's early one act farce, *Le Médecin Volant*, or for those scholars among us, *The Flying Doctor*. I can assure you that you will never have seen anything like it in the Entire Annals, ladies and gentlemen, the Entire Annals of the History of Entertainment. Forty-five minutes boiled down to five. On your marks, get set, go.

PLAYERS (*sing*). Roll up, roll up for an old, old story.
       It could be of honour, it could be of glory,
       It could be of vengeance from heaven above;
       But, as it happens, this time it is love.
       We make no excuse if you've heard it before
       For there's just seven plots on which we can draw.

LUCILE *and* VALERE. LUCILE *is crying in* VALERE's *arms.*

Enter SABINE.

SABINE. What's the matter?

LUCILE. My father wants to marry me off to a rich old twit today.

VALERE. And we want to marry each other. What shall we do?

SABINE. I must think. I've thought. You pretend to be ill.

LUCILE. Pretend to be ill?

SABINE. Lie on the floor and groan.

VALERE. What's the point of that?

SABINE. You get your servant . . .

Enter SGANARELLE.

SGANARELLE. Me.

SABINE. Sganarelle, to dress up as a doctor. He'll prescribe her fresh air. Her father will put her in the summerhouse at the bottom of the garden, and . . .

LUCILE. . . . and . . .

VALERE. . . . and . . .

SABINE. . . . and you can do as you please. I'm going to get your father.

SABINE *goes.*

SGANARELLE. I can't do it.

VALERE. I'll give you five francs.

SGANARELLE. I can do it. What do I say?

VALERE. Just witter on about Galen . . . .

SGANARELLE. Galen . . .

VALERE. And Hippocrates . . .

SGANARELLE. Hippocrates . . .

VALERE. And throw in some Latin.

SGANARELLE. . . . some Latin.

VALERE. They're coming. My love, I'll meet you in the summerhouse.

VALERE *goes.*

SGANARELLE. Lie on the floor.

    LUCILE *does so.* SGANARELLE *does a costume change into a doctor.*

    Enter SABINE *and* GORGIBUS.

SABINE. Look, there she is.
GORGIBUS. What, my daughter, ill?

    LUCILE *shrieks and throws herself around.*

GORGIBUS. We must get a doctor.
SABINE. Funny you should say that, there's one here.
GORGIBUS. Is he good?
SABINE. He's the tops.

    SGANARELLE *as a doctor to* GORGIBUS.

GORGIBUS. I want you to look at my daughter. She's ill.

    LUCILE *shrieks and throws herself around.*

SGANARELLE. Have you come to the right person? Galen says, and Hippocrates agrees with him, that when a person is ill they are not well. *Ars longa vita brevis; delenda est Carthago; e pericoloso sporgesi.* Let's have a look at you.

    He lunges at GORGIBUS.

SABINE. He's not ill.
SGANARELLE. Who is?
SABINE. His daughter.

SGANARELLE. Can I see the patient's urine?

LUCILE and SABINE go out behind door.

GORGIBUS. She's not going to die is she?

SGANARELLE. Of course not. No one's allowed to die under the doctor.

Enter LUCILE and SABINE with a bottle of amber liquid.

SGANARELLE. Yes, she's ill all right, but not that ill.

He drinks it.

GORGIBUS. You've drunk it.

SGANARELLE. You find out more than by just looking at it. Mmmmm. If all patient's piss was like this, I'd be doctor for life. More.

SABINE. There isn't any.

SGANARELLE. What, is this all she can do? What a poor pisser. Your daughter must get lots of fresh air.

GORGIBUS. There's a summerhouse at the bottom of the garden. Would that be all right?

SGANARELLE. Take her there, immediately.

LUCILE and GORGIBUS go. SABINE and SGANARELLE shakes hands. SABINE goes. SGANARELLE takes off the doctor costume.

SGANARELLE. Everything's going to plan. The old man must be thick to be taken in like that. Oh God, here he is again.

Enter GORGIBUS.

GORGIBUS. Morning.

SGANARELLE. Evening.

GORGIBUS. Haven't I seen you some where before?

SGANARELLE. In a manner of speaking. You don't happen to know if a famous doctor's just hit town?

GORGIBUS. Funny you should say that.

SGANARELLE. I'm his identical twin. We've had a dreadful row and he's thrown me out of the house. I'm completely on my uppers.

GORGIBUS. I'll make it up for you. I'll go and talk to him.

SGANARELLE. I'm very much obliged.

GORGIBUS *turns*. SGANARELLE *puts on the doctor kit.*

SGANARELLE. When patients refuse to obey their doctors they've taken the first steps on the primrose . . .

GORGIBUS *turns*.

GORGIBUS. Monsieur . . .

SGANARELLE. What is it?

GORGIBUS. I've just met your brother.

SGANARELLE. He's a total washout.

GORGIBUS. He says he's very sorry for having upset you. Forgive him, just for me?

SGANARELLE. Your arguments are overwhelming. Put it there.

They shake hands.

SGANARELLE. He's forgiven.

GORGIBUS. I'll go and tell him the good news.

GORGIBUS *turns*. SGANARELLE *takes off the doctor kit.*
GORGIBUS *turns*.

GORGIBUS. I've been looking for you everywhere. Your brother's forgiven you, but to make sure, I'll get him to embrace you in front of me. You stay in the house and I'll go and find him.

SGANARELLE. I can't.

GORGIBUS. You must.

SGANARELLE. You won't be able to. I'll come with you.

GORGIBUS. You're staying here.

He pushes him inside whatever represents the house.

GORGIBUS. I'm locking you in.

He does so and goes.

SGANARELLE (*from the window*): Hoist with my own petard. When they find out there'll be hell to pay. Still, in for a penny, in for a pound as the English say.

He jumps out of whatever represents the window and goes.

Enter GROS-RENE.

GROS-RENE. There's something funny going on here. Someone's just jumped out of that window. I'm staying to watch.

Enter GORGIBUS.

GORGIBUS. I can't find the doctor anywhere. Ah, here he is.

Enter SGANARELLE *as the doctor*.

GORGIBUS. Monsieur, embrace your brother, just for me. He's in the house. Here's the key.

SGANARELLE. Very well, just for you.

He unlocks the door and goes in.
In the following, he fights himself, bobbing up and down
taking his hat on and off.

SGANARELLE (*doctor*). So there you are, wretch.

SGANARELLE (*brother*). I'm sorry, it wasn't my fault.

SGANARELLE (*doctor*). I'll learn you.

SGANARELLE (*brother*). Honestly, I didn't mean . . .

SGANARELLE (*doctor*). Shut up.

SGANARELLE (*brother*). But . . .

SGANARELLE (*doctor*). I said shut up.

GROS-RENE. What's going on?

GORGIBUS. It's the doctor and his brother. They're making
it up.

SGANARELLE (*doctor*). Take that.

GROS-RENE. They're both the same person.

SGANARELLE (*doctor*). And that.

GROS-RENE. Ask to see them both at the window.

GORGIBUS. Monsieur, would you embrace your brother at
the window?

SGANARELLE (*doctor*). Very well. You come and apologize for
all the trouble you've caused.

SGANARELLE (*brother*). I'm very sorry. I'll turn over a new
leaf.

He embraces his hat.

GORGIBUS. You see, there are two of them.

GROS-RENE. He must be a magician.

SGANARELLE *as the doctor comes out of the house.*

SGANARELLE. Here's the key. I don't want to be seen in town with him. It would ruin me.

He runs round the back of the house and dumps the doctor kit.

GORGIBUS. I must let the poor boy out. He's been punished enough.

He unlocks the door. SGANARELLE (*brother*) *comes out.*

SGANARELLE. Monsieur, thank you for all your help. How can I ever repay you?

GROS-RENE *grabs* SGANARELLE.

GROS-RENE. Where's the doctor now?
GORGIBUS. Gone.
GROS-RENE. I've got him here. While we were watching this farce, Valère and Lucile were together, in the summer-house, alone.
GORGIBUS. You'll hang for this.
SGANARELLE. There's no need to get upset. I haven't harmed you. He's the perfect husband; good birth and stinking rich. If you make a fuss, you'll just look stupid. Here they are.

Enter VALERE *and* LUCILE.

VALERE. We throw ourselves at your feet.

They do so.

GORGIBUS. I forgive you, in fact I'm happy to be fooled. Everyone come to the wedding and toast the happy couple.

PLAYERS (*sing*). Like most entertainments this play has a
moral.
Its not about duty, a father, a quarrel.
We think all of you will agree when we say:
Gather ye rosebuds while yo may
Young girls under Cupid's sway;
The springtime of your life's the chance
To give yourself to sweet romance.

The PLAYERS *pack up and go during the following.*

ARGAN *goes up to* MOLIERE.

ARGAN. Are you Monsieur Molière, the author?
MOLIERE. I am.
ARGAN. You ought to be ashamed of yourself.
BERALDE. Brother.

They go out.

TOINETTE *goes up to* MOLIERE.
TOINETTE. Thank you. You've given me an idea.

She goes.

The set changes.

Act Three

ARGAN's *study. Enter* BERALDE, ARGAN *and* TOINETTE.

BERALDE. Well, brother, and what do you say to that? Went
down better than a dose of salts.

ARGAN. There's nothing wrong with a good dose of salts.

BERALDE. Anyway, shall we have our little chat now?

ARGAN. Bear with me, brother; I'll be back soon.

TOINETTE. Just a minute, M'sieur. What about your stick?
You're surely not thinking you can walk without it.

ARGAN. You're quite right. I'll be forgetting my own head
next. (*Exit.*)

TOINETTE. Please Monsieur, don't leave your niece in the
lurch.

BERALDE. I'll do my best to get her what she wants.

TOINETTE. We've got to stop this absurd marriage he's got
into his head. I was thinking of getting a doctor onto our
side. He could put him off his Monsieur Purgon and generally read him the Riot Act.

BERALDE. Really.

TOINETTE.But I couldn't find one. So, I've decided on a
scheme of my own.

BERALDE. What?

TOINETTE. It's an old trick, but it might just work. Here's
our man. You play your part and I'll play mine.

Enter ARGAN. *Exit* TOINETTE.

BERALDE. Now, brother, we're going to have our little chat.

ARGAN. Yes.

BERALDE. And it's very important you don't get worked up.

ARGAN. Yes.

BERALDE. And that you answer any arguments I advance without acrimony.

ARGAN. That goes without saying.

BERALDE. And that you consider the pros and cons in a completely disinterested fashion.

ARGAN. Yes, yes, yes. Get on with it.

BERALDE. Brother, you're rich, and you've only got one daughter; I don't count the little one. Why, then, are you thinking of putting her in a convent?

ARGAN. Why, brother, am I master in my house, if not to do as I please?

BERALDE. Your wife is always on at you to get rid of the two girls, out of the milk of human kindness, I'm sure. She'll be over the moon to see them both nuns.

ARGAN. So that's the way the wind's blowing. The poor woman's been brought into play already. Every time she opens her mouth she puts her foot in it.

BERALDE. All right, we'll put her to one side. I'm sure she wants the best for everyone. She hasn't a thought for herself; she's very much in love with you, and she shows her feelings for your children in ways you wouldn't dream of. We won't mention her again, and get back to your daughter. Why on earth, brother, do you want to marry her off to a doctor's son?

ARGAN. So, brother, I can get the son-in-law I require.

BERALDE. But what about your daughter? Someone else has turned up who is far more suitable for her.

ARGAN. Yes, but this one is far more suitable for me.

BERALDE. But should she marry for her sake or for yours?

ARGAN. She should marry for her sake and for mine. I'm going to get all the people I could possibly need into the family.

BERALDE. So, you'd palm your little girl off onto an apothecary if she was bigger.

ARGAN. And why not?

BERALDE. Are you going to be entangled with your doctors and your apothecaries for ever? Are you going to insist on being ill, despite all people say and in the teeth of all the evidence?

ARGAN. What do you mean?

BERALDE. I've never seen anyone less ill than you in my life. You're as strong as a horse. You've not spoilt your health in the least, and despite all the trouble you've been to. All the stuff you've taken, by rights you ought to be dead.

ARGAN. But don't you realize that's what keeps me going? Monsieur Purgon says if he stopped taking care of me, I'd be dead as a doornail in three days flat.

BERALDE. If you're not careful, he'll take such good care of you you'll end up in another world.

ARGAN. Let's talk this through a little, brother. Don't you believe in medicine at all?

BERALDE. No, brother, I do not. I can save my soul perfectly well without it.

ARGAN. But it's an established fact. Medicine is practised throughout the world and has been revered down the centuries.

BERALDE. Established fact? Between you, me and the gatepost it's the biggest joke out. I can see nothing more ridiculous, nothing more farcical than one man trying to cure another.

ARGAN. Why won't you accept it's possible?

BERALDE. Because the workings of that sublime machine, our body are so enshrouded in mystery, we cannot possibly fathom them. Nature in her wisdom holds a veil in front of our eyes, that's too thick for mortal vision to penetrate.

ARGAN. So, according to you, doctors know nothing.

BERALDE. Oh, most of them know something. They know the Classics; they know how to talk nicely in Latin. They know how to name all the diseases in Greek. They know how to diagnose them and classify them. They can even tell one from another. But when it comes down to curing them, they know nothing.

ARGAN. But even you have to admit doctors know more about all this sort of thing than normal people.

BERALDE. They know no more or less than what I've just said, and that's not much help when it comes to curing people. Their so-called professionalism is just mumbo-jumbo, a smokescreen. They give you words instead of reasons and promises for results.

ARGAN. But even people as clever as you run for the doctor when they're ill.

BERALDE. That's a mark of human frailty, not the truth of the doctor's art.

ARGAN. But the doctors must believe in it. After all, they treat themselves.

BERALDE. All doctors are divided into two types. There are those who believe in it all, and make money out of it; and there are those who don't, and make money out of it anyway. Your Monsieur Purgon, for example, makes no bones about it. He's the compleat doctor from the top of his head to the tips of his toes. He believes in his rules more than any mathematical proof. He even thinks it a crime to wish to test them. He sees nothing obscure in medicine, nothing doubtful, nothing difficult. Out of blind faith and ignorance, a complacent self-satisfaction, and all the commonsense of an ox, he bleeds and purges at random and baulks at nothing. He isn't out to harm you when he does what he can for you; he disposes of you with a smile on his face and a song in his heart. In killing you, he's only doing what he'd do to his wife, his children and even, if necessary, himself.

ARGAN. You've always wanted to get your teeth into him. But let's get down to basics. What should one do when one's ill?

BERALDE. Nothing, brother.

ARGAN. Nothing?

BERALDE. Nothing. All you have to do is rest. Nature herself, when we let her, will take care of everything else. It's our impatience spoils things. Most men die of their cures, and not of their diseases.

ARGAN. But you just admit, brother, there are certain things help nature on her way.

BERALDE. My God, brother, all that's just theory, which we love to trot out parrot-fashion. There are always clever men around, sliding these ideas into circulation so that they're believed by everybody. That's because they flatter us, and so we want them to be true. When a doctor talks to you of helping, succouring, assuaging nature, of removing what harms her and supplying what she lacks; when he talks to you of rectifying the blood, tempering the bowels and brain, deflating the spleen and inflating the chest, of overhauling the liver, fortifying the heart, restoring and conserving the natural warmth, and of having the secret of long life; when he says all this he is just spinning you a story: the romance of medicine. When you get to the truth of the matter, you find there's nothing there. It's like being taken in by a wonderful dream.

ARGAN. So, you're saying you know more than all the great doctors of the age put together.

BERALDE. There's two sides to your great doctors; there's what they say and what they do. To hear them talk, you'd think them the most skilful of men; to see what they do, the most ignorant.

ARGAN. My word! You're getting quite the great doctor yourself. I very much wish some of them were here. They'd soon put you in your place and stop your idle tongue.

BERALDE. Me, brother? I've got nothing against medicine, as such. A man can believe whatever he likes, come hell or high water. However, I'm not in a minority of one about this. That Molière play we've just seen; I would have thought that would have put you on the right track as well as given you something to laugh at.

ARGAN. Your Molière is an impertinent fellow with his so-called comedies. It's a fine thing to make fun of honest men, like doctors.

BERALDE. He doesn't make fun of doctors, but ridicules medicine. He condemns the fault but not the actor of it.

ARGAN. What right has he to meddle in medicine? What does he think he's up to, sniping at consultations and prescriptions, attacking the Faculty of Doctors; putting venerable gentlemen like these on stage?

BERALDE. What should he put there, but the different professions of men? One sees princes and kings there everyday, and done very well too, and they're a far better class of person than doctors.

ARGAN. Jesus, Mary ...... I mean damn it. If I were a doctor, I'd be revenged for his impertinence. When he was ill, I'd leave him to die without help. He could do and say all he liked; I would not deign to prescribe even a bleeding, not even the least little enema. I would say to him, 'Die, die, die like a dog; that will teach you to trifle with the Faculty another time'.

BERALDE. My, my, you're getting quite steamed up about him.

ARGAN. He's a complete fool. If the doctors have their heads screwed on, they'll do as I say.

BERALDE. But Molière will be one step ahead of them. He won't ask for their help at all.

ARGAN. Then he deserves all he gets.

BERALDE. He has his reasons. He says only people in perfect health have enough strength to stand up to both the disease and the cure. He's only strength enough for his illness.

ARGAN. How stupid. Enough, brother, let's not discuss this man any longer. It inflames my bile, and makes me even iller.

BERALDE. Very well, brother, we'll change the subject. I've this to say to you. There's no need to swear blind you'll put your daughter in a convent just because she's a little reluctant. You shouldn't let your obsession run away with you when choosing a son-in-law. You ought to take your daughter's feelings into account a little. After all, the happiness of her marriage depends on them. It's her life.

Enter MONSIEUR FLEURANT *with a syringe.*

ARGAN. Oh yes. Brother, with your permission.

BERALDE. And what are you up to now?

ARGAN. Just having a little enema. It won't take long.

BERALDE. Is this some kind of a joke? Can't you survive a single solitary moment without some kind of enema or medicine? Send it back. Take it some other time and give yourself a rest.

ARGAN. Monsieur Fleurant, I'll have it either this evening or tomorrow morning.

M. FLEURANT. May I ask on what authority you presume to oppose doctor's orders, and prevent Monsieur from taking my enema? You have not been backwards with your forwardness.

BERALDE. Be off, Monsieur. It's very clear you're not used to talking to people's faces.

M. FLEURANT. You shouldn't mock medicine, or make me waste my time. I wouldn't be here, except in a good cause. I'm going straight to Monsieur Purgon and I'll tell him a certain someone is usurping my function and preventing me from carrying out his orders. You'll see, you'll be sorry . . .

Exit MONSIEUR FLEURANT.

ARGAN. Here's a fine mess you've got me into.

BERALDE. What mess? Not taking Monsieur Purgon's enema? Brother, is there no way of curing you of this doctor's disease? Do you want to be caught in their web for ever?

ARGAN. Brother, when you say things like that, you're talking as a man with his health. If you were me, you'd soon change your tune. It's easy to rail against physic when there's nothing wrong with you.

BERALDE. But what, exactly, is wrong with you?

ARGAN. You're making me angry. I wish you'd got my illness, then we'd see if you'd chatter so much. Ah, here is Monsieur Purgon.

Enter MONSIEUR PURGON *and* TOINETTE.

M. PURGON. As I came in, I was given some very disturbing news. It seems my prescriptions are made fun of here. In this house my remedies are refused.

ARGAN. Monsieur, it's not that I . . .

M. PURGON. Here's effrontery indeed; the unnatural rebellion of a patient against his doctor.

TOINETTE. How absolutely appalling.

M. PURGON. An enema I have taken the pleasure of making up myself . . .

ARGAN. It's not my fault.

M. PURGON. . . . devised and formulated according to all the rules of the art . . .

TOINETTE. It is his fault.

M. PURGON. . . . and that would have had an unprecedented effect on your bowels . . .

ARGAN. My brother . . .

M. PURGON. Is thrown back in my face, with contempt.

ARGAN. It's him . . .

M. PURGON. This is an outrageous slander . . .

TOINETTE. It is.

M. PURGON. . . . a criminal outrage against Medicine herself . . .

ARGAN. He's the reason I . . .

M. PURGON. . . . an insult against the Faculty that cannot be punished enough.

TOINETTE. You're right.

M. PURGON. I solemnly declare I hereby break all commerce with you . . .

ARGAN. It's my brother . . .

M. PURGON. That I crave no further alliance with you . . .

TOINETTE. You're doing the right thing.

M. PURGON. And, to terminate forthwith all liaisons entered into with you, here is the deed of gift I made in favour of my nephew's marriage. (*He rips it up.*)

ARGAN. My brother's caused all the trouble.

M. PURGON. He dares to scorn my enema.

ARGAN. Call it back; I'm going to take it.

M. PURGON. I would have given you a happy issue out of all your afflictions.

TOINETTE. He doesn't deserve it.

M. PURGON. I was going to cleanse your body entirely and get rid of all its ill humours.

ARGAN. Ah, brother.

M. PURGON. Only a dozen of so more purges and we'd get to the bottom of it.

TOINETTE. He isn't worth the trouble.

M. PURGON. But, as you do not wish to be cured by my hands . . .

ARGAN. It's not my fault.

M. PURGON. As you have broken the bond of obedience owed to one's doctor . . .

TOINETTE. Heaven cries for vengeance . . .

M. PURGON. As you have presumed to rebel against the remedies I prescribed for you.

ARGAN. I haven't. I haven't.

M. PURGON. I say to you that I abandon you to the vagaries of your constitution; to the intemperance of your bowels, the corruption of your blood, to the accidity of your bile, and to the impure feculency of your humours.

TOINETTE. Bravo. Encore.

ARGAN. My God.

M. PURGON. And I prophesy that ere four days are done you will fall into an incurable state.

ARGAN. Ah, have mercy on me.

M. PURGON. That you will fall into a bradyspepsia.

ARGAN. Monsieur Purgon.

M. PURGON. And from a bradyspepsia into an apspepsia.

ARGAN. Monsieur Purgon.

M. PURGON. And from an apspepsia into a dyspepsia.

ARGAN. Monsieur Purgon.

M. PURGON. And from a dyspepsia into a diarrhoea.

ARGAN. Monsieur Purgon.

M. PURGON. And from a diarrhoea into a dysentery.

ARGAN. Monsieur Purgon.

M. PURGON. And from a dysentery into a dropsy.

ARGAN. Monsieur Purgon.

M. PURGON. And from a dropsy into that deep, dire deprivation of life whither your folly shall have driven you.

Exeunt MONSIEUR PURGON *and* TOINETTE.

ARGAN. My God, I'm as good as dead. Brother, brother, you've done for me.

BERALDE. What's the matter now?

ARGAN. The end is nigh. Already I feel Medicine wreaking her revenge.

BERALDE. Brother, you're mad. I wouldn't like anyone to see you like this. Why don't you calm down a little; take

your own pulse; gather yourself together. You shouldn't
give in to your imagination so much.

ARGAN. Brother, you heard the strange diseases he threatened me with?

BERALDE. What a simple man you are to be sure.

ARGAN. He said that ere four days were done I would fall
into an incurable state.

BERALDE. Just because he's said it doesn't mean he can do
it. Has an oracle spoken? It would appear from you Monsieur Purgon holds the thread of your days in his hand to
length or shorten at will. You're responsible for your own
life. Monsieur Purgon's anger is as little capable of making
you die as his medicines are of making you live. Here's a
chance, if you want, to get rid of doctors altogether; or if
you absolutely can't live without them to get another with
whom you'll run a little less risk.

ARGAN. Ah, brother, he knew me inside out and exactly
how to treat me.

BERALDE. Sometimes I think you live in a world of your own.

Enter TOINETTE.

TOINETTE. M'sieur, there's a doctor wants to see you.

ARGAN. Which doctor?

TOINETTE. No, a doctor, doctor.

ARGAN. I asked you who he is.

TOINETTE. I don't know, but he and I are as alike as two
peas in a pod. If I didn't know my mother was an honest
woman, I'd say he was a little brother she'd had since the
death of my father.

ARGAN. Ask him to come in.

Exit TOINETTE.

BERALDE. Who could ask for anything more? As one doctor
leaves you, another arrives.

ARGAN. I'm frightened you're going to cause another unpleasantness.

BERALDE. As if I would.

ARGAN. You see, I get very worried about all these illnesses I've got that I don't know about. You can't be too . . .

Enter TOINETTE *disguised as a doctor.*

TOINETTE. Monsieur, please allow me to introduce myself and offer you my humble services for any bleedings or purgings you might require.

ARGAN. Monsieur, I'm greatly obliged to you. Good heavens, it's Toinette to a T.

TOINETTE. Monsieur, I must beg you to excuse me; I've forgotten to send my servant on an errand. I shall return immediately.

Exit TOINETTE.

ARGAN. Eh, it's Toinette as near as damn it.

BERALDE. It's true there's a strong resemblance, but it's not the first time I've seen this sort of thing. Indeed, plays make great use of these freaks of nature. That Molière play we saw, you remember, had someone pretending to be twins in it, but you wouldn't get away with it in real life.

ARGAN. Well, anyway, it's almost unbelievable, and . . .

Enter TOINETTE *as herself.*

TOINETTE. What do you want, M'sieur?

ARGAN. What?

TOINETTE. Didn't you call me?

ARGAN. Me? No.

TOINETTE. I must have been hearing things.

ARGAN. Don't go. I want you to see how much this doctor looks like you.

TOINETTE. Yes, I know. I've got things to do downstairs and besides I've already met him.

Exit TOINETTE.

ARGAN. If I hadn't seen the two of them I'd think they were both the same person.

BERALDE. I've read the most surprising things about this sort of thing. We can all name cases when everyone was taken in.

ARGAN. Yes, I'd've been completely fooled. I would've sworn they were one.

Enter TOINETTE.

TOINETTE. . . . and don't forget to bring the change. Monsieur, I do apologise.

ARGAN. It's incredible.

TOINETTE. I trust you will not take offence at the curiosity I had to see such a celebrated invalid as yourself. Your reputation alone, which spreads far and wide, will excuse any liberty I may have taken.

ARGAN. Monsieur, I am your servant.

TOINETTE. I see, Monsieur, you look at me closely. Honestly now, how old would you say I am?

ARGAN. I think you must be twenty-six or twenty-seven at the most.

TOINETTE (*laughs*). I'm ninety.

ARGAN. Ninety?

TOINETTE. Yes. You see, in keeping me so young and active, the effects of just one of the secrets of my art.

ARGAN. Yes indeed, you're not bad looking for ninety.

TOINETTE. I am a travelling doctor. I go from town to town,

province to province, from kingdom to kingdom, putting
my skills to the severest test, finding patients worthy of
my attention and capable of putting to the proof the great
and glorious secrets Medicine has revealed to me. I dis-
dain to amuse myself with piffling detritus of common or
garden diseases; trifles like rheumatism, fluxions, all those
little fevers, attacks of the vapours and migraines. No, I
am on the lookout for diseases of consequence; raging
chronic fevers, brain seizures, livid suppurating purpura
fever, a nice plague or two, full-grown dropsies, deep-set
pleurisy with inflammations of the chest; that's the sort of
thing that gets me going and brings out the best in me. I
wish, Monsieur, you'd got all the diseases I've just mentioned, and you'd been abandoned by all the doctors, and
you were despairing, at death's door. Then I could prove
to you how good I am, and the desire I have to render
you service.

ARGAN. I'm obliged, Monsieur, for your good wishes.

TOINETTE. Show me your pulse. Let's see if it knows how
to beat properly. Aha! It obviously doesn't know me yet.
My word, it's being very impertinent indeed. I'll soon
have it back in line. Who's your doctor?

ARGAN. Monsieur Purgon.

TOINETTE. That man is not on my list of great physicians.
What does he say is the matter with you?

ARGAN. He says it's the liver, while the others say it's the
spleen.

TOINETTE. Ignoramuses, the lot of them. It's the lungs that
are making you ill.

ARGAN. The lungs?

TOINETTE. Yes. What are your symptoms?

ARGAN. I get headaches from time to time.

TOINETTE. Exactly, the lungs.

ARGAN. It seems to me at times as if there's a veil before my
eyes.

TOINETTE. Exactly, the lungs.

ARGAN. Sometimes I get heartburn.

TOINETTE. Lungs.

ARGAN. I feel at times a lassitude pervades my limbs.

TOINETTE. Lungs.

ARGAN. And sometimes I get stomach ache, as if with the colic.

TOINETTE. Lungs. You enjoy your food?

ARGAN. Yes sir.

TOINETTE. Lungs. You like to drink a little wine?

ARGAN. Yes, sir.

TOINETTE. Lungs. You enjoy forty winks after a meal?

ARGAN. Yes, sir.

TOINETTE. The lungs, the lungs I tell you. What does your doctor advise in the way of diet?

ARGAN. Soup.

TOINETTE. Ignorance.

ARGAN. Poultry.

TOINETTE. Ignorance.

ARGAN. Veal.

TOINETTE. Ignorance.

ARGAN. Beef tea and calf's foot jelly.

TOINETTE. Ignorance, ignorance.

ARGAN. Fresh eggs.

TOINETTE. Ignorance.

ARGAN. And, every evening, a small helping of prunes to clear out the stomach.

TOINETTE. Ignorance.

ARGAN. And above all, drinking my wine strongly diluted.

TOINETTE. Ignoramus, ignorami, ignorantissimi. You should drink your wine neat; and as your blood is far too thin, you should eat good fat beef, succulent pork, full fat cream cheese, porridge, rice pudding, chestnuts and clotted cream, all to thicken and coagulate it. Your doctor's an arrant fool. I shall send you one I've trained myself, and I'll come to see you personally from time to time when I'm in town.

ARGAN. I'm very much obliged to you.

TOINETTE. What on earth are you doing with that arm?

ARGAN. What?

TOINETTE. I'd have that arm off at once if I were you.

ARGAN. Why?

TOINETTE. Can't you see it's drawing all the nourishment to itself and stopping the other one from growing?

ARGAN. Yes, but I like my arm.

TOINETTE. You've got a right eye there. I'd have that out as well if I were you.

ARGAN. Have my eye out?

TOINETTE. Can't you see how it gets in the way of the other one? Believe me, have it out as soon as possible. You'll see far more clearly with the left one.

ARGAN. I don't think it's that urgent.

TOINETTE. Goodbye. Sorry to have to leave you so soon. We're holding a full scale consultation on a man who died yesterday.

ARGAN. On a man who died yesterday?

TOINETTE. Yes, to find out how we could have cured him. Until I see you again.

ARGAN. Can you see yourself out? We poor invalids you know . . .

Exit TOINETTE.

BERALDE. Now that's what I call a real doctor. He's obviously very skilled.

ARGAN. Yes, but he does take things at a bit of a run.

BERALDE. All the truly great doctors do.

ARGAN. All the same, to cut off my arm and pluck out my eye simply to encourage the others. I'd look stupid. (*He covers his left eye with his hand and slips his right hand in his shirt* (Nelson)) No-one ever looked like that.

Enter TOINETTE *as herself.*

TOINETTE. Come, come, I'm your servant. Please don't make me laugh.

ARGAN. What is it?

TOINETTE. That doctor of yours. He wanted to take my pulse, in a most peculiar place.

ARGAN. You take a good look at him. You wouldn't think he was ninety.

BERALDE. Well, brother, since you and your Monsieur Purgon have fallen out shall we discuss the young man I have in mind for my niece?

ARGAN. No brother. Since she won't do what I want, I'm putting her in a convent. There's some love affair or other underneath all this, you mark my words. I've found out about a certain secret interview, and nobody else knows.

BERALDE. All well and good, brother, but is that so very bad when the couple are inclined towards each other anyway? Surely you can't take it amiss when it's all leading to something above board, like marriage?

ARGAN. Be that as it may, brother, she's going to be a nun. I've made up my mind.

BERALDE. You're trying to please someone.

ARGAN. I see what you're driving at. You're always harping on about that. You're just prejudiced against my wife.

BERALDE. Very well, yes, brother; if we're going to put our cards on the table I am. I can no more tolerate your infatuation with medicine than your infatuation with her. Neither can I stand by and see you run headlong into all the traps she sets for you.

TOINETTE. Monsieur, don't talk about Madame like that. She is above suspicion, like Caesar's wife. She's a woman completely without artifice and who loves Monsieur, who loves him . . . words can't say how much.

ARGAN. Ask her about the way she caresses me.

TOINETTE. Yes, yes, she does.

ARGAN. The way she worries about my illnesses.

TOINETTE. If only you could see her.

ARGAN. All the trouble and care she takes over me.

TOINETTE. It's absolutely true. (*To* BERALDE.) Do you want me to prove it to you; to show you how much Madame loves M'sieur? (*To* ARGAN.) M'sieur, let me show him what's what.

ARGAN. How?

TOINETTE. Madame has just returned. Lay yourself out in your chair and pretend to be dead. You'll soon see her grief when I tell her the news.

ARGAN. Very well then.

TOINETTE. Yes, but don't leave her too long in her despair. I'm afraid it might kill her.

ARGAN. You leave me; I'll get on with it.

TOINETTE (*to* BERALDE). Monsieur, hide behind this screen.

ARGAN. There's no danger in pretending to be dead?

TOINETTE No, no; how could there be? Now lay yourself out. (*Low.*) You'll enjoy proving your brother wrong for a change. Here's Madame. Keep still.

Enter BELINE.

TOINETTE (*crying out*). Oh, my God, oh woe is me, what an untoward accident.

BELINE. What is it, Toinette?

TOINETTE. Ah, Madame.

BELINE. What is it?

TOINETTE. Your husband is dead.

BELINE. My husband is dead?

TOINETTE. Alas, yes. He's shuffled off his mortal coil.

BELINE. You're sure.

TOINETTE. I'm sure. Nobody knows yet; I found him here by myself all alone. He passed away in my arms. Look, there he is, all stretched out in that chair, defunct.

BELINE. Heavens be praised. There's a millstone from round my neck. You're being silly, Toinette, letting his death upset you.

TOINETTE. I thought you were supposed to cry, Madame.

BELINE. Come, come, it's not worth the bother. Is he any loss to anyone except himself? What use was he when he was with us? He was an inconvenience to everyone. He was grubby, disgusting, never without an enema or a dose of something in his guts, always blowing his nose, coughing and spitting. There was nothing to him. He was bad tempered, tired people out the entire time, and scolded the servants night and day.

TOINETTE. Here's a nice funeral oration.

BELINE. You must help me, Toinette, to put my plans into action. You can rest assured if you play ball with me I'll see you all right. By a happy chance no-one yet knows of this. Let's get him into his bed and keep his death secret until I've finished what I've got to do. There are some papers and money I want to get my hands on. It's only fair; I've given him the best years of my life; I ought to get something in return. Come, Toinette, first of all let's get his keys.

ARGAN (*getting up suddenly*). Not so fast.

BELINE (*surprised and terrified*). Aaaaaargh!

ARGAN. So, Madame, my wife, this is the way you love me.

TOINETTE. Aha! He's shuffled it back on again.

ARGAN (*to* BELINE *who goes off*). I am very pleased to have witnessed your love, and to have heard your fine panegyric over me. This plain speaking will make me wiser in the future and stop me from doing a lot of things.

BERALDE. (*coming from his hiding place*). So, brother, there you have it.

TOINETTE. I would never have believed it. But I hear you

daughter. Get back as you were, and we'll see how she receives your death. It's not a bad idea putting all this to the test. You'll end up knowing what the whole family feels about you.

Enter ANGELIQUE.

TOINETTE (*crying out*). Oh heavens, oh catastrophe, oh unhappy day.

ANGELIQUE. What is it Toinette? Why are you crying out?

TOINETTE. Alas, I have sad news for you.

ANGELIQUE. What can it be?

TOINETTE. Your father is dead.

ANGELIQUE. My father is dead, Toinette?

TOINETTE. Yes, you see him there. He died just this minute of a sudden fainting fit.

ANGELIQUE. Oh heavens! What misfortune, what cruel blow. Alas, must I lose my father, the only thing left to me in the world? And, to add to my despair, must I lose him when he was angry with me? What will become of me, unhappy woman that I am? What consolation can I find for so great a loss?

Enter CLEANTE.

CLEANTE. What is it, my fair Angélique? What misfortune ails you?

ANGELIQUE. Alas, I weep for the most dear and precious thing I can lose in this life. I weep for the death of my father.

CLEANTE. Oh heavens, what sad twist of fate, what unexpected blow! I had asked your uncle to beg a favour from him for me. I was coming to present myself to him, and to endeavour, by my respects and by my prayers, to persuade him to bestow you according to my wishes.

ANGELIQUE. Ah, Cléante, let us talk no more of it. Let us

renounce here all thoughts of marriage. After the loss of
my father, I wish no longer to be part of this world; I shall
take the veil and renounce it forever. Yes, Father, if 'til now
I have resisted your wishes, now at least I shall follow one
of your intentions. I shall atone for the pain I accuse myself
of having given you. Let me, Father, give you my word,
and embrace you in witness of my daughterly contrition.

ARGAN (*gets up*). Ah, my daughter.

ANGELIQUE (*frightened*). Aaaargh!

ARGAN. Come, do not be frightened, I am not dead. Come,
blood of my blood, true daughter of mine. I am overjoyed
to have witnessed your good nature.

ANGELIQUE. Ah, Father, what an agreeable surprise. Since,
by a stroke of extreme good fortune, heaven restores you
according to my wishes, let me throw myself at your feet
and entreat you for one thing. If you are not favourable to
the leanings of my heart, if you refuse me Cléante for my
spouse, I beseech you not to force me to espouse another.
That is all I ask.

CLEANTE (*throwing himself to his knees*). Ah, Monsieur, let
yourself be moved by her prayers and by mine. Do not
oppose the mutual ardours of so worthy a love.

BERALDE. Brother, can you hold out to the contrary?

TOINETTE. M'sieur, can't you feel them tugging your heart-
strings?

Pause.

ARGAN. If he'll consent to be a doctor, I'll consent to the
marriage. Yes, make yourself a doctor, and I'll give you
my daughter.

CLEANTE. Willingly, if that's all it needs to be your son-in-
law. I'll make myself a doctor, an apothecary as well, if
you like. It's not much to ask, and I would do anything to
obtain the fair Angélique.

BERALDE. Brother, I've had an idea. Become a doctor your-self. Nothing could be more convenient than for the phy-sician to heal himself.

TOINETTE. That's very true. You'll completely cure yourself in no time. It's foolproof. No illness would dare tackle a doctor.

ARGAN. I think, brother, you're teasing me. Am I of an age to study?

BERALDE. You've no need to; you know enough already. There are many actual doctors who don't know as much as you.

ARGAN. But you have to speak good Latin, and know all the illnesses and the necessary cures.

BERALDE. When you receive your doctor's cap and gown you'll find you know all that. In fact, you'll find you know rather more than you want.

ARGAN. What? You know all about illnesses as soon as you put on the clothes?

BERALDE. Yes. Put on a cap and gown, open your mouth and all hot air sounds learned; all stupidity reason itself.

TOINETTE. Now, Monsieur, if only you had a beard you'd be almost there. A beard's more than half the battle for a doctor.

CLEANTE. I'm ready for anything.

BERALDE. Do you wish the induction to be performed im-mediately?

ARGAN. You mean now?

BERALDE. Yes. I've some friends in the Faculty who'll drop everything to perform the ceremony here and now in the square. It won't cost you anything.

ARGAN. Yes, but what do I say? How do I answer?

BERALDE. You'll be told all that. There's nothing to it, and they'll give you all you've got to say in writing. Go and put on some decent clothes while I send for them.

ARGAN. Yes. Yes. Yes.

Exit ARGAN.

CLEANTE. What are you talking about? What do you mean by friends in the Faculty?

TOINETTE. What are you up to?

BERALDE. Just setting up a little diversion for us this evening. The players have devised a little interlude about the induction of a doctor, with dances and music. I suggest we all take part in it, and that my brother be the principal character.

ANGELIQUE. Uncle, I think you're making too much fun of Father.

BERALDE. Niece, it's not so much making fun of him as indulging his fantasies. We will all take a character and pass the joke on from one to the other. It's carnival time; there is licence for all. Quickly, let's get things ready.

CLEANTE (*to* ANGELIQUE). Do you agree to this?

ANGELIQUE. Yes, since it's my uncle.

Exeunt.

Epilogue

Street. CELEBRANTS *in four groups, severally. They chant
a Latin sentence each.*

ONE. Gallia est omnis divisa in partes tres.
TWO. Timor mortis conturbat me.
THREE. Post coitum omni animal triste.
FOUR. Humani nil a me alienum puto.

Build severally, then together. Enter BERALDE *as President. Chanting stops.*

BERALDE. Wisestissimi doctores
        Medicinae professores
        Qui hic assemblitis estis,
        We're gathered here today
        To make in our own way
        A doctor of a man who's tried his bestist
        Vocat Argan.
VOICES (*courtroom style*). Vocat Argan.

Enter ARGAN *as initiatee.*

BERALDE. This is Argan who here comes?
ARGAN. Argan ego sum.
OMNES Argan suus est.
BERALDE. Prepare to take the test.
        Cave canem
        Take my manem.

ARGAN *takes his outstretched hand.*

BERALDE. Verbis dare, respondare
       Comprehendi?

ARGAN. Yes, effendi.

BERALDE. Mensa, mensa, mensam.

ARGAN. A humble postulant I am.

BERALDE. Amo, amas, amat.

ARGAN. To be a doctor, better that.

BERALDE. Noli me tangere.

ARGAN. Drive my ignorance away.

BERALDE. Quod erat demonstrandum.

OMNES. This is quite easily done.
       Ars gratia artem.

BERALDE. Tell me the doctor's art then.
       Festina lente.

ARGAN. Charge them plenty.

BERALDE. Nihil obstat.

ARGAN. Price no object.

BERALDE. Dulce et decorum est.

ARGAN. To flatter nobles, fleece the rest.

BERALDE. Nunc doctore suus est.

OMNES. May all his enemas be blest.

BERALDE. Novissimus doctore, hic est mali to curare.
       Acne, ague, anaphylaxis,
       Ankylosing spondylitis,
       Genu valgum, genu varum,
       Granuloma inguinale;
       Herpes zoster, impetigo,
       Myocradian infarction,
       Salpingitis, sinusitis,
       Coronary thrombosis.

The CELEBRANTS *file past* ARGAN *coarsely impersonating various diseases.* ARGAN *miraculously cures them. Their illnesses do not correspond to the below.*

BERALDE. Back ache, bad breath, bat ears, bed sores,
Flat feet, flatulence, flooding, flu,
Rabies, rash, rickets, ringworm,
Whitlow, wind and warts to you.

ARGAN *throws away his stick in his excitement.*

ARGAN. I can walk, I can walk, I can walk without my stick.
I'm cured.

He is chaired round the stage.

OMNES. Vivat, vivat, a century vivat
Novus doctor who cures all ills;
Mille annis may he eat and drinkat,
Bleedat, purgat and above all kill.

The cast discard their robes. Chain dance, led by ARGAN.

OMNES. Gather ye rosebuds while ye may
Young girls under Cupid's sway;
The springtime of your life's the chance
To give yourself to sweet romance.

The dance becomes wilder and more complex. ARGAN
*becomes detached from it, downstage centre. The cast end
up upstage, backs to the audience. Discord. Solo instrument
or electronics.* ARGAN *has a heart attack and dies. The
cast turn to face audience. They are wearing death's
heads.*

OMNES (*chant over slow fade*).
Timor mortis conturbat me . . . (etc.)

End

Note: Music goes on throughout.

For a Complete Catalogue of Methuen Drama titles
write to:

Methuen Drama
215 Vauxhall Bridge Road
London SW1V 1EJ